HOME OWNERSHIP
Differentiation and Fragmentation

RAY FORREST, ALAN MURIE AND PETER WILLIAMS

LONDON AND NEW YORK

First published in 1990 by the Academic Division of Unwin Hyman Ltd.

This edition first published in 2021
by Routledge
2 Park Square, Milton Park, Abingdon, Oxon OX14 4RN

and by Routledge
52 Vanderbilt Avenue, New York, NY 10017

Routledge is an imprint of the Taylor & Francis Group, an informa business

© 1990 R. Forrest, A. Murie, P. Williams © 2021 New Preface A. Murie, P. Williams

All rights reserved. No part of this book may be reprinted or reproduced or utilised in any form or by any electronic, mechanical, or other means, now known or hereafter invented, including photocopying and recording, or in any information storage or retrieval system, without permission in writing from the publishers.

Trademark notice: Product or corporate names may be trademarks or registered trademarks, and are used only for identification and explanation without intent to infringe.

British Library Cataloguing in Publication Data
A catalogue record for this book is available from the British Library

ISBN: 978-0-367-64519-9 (Set)
ISBN: 978-1-00-313856-3 (Set) (ebk)
ISBN: 978-0-367-67889-0 (Volume 5) (hbk)
ISBN: 978-0-367-67894-4 (pbk)
ISBN: 978-1-00-313327-8 (Volume 5) (ebk)

Publisher's Note
The publisher has gone to great lengths to ensure the quality of this reprint but points out that some imperfections in the original copies may be apparent.

Disclaimer
The publisher has made every effort to trace copyright holders and would welcome correspondence from those they have been unable to trace.

Revisiting Home Ownership in the UK 30 years later

Preface to the Re-issue of 2021

This book, *Home Ownership: Differentiation and Fragmentation,* published in 1990, provided an alternative to accounts of owner occupation that generalised about the tenure's security, ideology, meaning, politics and other attributes. The book emphasised differences between tenures - legal rights, the institutional framework, financing, policy, ownership and security of tenure. But, crucially, it also demonstrated that differences within owner occupation were profound. It emphasised that rather than having intrinsic characteristics the category, owner occupation, embraced a wide range of features and changed over time – transitions from early, middle and late stages of development. It argued that it was misleading to generalise about home-owners being in advantageous situations when compared with tenants: whether in terms of housing quality, security, access to mortgages, tax reliefs and other assistance. It was also inaccurate to generalise about a common or shared character as middle class, suburban, associated with specific life-styles, asset appreciation, ideologies and social conditioning. Tenures, including owner occupation, were mixed and stratified and tenure status did not define or determine class, occupation, income, wealth, life-style or health.

As we set out in the book, home ownership in the UK was never solely for the richest households: the most expensive private housing was almost completely the exclusive preserve of the most affluent households but there were also home-owners in the lowest value and least attractive dwellings. Many higher income households were not owner occupiers and although the proportion of owners increased as incomes increased there were significant numbers of home-owners in every income decile. It was only a minority of households for whom owner occupied housing was a positional good that defined status and wealth. Not all of the highest income owners lived in the most expensive dwellings and not all of the most expensive dwellings were occupied by households with the highest incomes. Many owner occupiers expressed high levels of dissatisfaction with their housing and the hierarchy of demand and satisfaction with housing was affected by factors beyond tenure. Owner occupiers had not all accessed home ownership through privileged and protected public finance networks dependent on retail savings and preferential tax treatment, benefitting from direct government subsidies and a special relationship between borrower and lender. There were always 'class', race, income and other divides among home-owners; and divisions about living conditions that presented risks to health and safety and generational experiences. There have always been a significant group of low-income owner occupiers and of owner occupiers who did not accumulate significant wealth that they could realise or access in their lifetime and who did not bequeath significant equity. The differences between tenures and within home ownership were linked with, but not determined by, social class, occupation or income and were affected by when households were formed, lifetime events and where people lived. Even at the level of legal rights there were divisions within home ownership between outright and mortgaged home-owners and leaseholders.

It is impossible to revisit this book and agenda without reflecting on the very sad and untimely death of our colleague Ray Forrest. As we have shown elsewhere (Housing Studies https://www.tandfonline.com/doi/full/10.1080/02673037.2020.1747754) many of the themes in the book remained of interest to Ray as well as ourselves. He would have been delighted to see this book republished. The perspective advanced in *Home Ownership: Differentiation and Fragmentation*, was informed by research and evidence mostly referring to the UK, much of it growing out of work undertaken at the Centre for Urban and Regional Studies, an active multidisciplinary research centre at the University of Birmingham between 1966 and 2010 and continuing in a different format since then. Some of the research was innovative: looking at mortgage lending and inner-city home ownership; processes and outcomes of private as well as public sector urban management; the local impacts of policies affecting levels of home ownership and their sustainability; and issues of housing wealth and inheritance. The research drew on different disciplines, used a variety of methods and embraced historical work on building societies and the growth of owner occupation, studies of different tenures, government policies affecting levels of home ownership (especially the sale of council houses), low income owner occupation especially in older, dilapidated, inner city neighbourhoods and among households from minority ethnic groups largely excluded from better quality public sector housing, and on changes in housing over the life cycle. Rather than reporting the results of a single research project the book attempted a synthesis that drew on a succession of projects over more than fifteen years. It also drew on other work and responded to an active debate between housing researchers at the time about housing tenure. Its distinctive contribution was to represent home ownership as diverse. It was differentiated and fragmented, segmented and stratified.

Has owner occupation become more homogeneous over the last 30 years? For the UK, the answer is 'No'. The tenure itself, the expectations of owners, the market context (and not least the mortgage market) and the way it is financed has changed. Importantly, and contrary to our expectations thirty years ago, the growth of owner occupation has been followed by decline in both the percentage of owners and within it, in the number of mortgaged home-owners. The associations between income and tenure have changed because of the decline of council housing and growth of private renting. But the outcome is still that owner occupiers own properties with different asset values and other attributes and have different incomes and other characteristics. Housing tenure is even less of a fault line than in the past. Emerging differences between places and generations make whole tenure generalisations as problematic as they ever were.

Since 1990 we have had two major market downturns – 1990/91 and 2007/08 but there have also been long periods of sustained price growth, in part reflecting the deregulation of the finance market in the 1980s and the expansion of mortgage credit. One consequence of that is affordability ratios for home ownership (price income ratios) have been stretched – almost to the point of breaking – compensated only to a modest degree by longer loan terms and much reduced interest rates. That last is perhaps one of the most striking changes over the last 30 years. In 1990 the average mortgage interest rate was around 15%, it came down to around 6.5% in 2000 and subsequently fell to just over 2% by May, 2020.

Those rate reductions reflect the evolution to low inflation in the wider economy, much intensified competition in the mortgage market and unprecedented levels of government and Bank of England intervention to drive rates down and keep them low. This has in turn fed house price inflation, albeit unevenly including since the 2007/8 downturn. These changes, deregulation of the private rented market and changes elsewhere in the economy have made property an attractive investment option: since the mid-1990s the private rented market has expanded, backed by Buy to Let mortgages. This has created new homes for renters and good returns for landlords but has also intensified competition for house purchase with investors sometimes squeezing out new and other owner occupiers.

In the UK Owner occupation has absorbed huge changes in access and affordability, visible in the rise of gifts and loans within family and kinship groups, changes in tax reliefs and subsidies, new forms of financing, including shared equity and new leasehold arrangements. The tenure has also become less spatially concentrated because of the Right to Buy and expansion of private renting. It is more differentiated in dwelling type because it includes flats sold under the Right to Buy, the sales of private rented homes into home ownership on a continuing basis and the larger numbers of apartments and other leasehold properties built since the 1980s. Regional and local variation in property values has also increased and negative equity following falling house prices after 2008 has remained for some while values have risen for others. Moreover, the temporal and spatial dynamics of this market are such that much turns on generational trajectories and inheritance in terms of propelling subsequent households into and up the so-called home ownership 'ladder'. The past now has a much bigger impact on home ownership than it did in previous decades.

The expansion and then stabilisation of home ownership is consistent with an emphasis on a tenure in constant transition. But, although the big gains in the size and scale of the tenure are over and there is no real prospect of universal home ownership, the later stages are still associated with differentiation and segmentation between owners. All of this underlines the weaknesses in generalisations about this tenure. From this starting point it appears essential that in the future researchers and housing commentators resist an agenda set by perspectives that assume a binary division or polarisation between tenures, or that treat tenure status as a key social division or determinant of behaviour. While these perspectives are simple and, for this reason, attractive, they lack a priori justification and are based on false assumptions. Hypotheses about whole tenures are likely to be spurious; and international comparisons, based on aggregate levels of owner occupation, rather than analysis of the dynamics and differences between housing systems internationally, are likely to be seriously flawed. The challenge posed by the reality of fragmented and differentiated tenures is to develop real world research questions that engage with local differences and segments within tenures. The divisions within owner occupation are not, however self-evident and will differ with spatial and temporal contingencies: they may relate to mortgage status, leasehold, different property types, values or levels of demand or to race, class and age. What is clear, however, is that research that starts off with grand hypotheses about whole tenures should be treated with great caution. In essence they are starting from the wrong premise.

Alan Murie and Peter Williams

Home ownership

Differentiation and fragmentation

RAY FORREST
ALAN MURIE
PETER WILLIAMS

London
UNWIN HYMAN
Boston   Sydney   Wellington

© R. Forrest, A. Murie, P. Williams 1990

This book is copyright under the Berne Convention. No reproduction without permission. All rights reserved.

Published by the Academic Division of
Unwin Hyman Ltd
15/17 Broadwick Street, London W1V 1FP, UK

Unwin Hyman Inc.,
8 Winchester Place, Winchester, Mass. 01890, USA

Allen & Unwin (Australia) Ltd,
8 Napier Street, North Sydney, NSW 2060, Australia

Allen & Unwin (New Zealand) Ltd in association with the
Port Nicholson Press Ltd,
Compusales Building, 75 Ghuznee Street, Wellington 1, New Zealand

First published in 1990

British Library Cataloguing in Publication Data

Forrest, Ray
  Home ownership: differentiation and fragmentation.
  1. Great Britain. Residences. Ownership by occupiers
  I. Title II. Murie, Alan, *1946–*   III. Williams, Peter,
  1946–
  333.3380941
  ISBN 0–04–445444–9

Library of Congress Cataloging in Publication Data

Forrest, Ray
    Home Ownership: differentiation and fragmentation / Ray Forrest
  Alan Murie, Peter Williams.
      p.   cm.
    Includes bibliographical references.
    ISBN 0–04–445444–9
      1. Home ownership—Great Britain. I. Murie, Alan. II. Williams,
  Peter, 1946- . III. Title.
  HD7287.82.G7F67 1990   90–12186
  333.33'8'0941—dc20   CIP

Typeset in 10/11 point Bembo
Printed by Billings and Sons, London and Worcester

Contents

	List of figures	ix
	List of tables	x
	Acknowledgements	xi
	Introduction	1
1	Understanding home ownership	7
	The focus of current debates	12
2	Home ownership: facts and fictions	19
	Patterns of ownership	19
	Aspects of the social structure of home ownership	32
	Prices, mortgages and tax relief	37
	The preference for home ownership	41
	Concluding remarks	54
3	Home ownership: a silent revolution?	55
	The growth of home ownership	56
	House prices	64
	A silent revolution?	64
	Conclusions	74
4	Property, class and tenure	78
	Home ownership and property ownership	78
	Consumption sector cleavages and the primacy of class	85
	Differentiation among home owners	88
	Changing meanings and associations	91
	Concluding comments	94
5	The fragmented market	98
	Fraying at the edges?	101
	Segmented markets, differential subsidies	108
	The housing histories of home owners	119
	Concluding comments	124

viii

6	Wealth: realizing the dream	127
	Housing in the distribution of wealth	130
	Definitions and statistics	134
	Rates of accumulation	136
	Realizable wealth	140
	Inheritance	145
	Wealth and power	152
	Speculation and investment strategies	154
	Conclusions	157
7	A tenure in transition	160
	The socialization of home ownership	160
	A bulwark against Bolshevism?	166
	Home ownership and the home	170
	Transitions	179
	New policies	188
8	Home ownership: deconstruction and reconstruction	191
	Key perspectives on home ownership	191
	The changing organization of home ownership	200
	The reconstruction of home ownership?	209
	Concluding comment	213
	References	218
	Index	228

List of figures

Figure 2.1	Tenure change, 1971–1986	22
Figure 2.2	Home owners: proportion in each income decile	35
Figure 2.3	Annual average house prices for the UK by country and region 1969–89	39
Figure 3.1	Size and age of the owner-occupied stock: England and Wales, 1938–88	67
Figure 5.1	Average regional house prices expressed as a percentage of average house prices in the South East (excl. Greater London), 1969–89	99
Figure 6.1	Gross personal wealth, 1985: asset composition by range	133

List of tables

Table 1.1	Perspectives on home ownership	8
Table 2.1	Growth in home ownership, 1976–1986	20
Table 2.2	Freehold home owners: household type, 1981	25
Table 2.3	Building societies: repossession and mortgage arrears: UK, 1982–1988	29
Table 2.4	Profiles of home ownership in 1977 and 1986: Great Britain	33
Table 2.5	Occupational group of home owners and council tenants, 1986: Great Britain	35
Table 2.6	Building societies: mortgage advances and deposits, 1986	40
Table 2.7	Current tenure and tenure preferences	43
Table 2.8	Main reasons for choice of home ownership as ideal accommodation	51
Table 2.9	Attitudes towards home ownership	52
Table 3.1	Housing tenure in Britain, 1914–1988	57
Table 3.2	Rates of home ownership in selected cities	59
Table 3.3	Home ownership in 24 towns in 1939	62
Table 3.4	Economic group and tenure, 1947	63
Table 3.5	House prices and inflation, 1954–1986	65
Table 3.6	Home ownership in England and Wales: components of change	66
Table 5.1	Value of mortgage interest tax relief for different income groups, 1988/9	111
Table 5.2	Relocation allowances for new and existing executives	116
Table 7.1	Home ownership: stages of transition	182
Table 8.1	Perspectives on home ownership: propositions about home ownership and the implications of market segmentation	193

Acknowledgements

This book has had a lengthy gestation period. Its subject has continued to be important and to change throughout this period and some of the ideas we have developed have been referred to in other publications. They have also been informed by work carried out in a variety of research projects including those by Ray Forrest and Alan Murie on council house sales, and on low-cost home ownership, both funded by the Nuffield Foundation – and in two projects funded by the Economic and Social Research Council – 'Housing Origins and Destinations' and 'Urban Change and the Restructuring of Housing Provision'.

Much of the final work on this text was carried out at the University of Utrecht by Alan Murie while he held the Belle Van Zuylen visiting professorship at that university in the Faculty of Geographical Sciences.

Our thanks are due to all of those who have typed various versions of the chapters in this book. Finally, our gratitude to the School for Advanced Urban Studies for providing the base from which this work has been carried out.

Ray Forrest
Alan Murie
Peter Williams

Bristol, October 1989

Introduction

In 1990 the majority of households in Britain own their own homes. This feature is in striking contrast to the position of previous generations. The growth of home ownership has involved substantial changes in the way housing is produced and consumed; in the way it is financed, exchanged, managed and controlled; and in housing costs and patterns of wealth, inequality and saving.

This major change in the way housing is consumed and produced is too easily presented as a natural product of increasing affluence reflecting consumers' demands and representing a straightforward and unambiguous change in society. But other countries with developed industrial economies do not have the same or even similar levels of home ownership and in these countries home ownership involves different financial, legal and other arrangements. There is no natural form of tenure associated with stages of economic development and no convergence of advanced countries towards the same structure of housing provision. Moreover, even in Britain, home ownership as a category embraces a wide range of different circumstances – of property types, sizes, values and locations – and it has been and still is changing. The growth in home ownership is rooted in the same processes as the production and consumption of other goods. While housing has particular attributes in terms of cost, fixed location, durability, status, security and the services it provides, it is nevertheless a commodity that is produced, consumed and exchanged through the same processes that apply in markets for other goods. What happens at different points in the housing market process – as in other markets – is determined by calculations about capital investment, rates of return, appreciation of asset value and asset stripping and switching. The growth of home ownership has occurred through these processes, and competition and market penetration have been important elements in the way the tenure has changed.

This book is about the growth and development of home ownership and the contemporary academic and policy debates that surround it. It is not concerned to make a case for or against home ownership, or to take a particular policy stance. Rather, it is concerned with widening perspectives beyond a simple imagery that equates home ownership universally with ladders, opportunity, mobility, the accumulation of wealth or with problems of disrepair or loan repayment. More abstractly, it seeks to engage with those commentators who claim that the growth of home ownership has involved a more equitable distribution of wealth in contemporary society and that the old social divisions of class have been reshaped and smoothed over. The book presents a reality of a form of housing provision characterised by unevenness and inequality rather than homogeneity and uniformity of benefit and experience.

In exploring these issues four initial elements are important in developing a perspective on home ownership. First, there must be a recognition that home ownership is a diverse and fragmented tenure deriving from and generating a diversity of experiences amongst owners. This differentiation within home ownership has increased as the tenure has extended to different groups of people and types of properties. In this century, home ownership in Britain has moved from being the tenure of less than 10 per cent of the population to over 65 per cent. By the end of the century, it may well stand at 80 per cent. The market has moved from youth to maturity and is perhaps entering its old age. As a mature market, segmentation, fragmentation and differentiation are all observable features of contemporary home ownership.

Second, and related to the first, home ownership is undergoing constant change. Home ownership today is not what it was in the 1930s. Then it had different meanings, a different context and a different set of outcomes. It had different sources of growth and different legal and financial arrangements. Yet the continuing unqualified use of the term home ownership implies continuity and consistency.

Third, change reflects the fact that the features and characteristics of home ownership are an outcome of market processes. Changes in the way the market for housing production and consumption works have affected features of the tenure. In particular, changes in taxation, subsidy and other regulations and the development of competition have had significant impacts. The market does not only respond and adapt to demand and to the individual home owner. The decisions of government, corporate and private landlords, builders and developers, and major financial institutions mould the market in ways that often have little to do with housing, the home or individual ownership.

Fourth, because of all of this, the utility of housing tenure as a sufficient analytic category must be questioned. It implies a unity within tenures that is no longer evident (if it ever was) and this implies a uniformity of circumstances and interests that

Introduction 3

hampers clear analysis and debate. It allows governments to talk in generalities about policy related to a specific tenure, even though it will have selective effects within that tenure.

Our starting point for this analysis of the tenure and of change is the process of commodification. In market economies, goods and services are provided in a market supply framework and become subject to market regulation. Home ownership is a commodified form of housing provision. Whilst this is a somewhat cumbersome term, it encapsulates the driving force within capitalist economies – namely the search for new areas of profitable activity. One of the central defining features of capitalist societies is of course the commodification of labour itself. Less abstractly, however, the term describes a society where the elements of everyday life – food, clothing, shelter, leisure – are provided as goods and services bought and sold in the marketplace. The market for consumer goods is increasingly sub-divided and extended. We buy our pleasure and leisure in neat packages targeted at particular lifestyles. Home cooking is now mass produced and marketed with mythical images of an earlier, simpler life. Home ownership is mass produced and marketed as the lietmotif of settled, affluent family life. We stress this perspective as our starting point, as the backcloth to our discussion of the growth of home ownership in Britain, in opposition to approaches that stress voluntaristic and demand-led explanations or pluralistic political processes. The choices and aspirations of individual households do matter. But those who make those choices and experience those constraints have their housing histories shaped in housing market conditions which are not of their own making.

Any market once established and reaching maturity tends to enter a phase of fragmentation and segmentation. In the home ownership market this means more than the development of new products to meet new market 'niches'. Indeed, it must be understood that the housing market has certain special features. The most important of these is the fixed location of the commodities that are bought and sold, i.e. the dwellings. These fixed locations produce variations in the market and the effects of changes in external social, financial and economic conditions will not be the same for all home owners, or even for all those owning similar dwellings. While there may be a rising demand for ownership, overall it is quite possible for specific sub-markets to emerge where demand is falling and where individual owners are trapped in a declining asset.

The complexities of any market economy, and more specifically the extent of reconstruction of the British economy, have meant that there are now a variety of markets or sub-markets for home ownership in Britain. Images of home ownership tend to be built

4   *Home ownership*

around a stereotype of booming prices and mobile owners. But this stereotype is not accurate for many periods, places or people. The contrast between the booming market conditions of the mid to late 1980s and the very different conditions prevailing at the end of the decade amply demonstrates the changing realities of the owner occupied market. Alternative realities of home ownership have a bearing on the overall direction, nature and function of the tenure. Home ownership in this book is treated as a complex good subject to market processes. The tenure is viewed as a product of changing structures of provision – of changes in the social context in which housing operates. This includes changes in the organization and finance of home ownership, in government policy and in the family and community. The sector is not insulated from the effects of market competition.

In recent years considerable attention has been given to the production of housing and to structures of provision. This book aims to complement that approach by reviewing issues relating to consumption. More and more, this has involved referring to the important contributions made to the sociology of housing and of consumption by Peter Saunders. Successive drafts of some chapters of this book have increasingly cited his work. While the book has not been designed as a response to Saunders, and reflects a previous plan, it does at some points involve detailed discussion of Saunders' work as published in various working and conference papers. Using such sources is problematic, but the arguments presented are sufficiently important to warrant a response. Some of these papers have been revised to be included in Saunders' book *A nation of home owners*, (1990). Our comments are based on the papers seen and cited.

This book seeks to shift the emphasis in images of home ownership. It draws upon new research evidence and links to established academic debates. It is not principally concerned with the supply side and does not focus on the literature on planning, architecture, the building industry or the environment. Important recent contributions are available on some of these issues (e.g. Ball, 1983, 1988). However, home ownership in Britain today is predominantly a second-hand market. New building and the factors determining the volume or cost of new building are not the critical factors.

Having briefly outlined the approach, it is appropriate to conclude this introduction by summarizing the content of the book. Chapter 1 offers a brief review of existing and changing perspectives on home ownership, focusing on the relevant academic literature. It emphasizes prominent themes relating to the production of housing and structures of provision as well as those relating to consumption and to consumption sector cleavages.

Introduction 5

Both of these themes, but particularly the latter, are returned to throughout. In Chapter 2 a range of basic facts about home ownership are discussed. This involves a presentation of data about contemporary patterns of tenure and the growth of home ownership, and key characteristics of home ownership and home owners. Data are provided about mortgage arrears, house prices, mortgages and tax relief, and differences within home ownership are emphasized. Finally, the chapter discusses evidence about tenure preferences, the interpretation of this evidence and about how far home ownership is a demand-led tenure. As well as having a clear picture of home ownership today, it is important to have some perspective on the historical background. Chapter 3 outlines the growth of home ownership, referring to local, as well as national, data on tenure. The movement of house prices and the role of transfers between tenures as well as new building are mentioned. Finally, three case studies are used to highlight issues of current relevance to the politics of home ownership.

Chapter 4 focuses on issues related to a property-owning democracy. It discusses perspectives on property and power. It refers to the debate about consumption sector cleavages and their relationship to social class. Finally, it discusses differentiation within ownership and changing meanings and associations in the context of this debate.

In Chapter 5 issues of differentiation within home ownership are developed further. In addition to referring to issues about marginal owners, different routes into home ownership and to house condition, it is argued that home ownership is more generally segregated. Differential subsidies, including occupational subsidies, are referred to, and the chapter ends by discussing links between housing and labour market position – drawing on research into the housing histories of home owners.

Chapter 6 addresses the key question of home ownership as a source and store of wealth. It outlines the evidence on the increasing importance of housing in personal wealth. It goes on to examine propositions relating to rates of accumulation, to how far housing wealth is realizable, to inheritance, to housing wealth and power, and to the importance of investment in housing decisions. In both Chapters 6 and 7 considerable reference is made to debate about consumption sector cleavages and Saunder's contribution to this debate.

Chapter 7 begins to draw together themes from the book, It emphasizes change in home ownership and argues that the tenure is increasingly subsidized and state supported. It also discusses data on tenure and voting behaviour, and addresses views that relate to attitudes to the home and to ontological security. It

6 *Home ownership*

ends by presenting a summary of home ownership in transition by referring to three stages of transition and new policies.

Finally, Chapter 8 examines a number of key arguments about the social and political impact of rising levels of home ownership. It draws on the material presented in the previous chapters to offer an overall assessment of: the links between housing tenure categories and class divisions; the place of housing tenure in explanations of social change; and the importance of spatial and temporal differentiation within the owner occupied market. The final sections of this chapter refer to the way the organization of the tenure is continuing to change and discusses the implications of these developments for the future of home ownership.

1 Understanding home ownership

Most people are now home owners. However, the range of individual experience within home ownership is widening. As home ownership has become more significant so it has attracted more commentary and analysis. These commentaries have different starting points, and emphasise different processes, explanations and implications. This chapter introduces and summarises major perspectives and identifies key themes and issues to be explored later in this book. It provides a brief account of the different types and levels of analysis in the literature and focuses in particular on two perspectives: structures of provision and consumption sector cleavages.

Home ownership is in transition. Its history has been and will continue to be one of change. There has been a transition in housing – from a situation in which home ownership was a minority tenure to a situation where it is dominant. In contrast, private renting has moved from dominant to minority status. It is an obstacle to understanding if the imagery of home ownership becomes fixed at a point in time, failing to communicate current realities and future prospects. The tendency for this unchanging imagery derives from the media and from policy advocacy by government, but it is also a consequence of a wider failure to stress elements of change and variation.

A variety of approaches and frameworks have been applied to the analysis of home ownership. Table 1.1 provides a summary of four key perspectives. No reference is made to the ecological tradition, which focused on the patterns of residential stratification but largely ignored the processes that led to this, or blended into those approaches that emphasize choice and make no reference to the structure of the housing market. The development of the debate is simplified in Table 1.1 by presenting it as a succession of approaches growing out of each other. This is a device to highlight particular elements in different contributions. Within this progression it is also argued that elements of previous contributions are incorporated in later contributions. Some brief reference to the major headings identified in Table 1.1 provides some flavour of the debate.

Table 1.1 *Perspectives on home ownership*

Focus	Process	Implications
I Individuals	Choice and preference. Competition involving large numbers of buyers and sellers seeking to maximize housing services within an income/budget constraint (and trade-offs with travel to work and other services).	Home ownership is demand led and supply responds to need expressed through the market. Preference is the main determinant of outcomes.

But no attention is paid to the social contexts in which choice is formed, or to the structure of the housing market and especially the effects of state intervention on market processes. Consistent inequalities exist between households with the same market power. Individual search and information behaviour is not a sufficient explanation for these patterns.

Focus	Process	Implications
II Social groups	Competition for housing is based on factors other than income and achieved housing status and processes involve bureaucratic allocation systems adopting non-market criteria.	Home ownership reflects unequal power and competitive position, which cuts across market position to form separate housing classes.

But identifying social groups with the same means of access to housing or in the same housing situation/class does not identify the process or the nature of constraints involved.

Focus	Process	Implications
III Institutions	Key decisions that mediate competition for housing are exercised by a range of public and private sector institutions and gatekeepers. Who gets what in the housing market is directly explained by this. The interests and actions of the state and of private	Patterns and constraints in home ownership reflect the activities of a range of state and exchange professionals and the choices and decisions of consumers are mediated by this. Home ownership is a product of ideological and political processes.

Understanding home ownership   9

Table 1.1 *Continued*

Focus	Process	Implications
	sector agencies operating within a framework of state policy are reflected in the structure of the market.	

But identifying front-line institutions and urban gatekeepers focuses on 'middlemen' rather than underlying processes. It implies a degree of power and discretion in decisions and in forming the market that is inaccurate. Too great an emphasis is placed on the state as the orchestrator and on questions relating to the consumption of housing.

Focus	Process	Implications
IV Political economy of advanced capitalism	Price movements and the structure of the market reflect the operation of the production process in a capitalist economy with decisions about investment in land and housing based on profit taking. The role of the state in this process is not neutral in conflicts between and within classes relating to housing production.	Home ownership is supply led and its structure and growth reflect the process of commodity production under capitalism.

But the emphasis on production in a capitalist economy caricatures the 'interests' of capital and implies a (common) functional logic, which underestimates shifting and conflicting interests and fails to explain differences in home ownership in different countries.

1. Individual choice and preference

The simplest models of individual choice present households as making rational choices relating to their incomes and seeking to maximize their housing situation. This involves trade-offs, particularly relating to travel time and costs (especially travel to work). Whether individuals seek to achieve an optimal level of service relating to some particular attribute or to satisfy a wider

10
Home ownership

range of criteria, and whether they have imperfect knowledge or information, the process that determines the social distribution of housing resources is seen to be the outcome of the individual's exercise of choice and preference. The distribution reflects differences in preferred lifestyles, culturally determined behaviour and the values attached to different factors. Differences in incomes, house prices and travel costs form the basic components of individual choices and the implication is that persons with similar incomes have the same housing choices open to them between and within tenures. While some approaches seek to refer to an unspecified notion of housing service, others specify tenure and other elements and recognize that decisions about tenure, location and other attributes of housing are influenced by factors other than income. Individual choice models may specify a wider range of attributes, refer to satisfying rather than optimizing and acknowledge the importance of sub-markets relating perhaps to particular neighbourhoods. Nevertheless, they continue to indicate that preference is the main determinant of outcomes.

2. *Social groups and competition*

The essential alternative to an individual choice model is one that emphasizes constraints. All choices are constrained choices reflecting differential bargaining power and position in relation to bureaucratic allocation systems. Groups of people share common positions in means of access to housing and differences will exist among those with similar incomes or sharing the same relation to the means of production. Rather than individual choice determining where people live, in Rex and Moore's words the central process of the city as a social unit 'is a class struggle over the use of houses' (Rex and Moore, 1967, pp. 273–4). People in the same labour situation may 'have differential degrees of access to housing and it is this which immediately determines the class conflicts of the city as distinct from those of the workplace' (p. 274). The concept of housing classes rather than individuals exercising choice has been particularly relevant because it acknowledges that the housing market does not conform to an equilibrium, unified or *laissez-faire* model. The British housing market, at least since 1915, has been affected by state intervention and regulation. Market pricing does not operate across the system and the relationship between housing costs and housing service is not the same throughout the system. Consequently, competition is not based on income and price alone. Different means of access to housing involve different resources and attributes. Rex and Moore's identification of housing classes involved a variety of problems, which are fully

Understanding home ownership   11

discussed elsewhere. From the perspective of a book about home ownership it is interesting that the ranking of housing classes by Rex and Moore in 1967 differentiated between three different groups of home owners: outright owners, mortgage payers, and home owners who must take in lodgers to meet loan repayments. The last group was ranked below both council and private tenants and only above lodgers in rooms.

3. *Institutions and gatekeepers*

Identifying constraints, the importance of bureaucratic allocation systems and differential access to housing leads to a focus on the allocators, the types of constraint and the rules of access rather than on social groups in common positions in terms of access. The search for a classification of groups of households is complemented by an examination of the institutions and policies affecting the experience of these groups (see e.g. Murie *et al.*, 1976; P. Williams, 1982; Karn *et. al.*, 1985). At this point the debate is much more specific and refers to the practices of organizations and managers.

For a tenure dominated by the language of choice, a discussion of access and allocation, rules and procedures may seem inappropriate. However, access to home ownership rests heavily upon the access to and allocation of mortgage finance, property and legal services, and aid and advice. Studies of first-time buyers and movers indicate that, at least until recently, specific groups were sometimes discriminated against by lenders. Examples included single women, minority ethnic groups, the self-employed, indeed anyone who did not appear to have a conventional, white, middle-class family lifestyle and/or a stable income. Such groups could be refused mortgages or offered lower percentage advances.

A similar pattern of discrimination was apparent within lending on properties and in areas. Houses without front gardens, leasehold flats and areas of inner city terraced property were often marked out as undesirable risks and even specifically red- or blue-lined on maps in the lenders' offices. Just as access to mortgage finance could be problematic, so too, can the issue of finding and buying or selling property. Estate agents have a clear sense of who might buy any particular property or live in any specific area. Potential purchasers are both knowingly and unknowingly screened for their appropriateness and by one means or another encouraged or deterred. Such practices restrict access to some areas by some groups, and there has been evidence that minority ethnic groups in particular have suffered from it. While these practices in relation to mortgaging and estate agency have changed, especially with increased competition in recent years, they have formed a feature

12 *Home ownership*

of home ownership in the past and few would argue that they no longer obtain.

4. *Political economy*

In essence this involves a recognition that the housing market and home ownership are structured by a capitalist system in which the search for profit is paramount and in which society is structured by a class system. At its most instrumental, this approach would argue that home ownership has been promoted strongly within capitalist societies because it fosters social stability, offers a stake in the system (however illusory), is based upon individualized family units and is strongly anti-collectivist. Such arguments have often led to a strong anti home ownership stance. Home ownership is represented as encouraging social stability or as anti-collectivist or as a 'dupe' that distorts political judgements and other identities of interest. However, the evidence advanced to suggest that the growth of home ownership has independently changed political attitudes and behaviour is limited and unconvincing and the instrumental version of a political economy approach does not stand up to close scrutiny. Moreover, working-class home ownership in the nineteenth century developed in some areas as a conscious collective defensive strategy by employees in communities dominated by a single employer.

Within a political economy perspective, home ownership does not have to be seen either as having an instrumental or functionalist relationship to capitalism or as developing separately and independently of it. What is essential is a recognition that, under capitalism, housing is a commodity produced for profit. Decisions affecting what housing is produced, where, when and at what cost are based on relative profitability. In Britain and other advanced countries, state intervention plays an important part in determining these judgements -through arrangements for taxation and subsidy. In this it is also important to acknowledge that housing has an exchange value as well as a use value. Consequently, it is affected not only by changes in demand for shelter, but also by its role as an investment. However, changes in its value as a financial asset will have an impact on those seeking to gain access for use.

The focus of current debates

Coneemporary debate relating to home ownership grows out of these perspectives but few recent contributions would regard any one as satisfactory. Two contrasting perspectives are widely adopted currently:

1. *Structures of provision.* This perspective emphasizes the production of housing and its integration into the financial and economic system of capitalism. The progress of inflation, competition for funds with other sectors of the economy and rates of interest have direct repercussions on housing production and home ownership. Housing is a commodity and key decisions affecting home ownership (about production and investment) reflect opportunities for capital accumulation. A structure of housing provision relates to those social relations that are necessary for the production of housing in a form suitable for use by households. Structures form the social context in which individuals operate. They are historically and spatially specific and the outcome depends on the specific conditions that apply. They will change over time.

2. *Consumption sector cleavages.* This perspective on home ownership emphasizes the significance of social divisions relating to consumption. Such cleavages relate to public or private use of various commodities or services including transport and housing. It presents these divisions as cutting across other social divisions and involving (more) significant differences in interests, behaviour and social meanings for individuals and households. This approach particularly focuses on the growth and significance of home ownership and seeks to identify attitudes and behaviour associated exclusively with that tenure. In emphasizing behaviour associated with home ownership and the consumption of housing, processes of individual choice and demand are often presented as of crucial importance to the nature and growth of the tenure.

These two perspectives represent very different focuses and understandings. They are increasingly presented as polarized perspectives, with the former emphasizing production and capital and the latter emphasizing consumption and divisions that are divorced from class relations, economic power and supply-led processes.

Major elements of these debates are discussed more fully later in this book. In particular, issues relating to the consumption of housing and consumption sector cleavages are discussed in Chapters 4 and 6. This book is not concerned to develop perspectives relating to the production of housing. These have been fully developed in a number of key publications that have established the ways in which the housing production process rather than demand affects housing supply and house prices (e.g. Merrett, 1982; Ball, 1982,

14

Home ownership

1983, 1988; Dickens *et al.*, 1985; Ball, Harloe and Martens, 1988).
For the purposes of this book it is appropriate to refer briefly to
this literature.

Housing production and home ownership

The market for new housebuilding has been characterized by boom
and slump and the housebuilding industry has adopted a structure
commensurate with such an uncertain market. It relies heavily on
subcontracting, and it has low levels of skills and training and of
investment in plant. It is undercapitalized and often makes more
money out of land-dealing than land development for housing
or housebuilding. Because of this, the industry does not respond
quickly to changes in housing demand. As a result, changes in
demand result in price surges rather than increased supply and
these price surges become a feature of the housing market. In
other words, the market is unstable, producing great unevenness
over time and over space. The boom and slump that have been
common in the postwar period are in part a function of government
policies producing credit squeezes followed by easy credit, and
this in turn is (in part) a product of Britain's position in the
world economy. The limited supply of new building and the
domination of second-hand property in the market place mean
existing owners have a considerable impact. During price rises
they enter the market, but often hedge until prices appear to
be at their peak. When they do move, they move up-market,
paying a part of their money gain and taking out a substantially
greater mortgage. Until recently, mortgage finance would itself
act as a restriction because that would become in short supply.

Deregulation and increased competition in the housing finance
market have resulted in the expansion of the supply of finance. The
most obvious consequence of this at present is that price booms
have begun to last longer. In the late 1980s it has been high interest
rates rather than shortage of mortgage funds that have inhibited
trading up and terminated the house price explosion.

Ball's authoritative accounts (1983, 1988) of the construction
industry emphasize its role as a major industry (employing around
1 1/2 million people in the mid-1980s), which has tended to be used
as an economic regulator. The contraction of the industry since the
mid-1970s and concern over product quality, project delays, cost
overruns, employment conditions, productivity and costs represent
a dismal catalogue. However, the speculative housebuilder has been
successful in squeezing out virtually all other forms of building organization from building for home ownership. In contrast,
in other countries, pure developers or the direct intervention of

Understanding home ownership 15

financial institutions are more common. In Britain, speculative builders profit from buying land when it is cheap and developing and selling it when prices are high. As a result they tend to hold land banks, which enable them to build at the best times without having to acquire new sites at times when prices are high. They can run down their land banks until market conditions swing in their favour. The turnover of capital depends not on steady production rates but on the successful manipulation of land purchases, development programmes and building sales. This pattern of fluctuating activity is compatible with the volatility of the property market in recent years – and exacerbates it. One method of adding to land banks is through mergers and takeovers involving those companies with such land banks. The pattern of mergers and takeovers completed for this and other reasons, together with bankruptcy and voluntary withdrawal, have contributed to the increasing concentration of the industry. Product or geographic diversification are of major importance in takeovers and Ball concludes that the UK market share in new construction work, and especially in speculative housebuilding, of the largest firms has increased over the past decade or so.

Ball highlights the changing nature of the construction industry. During the late 1940s and early 1950s speculative building was severely curtailed by building controls, and public sector contracting dominated. The major contracting firms, which had reached unprecedented sizes during the war, retained their dominant role. From the early 1950s to the early 1970s the position of the large building contractors was consolidated. It was with the collapse of workloads in the early 1970s that the major restructuring of the industry occurred. Large building firms survived relatively unscathed while other sectors of the industry (especially design professionals and building workers) were adversely affected. Diversification into overseas markets and into other construction and non-construction assets was important in this. The large firms are not dependent on speculative building for their survival or profit. The consequences of this pattern of change for home ownership can be stated briefly. Speculative housebuilding (and a greater proportion of all housebuilding in view of the decline in public sector building) is dominated by a smaller number of larger builders whose housebuilding decisions relate to judgements about movements in house prices and who can switch activities (e.g. into other forms of construction). These larger companies do, however, have longer-term strategic plans and company strategies. Problems of skill shortages and more limited opportunities for profit in the repair and maintenance sector of activity both have real consequences for home ownership. The organization of construction does not, however, mean that building rates are steady or that what is built, where, and at what price, is responsive to changing needs.

The approach adopted in this book involves an acceptance of the broad structural arguments relating to the production, distribution and consumption of housing. The arguments relating to structures of provision suggest that 'any aspect of housing related to its provision cannot ignore the social agencies involved in that provision' (Ball, 1986, p. 158). Ball defines a structure of provision as 'a historically given process of providing and reproducing the physical entity, housing focusing on the social agents essential to that process and the relations between them'. Ball's argument was developed in opposition to what he saw as an overemphasis upon consumption-related questions within housing research. He recognized the validity of such questions but only if they were treated as part of the wider social relations of provision. In other words, it was the failure to attach the outcome – a specific tenure – and its problems to their underlying roots in the social relations of provision that he saw as problematic and leading to an inevitable neglect of class relations. This book will continue to refer to issues of production supply, finance and investment. However, it focuses on consumption issues. The way that production of housing is organized and financed is an essential element in understanding home ownership, but it is important also to treat consumption of housing as more than residual.

Housing consumption and home ownership

The focus of this book is presented as an alternative to one that focuses solely on production. However, it is a complementary alternative rather than a substitute. Not all of the issues that are discussed in relation to home ownership are resolved through analysis of housing production. A number of the themes that are addressed in this book – home ownership as a constantly changing system; differentiation and fragmentation within the tenure; wealth and accumulation; the relationship between the tenure structure and class structure – are crucial to understanding home ownership. Home ownership is also increasingly referred to as an element in the process of social polarization. The positions of home owners as consumers are different and in many cases advantaged compared with those who are not home owners. This socio-tenurial polarization increasingly relates to marginalization of groups within society, and reinforces social differences generated elsewhere. But this is not the whole story and needs fuller analysis. As home ownership has grown, the divergence of experience within the

Understanding home ownership 17

tenure has become more apparent. These social cleavages between and within tenures are important elements in a growing fragmentation of society in which class and occupational position do not subsume all social differences. The varied experience of housing is an important dimension of the life history of all households. These concerns are not emphasized by an approach that defines them away and leaves tenure as a residual outcome of structures of provision and does little to recognize how the process of consumption feeds back upon those structures.

In contrast to accounts that regard tenure as a residual outcome, contemporary contributions that concentrate on the consumption of housing focus on housing tenure and particularly on the political and social role of home ownership. The most plausible accounts identify a sectoral cleavage between owners and non-owners. Because it is based upon the tenure and use of housing, it is referred to as a consumption cleavage. It is argued that the cleavage reflects and reinforces other social divisions and represents a major fault line in British society (Saunders, 1984, p. 203). Questions about the material bases for such divisions are answered by reference to issues of capital gains and the investment potential of property ownership, the level of control and freedom exercised by owners (both absolutely and in relative terms to tenants), and the opportunity to pass on an inheritance to children. All of these factors are seen to give owners a personal interest and a common interest in their own dwelling and the tenure of home ownership in general. And these are interests that do not apply to those in other tenures.

There can be little doubt that all these factors are of importance in our understanding of home ownership. However, the view that particular behaviour and interests are common to all owners (and thus a source of solidarity between owners against others) is open to challenge. Part of the task in this book is to consider the extent to which these perspectives on the consumption of housing and on home ownership are accurate. It is ironic that, within a range of disciplines, there is a growing interest in housing in general and housing tenure specifically. Home ownership has attracted a great deal of attention within political science, economics and sociology at the very time when within mainstream housing studies the limitations of tenure as a concept (see also Barlow and Duncan, 1988; Ball, 1986) are being re-emphasized. These disciplines seem destined to make the same mistakes, picking up on the issues but failing to absorb the key arguments about tenure as an outcome.

The response to crude political economy arguments has been a development of both production- and consumption-based arguments. Ball's work is part of the former and the growing interest

18 *Home ownership*

in the sociology of consumption is part of the latter. The sociology of consumption has been neglected within housing. Stretton (1976) was an early exponent of the view that housing, and home ownership in particular, assisted people to develop their lives outside of the workplace. There is a growing interest in the meaning of the home. This in turn has linked into broader arguments about consumption issues in general and their neglect within mainstream social analysis. Just as discussion of meanings of the home has been overshadowed by debates about tenure, so consumption has been overshadowed by production and the world of work. Key issues about the home include its role in building and reproducing relationships between men, women and children, between neighbours, between social classes and between different racial groups. People spend a lot of time in their homes – indeed the amount of time is increasing. The home is seen as a private domain endowed with a variety of meanings and realities. For some home owners, home is not only a social and physical setting over which they may have greater control than a tenant, but also a source of wealth as the market value of the property increases. For some other home owners, perhaps because of age, income or health status, home ownership does not so much represent these positive values, but involves problems that are reflected in demands to move to rented housing.

Developing an understanding of home ownership involves a recognition and response to the perspectives outlined above. These perspectives and others focusing on individuals, social groups and institutions remain relevant. But there are other important elements. In this book emphasis is placed on increased commodification, and growing competition and penetration of market relationships in housing. Centrally, however, it is argued that an understanding of home ownership will only develop if the tendency to treat it as a static, homogeneous or unified tenure is replaced by an emphasis on change and differentiation. While it is important to re-examine issues around the consumption of housing, this examination should be set in the context of commodification and changes in the financing, production and organization of housing, and not start with a view that the consumption of housing through home ownership is demand or preference led.

2 Home ownership – facts and fictions

What sort of people are home owners? What sort of dwellings do they own? Where do they live? And to what extent do dominant images of the tenure correspond to reality? This chapter provides a general profile of home ownership and reflects upon important components of it. Home ownership conveys a complex package of messages and the message has changed over time and varies between individuals and places.

Patterns of ownership

Just over 10 million dwellings were classified as owner occupied in 1981, representing some 58 per cent of all dwellings in England. Of those, the vast majority were freehold (85 per cent). Taking Great Britain as a whole, the figure was 11.8 million, some 57 per cent of all dwellings. By the end of 1986 there were almost 14 million owner-occupied dwellings in Great Britain, 63 per cent of the total stock. The percentage figures for England, Wales and Scotland were 65, 67.5 and 42 respectively (Department of the Environment, Scottish Development Department and Welsh Office, 1987).

Strong regional variations remain in the pattern and growth of home ownership. As Table 2.1 indicates, Scotland stands out in 1986 with the majority of households in the rental tenures. Just over a decade ago, only a third of dwellings in Scotland were owner occupied. Since then the UK as a whole has experienced over a 9 per cent increase in the level of home ownership. It might have been expected that it would be in those areas with the lowest levels of owner occupation that growth rates would have been highest. However, at the regional level there has been a tendency for those areas with high home ownership rates to pull further away. Undoubtedly, the sale of council dwellings has been a significant factor in this process and in the general increase in

Home ownership

Table 2.1 *Growth in home ownership, 1976–1986 (percentage of dwellings)*

	1976	1981	1986	Increase % 1976–86
UK	54	57	63	9
North	46	49	56	10
Yorkshire and Humberside	54	57	63	9
East Midlands	57	61	68	11
East Anglia	56	60	67	11
South East	55	59	65	10
Greater London	47	50	56	9
Rest of SE	61	65	71	10
South West	62	65	70	8
West Midlands	55	59	64	9
North West	58	61	66	8
ENGLAND	56	59	65	9
WALES	59	63	68	9
SCOTLAND	34	36	42	8
NORTHERN IRELAND	51	54	61	10

Source: Central Statistical Office (1988).

home ownership levels. The available evidence shows that council house sales between 1979 and 1988 have been disproportionately high in the South East of England (excluding Great London), in the Eastern region, in the South West and in the East Midlands. They have been disproportionately low in Greater London (and especially Inner London), in the North West, in Yorkshire and Humberside in the Northern region of England, and in Scotland.

Owner-occupied dwellings vary considerably and include a wide range of sizes, types and conditions. In 1985 just under a third of all outright owners lived in dwellings built before 1919, compared with 22 per cent for owners with a mortgage. There is a larger proportion of detached houses and a smaller proportion of flats and maisonettes than in the council housing or other rental sectors. Whereas over a third of council tenants occupy flats or maisonettes this is true of only 6 per cent of owners. The dominant image and experience of owner occupation is of detached or semi-detached living. However, the proportion of terraced houses has increased

Facts and fictions

over the last decade as a consequence of transfers from the privately rented and council sectors and new building at the lower end of the market. For 44 per cent of first-time buyers in 1988, the initial purchase was of a terraced dwelling. In contrast, for those involved in a second or subsequent purchase, 26 per cent purchased a detached dwelling and only 25 per cent a terraced house (Building Societies Association, 1988). This pattern relates to stage in the family life cycle and corresponds with the image of a progression from small terrace to spacious detached over the home owner's housing history. To what extent this is an accurate representation of the housing route for the majority of owners we shall explore in later chapters. Unlike most household purchases (the closest parallel being cars), it is far more likely that the dwelling will be second-hand rather than new. The general longevity of dwellings, the cost of production and purchase and the relatively small number of new additions that occur annually have meant that as home ownership has expanded it has inevitably encompassed more and more older second-hand dwellings and dwellings with substantial maintenance and repair problems. Taking the UK as a whole, almost 19 per cent of dwellings mortgaged in 1976 were newly built. By 1986 the comparable figure had fallen to 10 per cent (DOE, SDD, WO, 1987).

How much did people pay to become home owners in 1988? The majority of first-buyers obtaining building society mortgages paid less than £30,000. Some 28 per cent paid £40,000 or more. Previous owners moving to buy a different house in 1988 bought further up-market: 60 per cent paid in excess of £40,000. These average figures obscure a very wide regional variation. In 1988, average regional house prices ranged from £69,000 in Greater London to less than £30,000 in Scotland, Wales and northern England (BSA, 1988). These averages conceal massive variations in the prices of dwellings and their quality within regions. A Victorian terraced house in the North West can change hands for as little as £6,000. By the way of contrast, in London a converted ex-Metropolitan Police flat described as having 'an inner sanctum of privacy and high security' as well as a gymnasium, sauna and whirlpool spa (quoted from a Regalian brochure) sold for upwards of £170,000.

It is important to note that the majority of home owners own their property but have an outstanding debt associated with it. In order to raise the finance to buy it, they have mortgaged their property. Only 39 per cent of home owners in 1985 were outright owners, the remainder owing sums of money, sometimes substantial, to a building society, local authority or other financial institution. This is an important distinction within owner occupation, particularly in relation to the perceived political consequences of interest rate increases or changes in the structure of tax relief on mortgage interest. Increases in the cost of borrowing for house purchase affect a substantially smaller proportion than the crude figures on tenure patterns suggest and affect some owners more than others. Outright owners may benefit from more expensive borrowing, which translates into a higher rate of return on their building society savings. It is worth pointing out that, whilst the proportion of total households who are outright owners has remained relatively stable over the last decade, mortgaged home ownership has continued to expand – particularly in the last five years (see Figure 2.1). This is a general consequence of the expansion of the tenure as it takes in more and younger households.

The dominant image of home ownership remains that of a nuclear family living in a semi-detached dwelling in relatively affluent suburbia. Housebuilders and building society advertisements contrive to present such a picture to the potential buyer. More than 1 million families are buying their own homes 'with a little Xtra help from the Halifax!' The symbol for the Peterborough Homebuyers' Centre is of two children (one of each sex) hand in hand with their parents. Phrases such as 'designs for comfortable

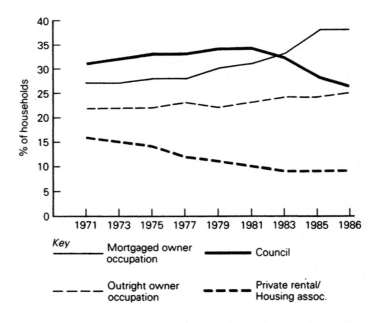

Figure 2.1 Tenure change, 1971–86.
Source: OPCS (1989)

Facts and fictions

family living' or 'houses for happy and contented families' are almost inevitable in advertisements for new housing estates. Home owners either have a family (preferably two children with the requisite balance of the sexes) or they are about to start one, or they used to have one but they've now grown up and left home. An advertisement for Laing Homes offers the description of themselves as 'family builders for over 140 years' (all quotations from *What Mortgage* and *Home Finder*). And those families, nascent or mature, tend to live in leafy suburbs. Whilst the market for the gentrified or newly constructed town house has expanded, it still remains a marginal demand – typically associated with middle-class professionals with few or no children, a sort of up-market Bohemianism, an attempt to retain the street credibility of student days and be among 'real' people rather than in the sanitized suburbs. But in the main the owner-occupied product is marketed much as it was in the interwar boom: the clean healthy family life in a stable, semi-rural environment (see, for instance, Jackson, 1973, for an account of the promotion of home ownership in London in the 1930s). This image is well conveyed in a consumer journal's advice on selling your home. In its 'useful 10-point drill' it suggests.

> Keep the garden in good order. A couple of hours spent tidying it is time well spent. See that the hinges are well oiled on the garden gate, the grass is mown, the flower beds weeded, the path swept, the dustbin tucked away, toys and bikes put away too. (*What Mortgage*, August 1988)

Elsewhere there are references to 'sunny passageways', 'family pets' and 'a fire in the grate'. It is cosy, safe, suburban affluence.

This dominant image of family home ownership is increasingly at odds with contemporary demands. The housebuilding and housing finance industries are aware of this. The conventional family market offers only limited scope for the further expansion of home ownership. Divorce and remarriage, later marriage and the expansion of the elderly population are making new demands on the home ownership product, particularly given the contraction of alternative rental opportunities. This is evident in increasing market segmentation, with specialist builders constructing dwellings aimed at the young singles market and elderly persons. It is also reflected in more flexible lending criteria by many building societies faced with demands for mortgage finance from less conventional households. Multiple, as opposed to joint mortgages, are now possible, albeit that they no longer qualify for multiple tax relief. The building societies too have had to move with the times and informally if not formally relax their constraints on owners taking in paying tenants. For single owner occupiers in high house price areas this has often been a necessary strategy for coping with mortgage repayments. Also many people simply do not like living alone. Available statistics do not provide reliable evidence on this form of household. The home owner with a tenant will typically appear in official statistics as a single household. However, there is enough evidence to warrant the suggestion that certain sub-sectors of home ownership are making a contribution to the survival of residential landlordism. In high house price areas some rental income may be a critical factor in affordability calculations. As a result, it is likely that in a number of cases a private tenant and the home owner form one household. Such a household does not conform to the stereotype of the elderly resident landlord and the young tenant – it may well be a household with two or more unrelated individuals of similar ages and in very similar socioeconomic circumstances. The point is that we assume that households and dwellings have unambiguous tenure status. Undoubtedly, the vast majority of home owners *are* unambiguously separate households but, on occasion, tenancy and home ownership coexist in the same dwelling.

People in the UK enter home ownership at an early stage in the family life cycle. It is much more typical in Western Europe for people to become home owners in their early to late thirties, when they are more geographically established and financially secure. The reasons for this difference are primarily connected with subsidy structures, which in other countries are geared to new rather than second-hand dwellings, and with the greater availability of high percentage of value loans in the UK. Typically, in most of Western Europe loan finance has been more expensive in real terms, has had to come from more than one source and a large deposit has been required. A much more protracted period of saving has therefore been necessary for a household to enter the owner-occupied sector. This situation is changing as many governments favour higher rates of home ownership and as financial deregulation proceeds. Nevertheless the idea of 95 per cent or a 100 per cent mortgage would be alien to many borrowers and lenders elsewhere (for a fuller discussion, see, for example, Ball, Harloe and Martens, 1988; Boleat, 1985). The relative ease of access to mortgage credit in the UK, combined with the increasing lack of rental alternatives, is reflected in the fact that almost a third of first-time buyers are aged under 25 (BSA, 1988). By contrast, the comparable figure for the Netherlands is 16 per cent (1981/2), for West Germany 4 per cent (1982) and France 7 per cent (1982) (BSA, 1985b).

The average age of first-time buyers in the UK has been relatively stable for at least a decade – fluctuating at around 30. Indeed, the

Facts and fictions 25

early 1980s saw a slight age increase with the impact of council house sales, which generally brought a middle-aged group into home ownership.

Table 2.2 summarizes the varied household types among freehold home owners. Single males or females of pensionable age represent 10 per cent of owners, and more than 16 per cent of households contain only one adult. Just over half of freehold home owners are married couples. Home ownership spans the whole family life cycle. As home owners age, we can expect the numbers of older people in the tenure to grow. Whether groups at the start of their

Table 2.2 *Freehold home owners: household type, 1981*

	Number
Total adults	8,776,557
Single adults	%
One male aged 65 or over with no children	2
One female aged 60 or over with no children	8
One adult under pensionable age with no children	5
One adult with one child	★
One adult with two or more children	1
Married couples	
Both under pensionable age with no children	15
One or both of pensionable age with no children	13
With one child	8
With two children	13
With three or more children	4
Two other adults	
Both under pensionable age with no children	2
One or both of pensionable age with no children	3
With one or more child(ren)	1
Married couple with one or more other adults	
With no children	14
With one or two children	8
With three or more children	1
Three or more other adults	
With no children	2
With one or more children	★

★ Less than a half per cent

Source: OPCS (1983b)

26 *Home ownership*

housing history become more represented among home owners depends on a range of factors.

Home ownership is expanding at a time of significant demographic change, with a substantial projected growth in very old (75+) persons and with processes of divorce and remarriage creating peculiar hiccoughs in the conventional family life cycle. These processes are by no means limited to the British context and are recognized in market strategies that identify distinct sub-groups with distinct lifestyles (see, for example, Murphy and Stopes, 1979). Terms such as 'mingles' have been applied to non-related adults sharing in the Australian context, and the 'empty nester' household occupying an oversized dwelling has been seen as a lucrative market by the housebuilding industry in the United States.

> Empty nesters are emerging as the builder's most constant buyers. They are ideal prospects because they are ready to leave large homes rich in equity, for luxurious attached quarters. (Quoted from the *Professional Builder* in Miron and Schiff, 1982)

And a consultants' report on the British house building industry noted that:

> The three main areas of growth look to be young singles of both sexes, single parent females in their thirties and women of post retirement age living on their own. (Laing and Cruickshank, 1982, p. 13)

So part of the shape of things to come is the expansion of new building and conversion geared to the young singles market, itself segregated into sub-markets according to level of affluence. At the other end of the life cycle, marketing strategies are designed to encourage movement of elderly owners into accommodation designed to suit their current and future circumstances. Whilst this may involve a move to a smaller dwelling, such specialized accommodation may also include a range of services and equipment specifically geared to the needs of elderly people and those with physical mobility problems. Payment for these services may absorb substantial amounts of the equity released by sale of the previous property and seriously disrupt assumptions about patterns of inheritance. 'Woopies' (well-off older people) are fast replacing Yuppies (young, upwardly mobile people) as a prime target group for marketing strategies.

But these are new forms of differentiation within home ownership. There are a range of existing variations within the tenure. For example, around 1.5 million owners (around 10 per cent of owners) own their dwelling but do not own the land on which it is situated. This leasehold tenure poses particular problems, and is concentrated in particular areas, e.g. South Wales. As leases approach expiry, confidence in an area often diminishes and households and agencies become unwilling to invest in the fabric of the property. The Leasehold Reform Act of 1967 gave households with more than five years' residence the right to buy the lease if it was below a specified rateable value limit, but this really only addressed areas where long-term leasing had been common. It did not resolve the problem of households on short leases at the margins of ownership.

In parts of Britain, particularly in the north of England, rental purchase schemes have been marketed as a way for low income households to purchase their own homes. Rental purchase agreements typically involve the payment of high interest loans over a ten year period. Only when the loan has been fully paid does the property come into the legal possession of the occupant. Whilst the numbers involved are not huge, such schemes illustrate the blurring of the distinction between ownership and tenancy.

In 1981, 42,208 households were living in caravans. Of these 69 per cent were home owners. A further 80,000 households were home owners in non-permanent accommodation. This includes towable caravans, converted railway carriages and houseboats. There are also a substantial number of home owners in non-self-contained accommodation (OPCS, 1983a). Moreover, there are still almost 100,000 home owners in properties without an inside bath and WC. The 1986 Welsh House Condition Survey revealed some 32,000 unfit owner-occupied dwellings within the Principality requiring repairs expenditure of £818 million (Welsh Office, 1988). Of those found to be unfit, 33 per cent lacked one or more basic amenities.

There is a further issue of home owners living in properties with other defects. For example, a group of former council houses including Cornish Units, Woolaways and Airey houses became unmortgageable and therefore a liability to their owners. To respond to this, government developed policies to provide aid to anyone who had purchased such a house before 1984. Other owners may be less fortunate. A range of dwellings built especially by the private sector in the inter-war period are vulnerable to 'concrete cancer'. The extent of this is difficult to ascertain and is only revealed as dwellings are surveyed when they are put up for sale. At the extremes the dwelling itself, as opposed to the site, may have little or no value. Consequently (and as an example), owners of dwellings built in the 1930s from Mundic block (concrete blocks made from mining waste) may find themselves in a very different

28 *Home ownership*

set of circumstances from the majority of owners. Moreover, these problems are not confined to older dwellings as evidenced by recent concern over modern timber frame constructions.

It would be a mistake to exaggerate the numerical importance of these elements in home ownership. Nevertheless, they serve to illustrate some of the extremes contained within such an all-encompassing category as home ownership, and the dangers of treating it as homogeneous. Such differentiation is evident in any major British city. Commuter villages with their gentrified artisans' cottages and carefully sculptured rustic gardens exist beyond the large detached houses of the upwardly mobile with their double garages and array of cars. Further in towards the city centre, high-rise council housing dwarfs the down-market home ownership terraces, and in the inner area are pockets of up-market gentrification – rows of sandblasted Georgian town houses with BMWs cluttering the narrow roads. Such a picture is particularly evident in London where comparisons between the 1971 and 1981 Census indicate the rapid growth of the inner urban middle class and the first increase in the population of inner London for 25 years (CES, 1987; Champion and Congdon, 1988).

The everyday experience of the residential environment and of home ownership is of a hierarchy of locations, dwelling types and conditions. Yet home ownership is often presented as a mode of consumption that confers a set of universal benefits, and in which upward mobility is smooth, unproblematic and inevitable. The notion of a 'starter' home, for example, contains an implicit assumption of an inevitable movement up the rungs of the home ownership ladder. But this is by no means assured, nor can we assume that all home owners have the same set of aspirations. Everyday experience suggests that different groups are on very different ladders, or at least if there is one ladder it is almost infinitely extendable.

Typically, it is the evidence of rising numbers of households experiencing mortgage repayment problems that is referred to in discussions of differentiation within home ownership. There is no disputing the fact that arrears and repossessions have risen substantially over the last few years and that statistics on this under-represent the numbers of home owners who are struggling in various ways to maintain their mortgage commitments. Households experiencing such problems may trade down or move to resolve the problem or may cut back on other expenditure or neglect the repair and maintenance of the dwelling. In 1979, fewer than 9,000 outstanding loans were 6–12 months in arrears and fewer than 3,000 properties were taken into possession by building societies. As Table 2.3 indicates, in the period 1982–1988 arrears cases of up

Facts and fictions

Table 2.3 *Building societies: repossession and mortgage arrears: UK, 1982–1988*

	Total no. of loans at the end of period '000	Loans in arrears by 6–12 months at end of period '000	Properties taken into possession during period '000
1979	5,264	8.4	2.5
1980	5,396	13.5	3.0
1981	5,505	18.7	4.2
1982	5,664	23.8	6.0
1983	5,949	25.6	7.3
1984	6,354	41.9	10.9
1985	6,705	49.6	16.8
1986	7,071	45.3	20.9
1987	7,197	48.2	22.9
1988	7,475	37.4	16.2

Source: Council of Mortgage Lenders (1989)

to 12 months' duration and actual repossessions showed a general upward movement. The fall in 1988 reflected the initial decline in interest rates in that period. By 1990 rising interest rates were being reflected in rising mortgage arrears. They had not led to a growth in repossessions by building societies. Changes in pratice relating to the management of mortgage debt in a stagnant housing market may be an important factor in this. This may include increasing the size or term of the loan rather than taking legal action.

The Building Societies Association, and others, quite justifiably point out that even 50,000 arrears cases represent a tiny fraction of all home owners. They also refer to earlier criticism levelled at lending institutions for operating overly conservative lending criteria, which effectively excluded particular social groups and properties from entry to home ownership. While arrears cases are not exclusively made up of those on the margins of home ownership, it is evident that they are the major group (not least because others can trade down to avoid the situation). All this is fair comment but should not disguise the dismay and despair experienced by many households who experience these problems, especially at a time when the alternatives of public or private renting are severely restricted. It also underlines the fact that getting on the ladder does not guarantee an upward trajectory or even a secure foot on the initial rung. The coincidence of rising home ownership and rising unemployment in the early to mid–eighties

30   *Home ownership*

was bound to produce a rising casualty list, just as in the last part of the decade high interest rates and rising inflation brought additional pressures. Whilst it is true that unemployed heads of households are overwhelmingly concentrated in the rental sectors (63 per cent), and especially in council housing (52 per cent of these), in 1986 a third of all unemployed heads of household were in home ownership. A fifth were home owners with a mortgage (Department of Employment, 1986).

Discussion of statistics on mortgage arrears has included reference to arrears of less than six months' duration. It is argued that many lending institutions may take action for possession following arrears of less than six months. In addition, arrears among agencies other than building societies may be higher. Data on these and related issues are sketchy (Doling and Stafford, 1989). Those in arrears are more likely to be lower income borrowers in junior, non-manual, skilled or semi-skilled jobs, and first-time buyers with higher than average percentage loans. However, age and social class seem likely to vary according to local circumstances. Doling and Stafford conclude that:

> the incidence of arrears, together with the large proportionate increase in their incidence over the period since 1979, is such that the failure cannot be thought of as a minor or residual one – short and long term failure to meet entry costs has become a widespread feature of home ownership. At any one time perhaps 5% of borrowers are in arrears, with a higher percentage having been in arrears at some time since purchase. (p. 81)

They emphasize the importance of unemployment and related phenomena such as loss of overtime earnings, and refer to marital and relationship breakup. But they conclude:

> much of the evidence indicates a more general factor in the extension of home ownership to groups of the population who are marginal to the tenure. Arrears are particularly prevalent amongst young, first time buyers who have borrowed to the limit in order to get a foot on the ladder. To this extent arrears are the consequence of, or the price to be paid for, extending the tenure to marginal groups and perhaps indicate a limit of the size of the tenure under existing circumstances. (p. 81)

Doling and Stafford also argue:

> there are implications for security of tenure. Clearly not all those who go into arrears subsequently lose their homes or indeed are

Facts and fictions 31

in any real danger of doing so. Equally clearly, getting a foot on the home ownership ladder is no guarantee of not slipping off again. Many people are evicted as a consequence of court action. Many, also, lose their homes as a 'voluntary' response to meeting present or impending financial difficulties. The point therefore is that just as arrears have become a feature of home ownership in Britain in the 1980s, then so has insecurity of tenure. This can no longer be thought of as the exclusive preserve of the tenant. (pp. 81–2)

It should not be assumed however that outright home ownership is for the majority a relatively unproblematic state reached after a lifetime of mortgage payments. Sullivan and Murphy (1987) have shown that there are a substantial number of young, outright owners. Whilst for some this has been achieved through receiving an inheritance from parents or other relatives, for many it would appear to have been a strategy for coping with a lack of rental alternatives or difficulty in raising mortgage finance. One of the conclusions drawn by Sullivan and Murphy is that:

> younger outright owner occupiers are, with the exception of some rather specialised groups – that is, professionals, large employers and farmers – relatively disadvantaged when compared to mortgagors with respect to a number of indicators such as quality of dwelling, crowding, social class and employment status. It is also evident that outright owners and mortgagors are differentiated with respect to spatial distribution and ethnicity, with outright owners displaying both a greater concentration of Asian and other ethnic minorities, and a greater propensity to be located in 'peripheral' areas of the country. (p. 187)

The purchase of a low-price, low-quality dwelling as a coping strategy is a more viable option in areas where housing markets are depressed. Aspirations to early outright ownership also appear to be linked to generation and class differences regarding attitudes to indebtedness. The rational, economic executive may strive to maintain a high level of indebtedness to maximize tax benefits. Many working-class home owners, however, will aspire to paying off the mortgage at the earliest possible opportunity so that their home is secure if they experience a drop in earnings, redundancy or unemployment. A recent survey on the Right to Buy discovered that some potential buyers saw mortgage payments as equalling indebtedness. The report comments that 'buying with a mortgage was thus alien to those who had always believed in immediate payment for purchases' (Kerr, 1988, p. 34).

32   *Home ownership*

Aspects of the social structure of home ownership

Without overburdening this chapter with statistics, it is appropriate to elaborate briefly on some of the issues raised earlier regarding the characteristics of owners. Table 2.4 provides a profile of mortgaged and outright owners on selected indicators. There are the obvious and predictable contrasts between outright and mortgaged owners. In general, these stem from age and life cycle differences. Some 63 per cent of outright owners were economically inactive in 1986 and 55 per cent of them were aged 65 or over. By contrast, only 6 per cent of mortgaged owners were economically inactive and two-thirds were aged below 45. Age differences are also reflected in length of residence. More than two-thirds of outright owners had been living in their current dwelling for more than 10 years – 22 per cent for over 30 years. Owners with a mortgage generally had been in their dwelling for less than 10 years – 31 per cent for less than three years. Levels of car ownership also indicate the relative affluence of home owners with a mortgage and the lower incomes and greater age of outright owners. Almost a third of mortgaged owners had two or more cars, compared with 18 per cent of the population as a whole.

The overwhelming majority of mortgaged owners are reasonably expected to become outright owners. However, it would be an oversimplification to see current differences simply in terms of the life cycle stage. As cohorts of home owners progress into old age, the profile of outright owners will reflect different periods in the growth of home ownership and broader changes in the social and economic structure. Most obviously, a higher proportion of elderly people will be home owners in 1995 than in earlier years. Current statistics show that among older persons the likelihood of being a home owner declines with age. The proportion of heads of households who are home owners is 61 per cent among those aged 60–64, 55 per cent for those aged 65–69, 51 per cent for those aged 70–79, and 47 per cent for those aged 80 and over (OPCS, 1987). A more elderly population combined with rising home ownership rates will inevitably result in more elderly owners, with implications for patterns of wealth, inheritance, mobility and repairs and maintenance of dwellings. Currently many lower-income outright owners occupying older properties may have bought their dwellings as sitting tenants from private landlords during the 1950s and 1960s. Subsequent groups will include large numbers of former council tenants who bought their dwellings from local authorities in the 1980s.

Comparisons over a relatively short timescale (1977–1986) reveal the ageing of the home ownership sector. This is most clearly seen

Table 2.4 *Profiles of home ownership in 1977 and 1986: Great Britain (heads of household)*

	Outright Owners		Mortgaged Owners		All households	
	1977 %	1986 %	1977 %	1986 %	1977 %	1986 %
Age:						
Under 25	0	0	4	4	4	5
25–29	1	1	15	13	8	8
30–44	8	7	48	50	25	28
45–64	40	38	31	31	35	31
65–74	32	32	2	2	17	16
75 and over	19	23	0	0	10	12
Education:						
Degree or equivalent	8	7	13	15	7	10
Below degree, higher educ.	10	9	23	15	14	10
GCE 'A' level or equiv.		5		12		8
Other	25	33	31	33	26	31
None	57	46	33	25	53	40
Socio-economic group:						
Professional	13	3	33	10	15	5
Employers/managers	10	8	22	25		13
Intermed. non-manual		4		12	14	7
Junior non-manual		3		8		5
Skilled manual	15	14	32	31	26	22
Semi-skilled	7	4	8	8	11	8
Unskilled	2	1	1	1	3	2
Economically inactive heads:	53	63	4	6	32	37
Length of residence (years):						
Under 1	3	4	9	12	8	10
1, under 3	6	6	20	19	14	14
3, under 5	6	6	14	16	11	12
5–10	21	15	32	28	26	22
11–20	26	24	19	20	21	21
21–30	16	23	4	5	10	11
Over 30	23	22	1	1	10	10
Car ownership:						
None	43	36	14	11	44	37
One	44	48	62	56	44	44
Two	10	17	21	32	11	18
Three or more	2		2		1	

Note: GHS underestimates one year movers prior to 1983

Source: OPCS (1979, 1989).

in the rise by 10 per cent of economically inactive heads of households who own outright and the 4 per cent increase in home owners aged 75 and over. Other changes parallel more general shifts in the socio-economic make-up of the population. Home owners with a mortgage are, however, more affluent, better educated and more mobile than the population as a whole. In part because of their disadvantaged position in the labour market, women also tend to be disadvantaged in access to home ownership. Thus, while 41 per cent of divorced or separated males were mortgaged owners, only 27 per cent of divorced or separated women were in this category. By contrast, 48 per cent of divorced women were in local authority housing but only 28 per cent of divorced men (this also partly reflects rehousing priorities). In general terms, women, whatever their marital status, are more likely to rent than own, whereas men are more likely to own (OPCS, 1989).

Table 2.5 and Figure 2.2 provide a more detailed picture of the income and occupational profile of home owners. As home ownership has grown in the postwar period those in middle-class, professional and white-collar jobs have been overwhelmingly drawn into the owner-occupied sector. Those in lower-paid and lower-skilled manual occupations and in the lower-paid parts of the service sector remain heavily reliant on the rental tenures. Whilst 75 per cent of people in professional/managerial occupations are mortgaged home owners, this is true of only 29 per cent of agricultural workers and 45 per cent of those in the personal service sector. The varied characteristics of outright home owners are clearly seen, with those in lower-paid occupations as likely to own their homes outright as the better paid. The housing histories of this group are, however, likely to be extremely diverse. Outright ownership for those in professional employment is likely to be of a high-status, detached dwelling achieved after a protracted, mobile history of highly geared mortgage indebtedness. In contrast, the outright owning agricultural worker is more likely to have bought a low-value, low-quality cottage from her or his employer. Interpretations of Table 2.5 are complicated by the interactions of tenure change, life cycle change and broader shifts in the occupational structure. For example, those sectors that have expanded most rapidly in recent decades might have younger occupational structures and thus be under-represented in outright home ownership. Nevertheless, there is no consistent relationship between levels of mortgaged home ownership and levels of outright home ownership in the different occupational groupings.

The consistent relationship between income levels and home ownership is shown in Figure 2.2. Taking all owners (i.e. mortgaged and outright), the higher the income level, the higher the

Table 2.5 *Occupational group of home owners and council tenants, 1986: Great Britain (percentages of persons in employment)*

Occupational group	Outright Owners	Mortgaged Owners	Council Tenants
Professional – managerial/admin.	15	75	3
Professional – education/health	15	69	6
Professional – science/engineering	17	71	5
Literary/arts – sport	19	61	5
Managerial	22	59	6
Clerical	18	62	13
Selling	17	60	16
Security	8	55	14
Personal services	14	45	30
Agricultural	19	29	24
Processing – excluding metal/electrics	15	52	26
Processing – metal/electrics	15	59	20
Repetitive assembly work	15	49	31
Construction/mining	15	51	27
Transport/storage	14	48	32
Miscellaneous	15	34	43
Inadequately described	17	46	31

Note: (All percentages across)

Source: OPCS (1987).

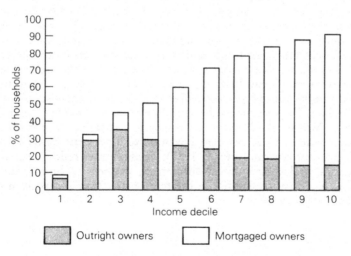

Figure 2.2 Home owners: proportion in each income decile.
Source: Department of Employment (1986)

level of home ownership. Fewer than 10 per cent of households in the lowest income decile are in home ownership, whereas this is true for more than 90 per cent of households in the highest decile. Three particular points are worth noting. First, there is a relatively rapid rise in the level of home ownership between the lowest and second lowest deciles. This could be interpreted as an indication that it is at this point in the income structure that households are excluded from the social consumption norms of the majority. Secondly, the relation between mortgaged and outright ownership changes markedly. In the lower deciles, greater numbers of households own outright (7 per cent as opposed to 2 per cent). The pattern is reversed in the higher deciles. Almost 92 per cent of households in the highest decile are home owners, of which 77 per cent have a mortgage. Thirdly, and related to the last point, the relationship between the level of outright ownership and income does not vary directly as it does with mortgaged home ownership. A higher proportion of households in the lower deciles (excluding the lowest) own outright. This relates to issues raised earlier. The vast majority of outright owners are in or nearing retirement, hence they are at a stage where their income will in most cases be markedly reduced. However, not all outright owners in the lower income deciles are at similar stages in the family life cycle or have experienced a 'successful' history of mortgaged ownership.

There are other aspects to this pattern. For example, the black population has overall a younger age structure than the white population. Single-parent families are less likely to be in home ownership and, for example, West Indian single-parent families are concentrated overwhelmingly in council housing (Brown, 1984). The more general pattern is of substantial tenure variation between the different ethnic groups. Whilst average figures for the period 1983–85 indicate that 57 per cent of white heads of household are home owners (Great Britain), comparable figures for minority ethnic groups are 39 per cent West Indian or Guyanese, 77 per cent Indian, 74 per cent Pakistani, 35 per cent Bangladeshi and 26 per cent African. And figures for outright ownership vary from 25 per cent white and 29 per cent Pakistani to 8 per cent Bangladeshi and 5 per cent African (OPCS, 1987). These figures reflect a variety of factors, including cultural differences, patterns of immigration and broader historical shifts in the tenure structure and pattern of housing opportunities.

Prices, mortgages and tax relief

The increased importance of home ownership has, particularly in recent years, coincided with a regionally differentiated pattern of house price inflation. Figures from the Building Societies Association/Department of the Environment 5 per cent sample survey of building society mortgage completions show that prices rose by 16 per cent in 1987. Regionally, however, this rate varied from 24 per cent and 23 per cent in Greater London and East Anglia respectively to 5 per cent in Wales and Northern Ireland and 3 per cent in Northern England. Whilst house price inflation is spreading out from the South east towards the two Midland regions, price inflation in the Northern, North West, Yorkshire and Humberside regions and in Scotland and Northern Ireland has remained stable or has fallen over the last year. Comparing the third quarter 1987 figures with the comparable figures for 1988 does indicate a further spreading of the 'ripple effect' of house price inflation from Greater London with higher rates of inflation being recorded in the Northern region (Building Societies Association, 1989). Nevertheless, absolute price differences remained substantial, with average house prices in the Greater London area being 2.5 times those in Northern England. We may well go through a period when rates of house price inflation are highest in the Northern region. At the end of the day, however, it may be that absolute price differentials will be greater than ever.

In the past, the pattern of house price inflation has tended to even out over time, with the north catching up (at least in percentage terms) as price inflation in the south slows. There are, however, some suggestions that the latest phase of regionally uneven house price inflation may be more deeply entrenched and longer term. It may be that special regional factors are at work that were less prominent in previous periods. The relative affluence of the South East appears to have increased and the centre of economic gravity may have moved further south. Financial deregulation has enhanced the importance of London in the world economy. The construction of the M25 and the electrification of the rail network has increased commutable distances around London. And there is general agreement that the Channel Tunnel will strengthen the southward pull and may already be affecting investment decisions (Ormerod quoted in Cowling, 1987). The intense pressure on the Green Belt and other planning restrictions in the southern part of the country reflects burgeoning effective consumer demand amidst severe supply constraints – thus adding to pressure on house prices. A striking feature of the changed spatial division of labour is an increased concentration of the managerial and professional classes and others in the fastest-growing sectors of the economy (e.g. electronics, private service sector) in the South East, South West and in East Anglia (see, for example, Massey, 1984). There is every sign that regional pay differentials may become more marked and widespread, thus accentuating differential effective demand. And the present regional pattern of levels of home ownership, its demography and relative value will be reflected in a geography of wealth accumulation and inheritance with striking north–south dimensions (see Forrest and Murie, 1989b, and Chapter 6 below). This is evident in regional variations in the market value of the housing stock. In 1986 it was estimated to be £697.5 billion for the UK as a whole. The South East, the South West and East Anglia, however, accounted for 60 per cent of the total value and 42 per cent of the total stock (Central Statistical Office, 1988).

The regional pattern of house price inflation has been broadly consistent over time. In absolute terms, house prices in the South East have been higher than elsewhere. They have pulled away fast in periods of growth to be followed by the other regions. As Figure 2.3 indicates, in recent years house price increases have shown a similar pattern across regions. One interesting feature of Figure 2.3 is that, contrary to popular belief, in real terms house prices only just returned to their 1973/4 levels in 1987. The graph also shows East Anglia beginning to pull away from the West Midlands by 1984. (see also Figure 5.1)

Three other features of house price differentials are of interest. First, the value of mortgage interest tax relief (MITR) has a regionally uneven pattern. The introduction of MIRAS in April 1983 has meant (according to the government) that regional information on the cost of MITR cannot any longer be extracted from Inland Revenue Records. In 1982/3, however, London accounted for 12 per cent of the cost of MITR, but reported just over 10 per cent of all mortgagors. Data from the *Family Expenditure Survey* for 1983–85 indicated that 14.5 per cent of MITR is attributable to London, which now contains 10.6 per cent of mortgagors (*Hansard*, 10 June 1988).

Secondly, house price levels in the south and particularly in London have meant that a significant number of borrowers and especially new borrowers have mortgages in excess of the £30,000 that qualified for mortgage interest tax relief. In Table 2.6 the figures for the regional pattern of deposits and advances underline the reasons for the disproportionate concentration of the cost of MITR in the south. In that part of the country a substantial number of mortgagors benefit from the full MITR allowance. In 1986 in Greater London, 65 per cent of all borrowers had mortgages that exceeded £30,000. This contrasts with less than 10 per cent in

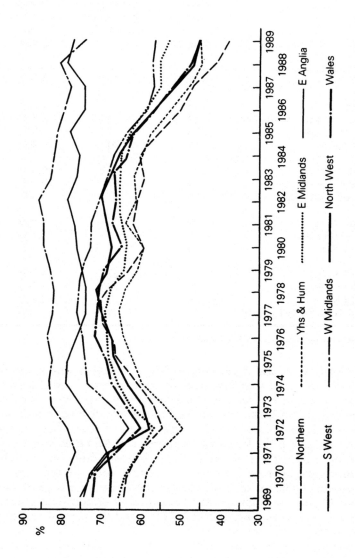

Figure 2.3 Annual average house prices for the UK by country and region 1969-89

40 Home ownership

Table 2.6 *Building societies: mortgage advances and deposits, 1986*

	All borrowers		
	Average percentage of price advanced	*Percentage of advances over £30,000*	*Average deposits of first-time buyers*
	%	%	£
UK	70	25	3,800
North	76	5	1,500
Yorkshire and Humberside	74	6	2,300
East Midlands	73	9	2,500
East Anglia	69	20	4,400
South East	67	52	6,400
Greater London	69	65	8,200
Rest of South East	66	47	5,300
South West	67	22	4,000
West Midlands	73	11	2,300
North West	73	9	2,500
ENGLAND	69	27	4,100
SCOTLAND	80	13	1,800
WALES	75	8	2,500
NORTHERN IRELAND	77	9	3,200

Source: Central Statistical Office (1988).

the North West and 8 per cent in Wales. Problems of access for low-income (or at least low 'wealth') borrowers is also shown by the relative sizes of deposits. Whereas average deposits in Scotland were less than £2,000, the average in the South East was £6,400 and in Greater London £8,200. One general feature that emerges from this table is the lessening importance of MITR as house price inflation erodes the real value of the £30,000 limit on tax relief on mortgage interest. This fact, combined with the reduction in the standard rate of tax and the abandonment of marginal rates above 40 per cent, indicates the likelihood of diminishing political resistance to the phasing out of MITR – and the present reality of its erosion by indirect means.

Finally, there is a tendency to talk of house prices as if all properties in an area are affected in the same way. A recent analysis by Nationwide Anglia (1989) reveals, however, that over the last twenty years prices have risen fastest at the upper end of the market. Between 1968 and 1988 the price of a terraced house rose 12.8 times.

Detached houses, however, rose in price by a multiple of 14.9. In other words, there is some evidence of a divergence between those at the top end of the market and those at the bottom. This is also compatible with a view of increasing social congestion at the top of the price pyramid with greater competition for dwellings with positional status (Hirsch 1977).

The preference for home ownership

Behind the general drive to extend home ownership are implicit and explicit assumptions regarding household preferences and aspirations. There is a popular view that the rise in home ownership over the last 50 years is at root an expression of an innate preference to own. Within this framework, it is argued that for some groups on low incomes and/or in particular positions in the family life cycle 'natural' desires for ownership are frustrated through price and deposit barriers to entry. But what is it that people seem to want in terms of housing? Does the desire for home ownership itself override everything else?

Two issues are of particular relevance to discussion of the demand for home ownership. First, there has been a shift in emphasis in the postwar period in Britain from a concern with housing shortage to a view that there is now a balance between the number of dwellings and households. In the 1970s, increasing reference was made to an emerging household surplus.

> There is no longer an overall housing shortage in Britain. As we are continually building more and more houses the gap between the number of households and the number of houses is increasing. The evidence suggests that only about 300,000 houses a year will need to be built in the foreseeable future in order to meet demand. (Boleat, 1976)

Similarly, in evidence to the House of Commons Environment Committee in 1981, Michael Heseltine, then Secretary of State for the Environment, remarked:

> I start off, and the Treasury knows I start off, from a situation where we have the largest crude surplus of houses over households that we have ever had in this country. (House of Commons, 1981, p. 44)

and later added:

Obviously, anyone who is interested in the problems of housing need is entitled to my attention. But I am pursuing, I would argue, within the constraints of an economy in decline, the housing policies most fitted to a situation where we have the largest crude surplus ever and where the essential challenge now is to make better use of the existing housing stock. (House of Commons, 1981, p. 48)

This view of the housing situation in Britain has been criticized as neglecting concerns over the quality of the available stock, its location and the problems of access experienced by particular groups. As the Environment Committee concluded:

This 'crude housing surplus' argument is, however, oversimplified and potentially misleading. The same National Dwelling and Housing Survey showed that in England in December 1977 there were 729,000 vacant and second homes as well as 1,445,000 households who lacked at least one basic amenity. To these should be added a further 1,000,000 or more dwellings which, by interpolation from the Housing Condition Survey 1976, can be estimated as either unfit or requiring repairs costing over £3,000 at today's prices in order to get some idea of how much the 'crude housing surplus' of 400,000 in England is dwarfed by other factors. In addition the measure of households excludes those 'concealed households' who are living as part of other persons' households and who were estimated in the NDHS 1977 to exceed 250,000 in England. This 'crude housing surplus' figure is heavily qualified not only by these far more substantial countervailing factors, but also by the substantial mismatch between our present housing stock and households' needs. This mismatch reflects both the problems of having already the wrong types of dwellings in the wrong places for people's requirements, and the constantly changing role of household formation which exceeds the present level of new housing starts and is changing significantly the national household profile. The Committee concludes that such an oversimplified and unreliable measure as the 'crude housing surplus' should not weigh heavily in the formation of housing policy and that this surplus does not undermine the case for a higher level of housing output. (House of Commons, 1981, para 18)

Nevertheless, the changing perception of housing shortage has resulted in a shift from quantitative to qualitative concerns in housing policy. Rather than being concerned about the number of dwellings constructed regardless of tenure, politicians and other

Facts and fictions **43**

commentators have turned their attention to making better use of the available stock. The 'fit' between household size and dwelling size has been a dominant issue, and choice and preference rather than need and shortage have been the more contemporary preoccupations. In relation to the two main tenures it is home ownership that has been regarded as the preferred tenure.

The second issue that has increasingly confused and transformed the housing debate is changing demographic structure. Over the 1980s, factors such as increased longevity, divorce, remarriage, later marriage and changed patterns of childbearing have combined to produce, most noticeably, an increase in single-person households, in single-parent families and in the number of elderly and retired persons. As noted earlier, housebuilders are increasingly responding to demands from single-person households, both the young and the elderly, by providing smaller units. Similarly, more liberal lending policies have developed among banks and building societies to cater for single persons and unrelated joint and multiple purchasers (albeit that demand for the latter is now somewhat diminished by changes in tax relief).

Government policies towards home ownership tend to be presented as a response to natural preference and choice. A procession of surveys have shown the desire to purchase among a high proportion of public and private tenants and rising expectations of entry to home ownership among newly formed households. (For an excellent review of the validity of these surveys, see Jones, 1982). Table 2.7 shows the results of various surveys on tenure preferences compared with the existing tenure structure.

Table 2.7 *Current tenure and tenure preferences*

	Tenure distribution Great Britain 1988 %	Preferred tenure (various surveys)					
		1967 %	1975 %	1978 %	1983 %	1986 %	1989 %
Home ownership	65	66	69	72	77	77	81
Public sector renting	25	23	21	19	16	17	12
Private renting, other	10	11	8	5	5	4	8
Don't know	–	–	3	3	2	3	1

Sources: Housing and Construction Statistics (HMSO) and Building Societies Association (1983); British Market Research Bureau (1986; 1989)

44   *Home ownership*

Taken at face value the message is clear. Current tenure does not coincide with tenure preferences. In both the 1983 and 1986 surveys carried out by the British Market Research Bureau for the Building Societies Association, 77 per cent of households stated a preference for home ownership. Although the gap between expressed preference and the achieved rate of home ownership was smaller in 1986 than previously, it remains more than 10 per cent. If the proportion of households expressing a preference for home ownership achieved that position it would result in the highest home ownership rate in Western Europe and North America. Some comparable figures are as follows: USA (1979) 65 per cent; Canada (1981) 55 per cent; Denmark (1981) 55 per cent; Norway (1981) 59 per cent; France (1975) 47 per cent.

Translating these tenure preferences into actual housing circumstances begs a number of questions. Is there some kind of limit to the growth of home ownership? For example, Australia, with a current level of 70 per cent, experienced an apparent marginal decline in home ownership between 1966 and 1976. Are these stated preferences in fact a reflection of constraint rather than choice; do they simply reflect a lack of alternatives? In this context, Boleat referred to an 'unnatural' demand for home ownership in inner city areas, reflecting a lack of available private rented accommodation for the young and transient (Boleat, 1982). Similarly, commenting on two surveys of households moving from local authority to owner–occupied housing in Leeds and Manchester, Jones (1982) noted that, for some households, 'the act of house purchase derives more from dissatisfaction with the accommodation available in the local authority sector than from any desire for home ownership as a form of tenure' (p. 121).

Ineligibility for council housing among certain groups, long waiting lists, the prospect of being allocated an unpopular flat or maisonette, the lack of private rented accommodation, rising rents and a general decline in investment in public housing are all factors that can fuel the preference for owner occupation. It is not a matter of opinion that tenure preferences have been heavily influenced by government policy. It is a matter of fact. But too often the data from surveys are presented as if preferences lead policy and are formed in a vacuum. It is quite clear that survey data that show an increase in the preference for home ownership from (say) 69 per cent of households in 1975 to 81 per cent in 1989 reflect changes in the social, economic and policy environment. Far from consolidating the view that such preferences are natural, it shows precisely the opposite.

In this context it is instructive to look at other countries or at attitudes towards housing in Britain earlier in the century. For example, a study of housing by Mass Observation carried out in 1943 reveals a very different discourse about preferences and aspirations. Whilst there was a section on renting versus owning, it was far outweighed by discussion of space standards, gardens, privacy, independence and the quality of the neighbourhood. Indeed, although the discussion of the pros and cons of owning and renting has very similar dimensions to contemporary debates, tenure is given no greater importance than, say, the design of the kitchen. What is striking is how far discussion of privacy or independence and general housing quality is divorced from discussion of tenure. In contemporary literature it would be assumed by most people that the statement 'It's our own, isn't it? A home of our own' was being made by an owner occupier. Quite unremarkably for the time it was being made by someone living in a wholly rented area (Advertising Service Guild, 1943 p. 171). And the final discussion of the 'Dream home of the future' makes no reference to home ownership. The Bournville Village Trust's study of Birmingham published in 1941 shows a similar pattern with very little discussion of ownership and an emphasis on overcrowding, rent levels, open spaces, gardens and design. The authors of the report argued that home ownership which involved buying on a mortgage under a system of weekly payments 'should really be classed with tenants who pay rent, rather than with occupiers who own their houses outright' (p. 54). The possible reasons for living in the present house, for moving and the preferences in moving did not include reference to home ownership and preference for home ownership does not appear to have been added by respondents under 'any other reason'.

These surveys were conducted during wartime when extensive bomb damage had occurred and in a period when the majority experience was of renting. They serve, nevertheless, as a reminder that in the not so distant past in Britain discussion of housing tenure was relatively unimportant. Moreover, many of the dimensions of housing which are now inextricably associated with home ownership (e.g. independence, privacy, freedom, a garden) were seen then as quite separate and no more an inherent feature of owning than of renting. Without labouring the point, it is clear that the current overwhelming preference for home ownership is not natural, inherent or cultural but reflects the current realities of the stock of dwellings, the means of access to them, the way they are managed and the financial and policy framework. If and when these circumstances change preferences will change.

Unless attitudinal surveys take full account of the context in which such questions as posed, they expose themselves to the sort of criticisms made by Merrett (1982) when he refers to the

Home ownership

existing literature on tenure preferences as being 'marked by an excess of unstructured empiricism and ideological rubbish' (p. 56). In a thorough assessment of the preference for home ownership, Merrett has shown how preferences are structured according to predicates of choice. In the present circumstances, a household considering aspects of control, mobility, the dwelling's physical characteristics, location and finance will tend to favour home ownership. In opposition to the view that home ownership is something people want for its own sake, Merrett (1982) states:

> I propose that the evident desire of very substantial numbers of British working people to own their home rests entirely on an unmistakeable foundation. The material base for the superstructure of the desire for a specific property relation in housing consumption is that owner occupation, for households on average or higher than average wages and salaries, in general gives access to dwellings, that are ranked higher in terms of their use-value and which are perceived to offer greater housing mobility and long-term financial advantages. (p. 71)

This is not to suggest that expressed preferences for owner occupation are exaggerated or that the measures are false. But the preference for ownership is shorthand for a collection of housing attributes such as space, quality, a house with a garden, the desire for a particular location, as well as reflecting specific tax and investment advantages. In this sense the question is not whether people are becoming owners but whether their particular needs and aspirations are being satisfied. The two are not necessarily synonymous. The younger single person buying a three-bedroomed, older terraced property in an inner city area might have preferred to rent a smaller property, possibly a flat, which involved less of a financial commitment, had little or no maintenance problems and which could be vacated at short notice – if such a property had been available.

Referring back to the BSA survey, what is it about home ownership that makes it the preferred tenure for 81 per cent of households? The survey asked respondents to give their main reasons for their choice of ideal accommodation. The attributes mentioned most often in favour of home ownership are given in Table 2.8. Preferences fall into two main categories: aspects of finance and aspects of use. The former is heavily influenced by government policy towards the main tenures and by assumptions about continuing real gain through house price inflation. The latter, it could be argued, relate more easily to what might be regarded as 'natural' inclinations to have freedom and autonomy in the domestic

Table 2.8 *Main reasons for choice of home ownership as ideal accommodation*

Weighted sample	2,465
	%
Want to own/continue to own/buy/habit	25
Can do what you want with it/flexibility/DIY	7
Independence/achievement/pride of ownership	10
Investment/financial stability/security/an asset/ prices keep going up	20
Don't like/want to pay rent/cheaper than renting in the long run	18

Source: Building Societies Association (1989).

domain. But such attributes are not necessarily exclusive to the current system of home ownership. Much of the demand for home ownership must be attributed to the negative aspects of the other tenures. And those aspects, such as rising rents, high-rise uniformity, oppressive bureaucratic paternalism, are not inherent aspects of council housing but are socially constructed. Moreover, just as it is erroneous to universalize and overemphasize the accumulative and liberating aspects of home ownership, so it is wrong to exaggerate the negative experience of, say, council housing. After all, the drive to extend home ownership through council house sales was predicated to a considerable extent on the view that there were large numbers of tenants who were settled in their 'home' and could afford to buy. Indeed, the argument that the disposal of council houses would not affect transfers and exchanges because those tenants who bought would not have moved anyway begs the question of why they would not have moved if security, freedom and autonomy are so exclusively associated with home ownership. (For a fuller discussion of this issue see Forrest and Murie, 1988a).

For some people at least, it seems that the desire for ownership for its own sake is an insufficient attraction. However, Merrett's rejection of the view that home ownership is natural or innate and that it rests on a firm material foundation associated with higher use values, greater mobility and long-term financial advantages (Merrett, 1982, p. 71) is not the whole story. It is argued that feelings of belonging and security add to other factors that currently make home ownership more attractive than other tenures. It is also argued that such feelings cannot be explained solely in terms of economic rationale and the bias of state policies. Whether they are referred to as innate or instinctive or cultural is less important than whether such qualities are found only in home ownership. If this was the case it would be difficult to explain why anyone on a reasonable income would choose to remain in council housing for any length of time. Those who preferred to remain council tenants, rejected the option of moving in order to buy and only bought when they were able to buy their council house were not behaving in a way that attached overwhelming priority to home ownership. It is also important to bear in mind that, whilst the movement between the two main tenures is overwhelmingly in the direction of home ownership, there is a not inconsiderable demand for social housing among owners and this may increase with the expansion of home ownership and the changes in its demographic and social composition. This point is discussed briefly in Chapter 7.

Expressed preference for home ownership varies throughout the country. For example, Jones (1982) pointed to a rather lower level of interest among council tenants for purchase in Durham (24 per cent) than indicated by a national survey carried out a few months later (NEDO, 1975). And he observes that:

> Given that the Northern Region has a lower proportion of owner occupiers than any other English region, it is evident that we cannot presume that the highest unsatisfied demand exists in those regions where the supply is numerically smaller. (Jones, 1982, p. 117)

This was again evident from the BSA survey (Building Societies Association, 1989). Scotland, with the lowest level of home ownership, also had the lowest level of preference for it. Whereas in Scotland 64 per cent of all households said they would prefer to own in two years' time, in East Anglia and the South West the proportion rose to nearly 90 per cent. Various factors lie behind these variations. For example, current owners generally express a preference for home ownership. This means that where established levels of home ownership are high, there is likely to be a stronger preference for home ownership than where there is a high proportion of council tenancies. As the BSA survey showed, nationally only 48 per cent of all council tenants wished to be owners in two years' time. Age and social class are also significant factors. The desire for home ownership is strongest in the younger age groups and among professional, managerial and skilled workers. The relationship between mortgage costs and rent levels also varies and must affect the pattern of preferences. For example, high rent levels in an area of low house prices would tend to create a particularly favourable climate for the expansion of home ownership. What does the 1989 BSA survey say about household expectations as

Facts and fictions

opposed to preferences? Preferences and expectations are in fact closely correlated, suggesting that stated choices are influenced by perceived constraints. For example, of those in the highest income group (£25,000+), 96 per cent expect to be home owners in ten years. Of those with household incomes in the £3,000–4,999 category, only 61 per cent wish to own in two years and 62 per cent expect to in ten years (BSA, 1989 pp. 141 and 170).

A basic feature of attitudinal information on home ownership is that the preferences expressed and the attributes cited are shaped and influenced by the views of the alternatives. However, these mirror images, for example in relation to investment and accumulation, tend to be interpreted as intrinsic to home ownership. Interview surveys may also be structured in such a way that they may distort understanding of how people regard their homes in general and home ownership in particular. If people are asked what they think are the *advantages* of home ownership – or why they *chose* home ownership – the questions are posed in such a way as to draw out the investment aspects of that tenure. In recent years government and other surveys have been preoccupied with house prices, capital gains and investment returns, and those aspects of housing have tended to come to the fore. People, however, value housing in all sorts of other ways – and in ways that have no necessary connection with any particular tenure. A long tradition of surveys concerned with residential mobility and housing choice includes questions about the reasons for making a particular housing decision. Rather than assuming that the decision was about tenure, such questions can be more neutral and invite the respondent to say whether location, size, type . . . . or tenure was crucial. In these surveys tenure emerges as an important, but not dominant or independent influence (see Murie, Niner and Watson, 1976). A recent study by Marshall *et al.* (1988) examined *inter alia* what the home *meant* to people. Its importance as a financial asset and something to leave children certainly emerged, but well down the scale from 'the centre of family life', 'a place to retreat, to relax, to be oneself' and 'freedom, independence and a place of one's own'. Moreover, the rankings of responses were consistent across class and gender (pp. 213–14). Of course, these are crude measures of complex feelings with issues of freedom or independence inextricably bound up with financial matters. Nevertheless, available evidence suggests that people are not overly preoccupied with the investment aspects of housing. This is not to suggest that people have no interest in housing investment – a position attributed by Saunders and Harris (1988) to various commentators on home ownership (p. 33). That would indeed be 'absurd'. To accept that home owners have an active interest

50   *Home ownership*

in house price and property values is, however, quite different from suggesting, as do Saunders and Harris, that investment is the primary motivation in people's housing market behaviour.

The majority of households move short distances when they change house. This has long been the case, although there are important class differences. People move for various reasons, for employment, for a bigger house, for a better neighbourhood, to achieve a higher status and to increase their investment. Aspects of use value are of major importance. Not surprisingly people also make (or try to make) rational economic decisions regarding the investment potential of their dwellings. Saunders and Harris, however, at least imply that people move short distances primarily to make money out of housing. If that were not the case, they argue, households would stay put – otherwise what is the point of moving say, three streets. This is a view that takes no account of a wide range of survey data on residential mobility (e.g. Murie *et al.*, 1976). Without labouring this issue, our work in Bristol on two sectors of the owner-occupied market highlighted differences in the geography of moves between an affluent and a lower-income sector of home ownership (Forrest and Murie, 1988b, 1989a). The high accumulators in an up-market area had generally moved for employment reasons and had a highly diffuse mobility pattern. By and large they had also made extremely large sums of potentially realizable money in the housing market. Conversely, home owners in the area of working-class home ownership had made fewer moves and these were heavily clustered in the same part of Bristol. Very few of these moves were motivated primarily (and in most cases not at all) by what Saunders and Harris refer to as 'housing investment strategies' (1988, p. 33). In some cases the reasons for moving were to be nearer kin or friends. In others, it was to obtain a larger house because of children, or a better garden, or a better area. Status was a factor but in a more complex way than simply the achievement of a more valuable property. As Franklin (1986) has indicated, status achievement is very often about being equal to rather than superior to those around you.

One of the interesting features of the demand for home ownership is the way in which the ideology can override everyday experiences. For example, the belief that home ownership is a good investment (which in most cases it is) is expressed by those who have gained little in the housing market. In their study of home ownership in inner city Birmingham and Liverpool, Karn *et al.* (1985) state:

> The fact that many owners saw the house as an investment is particularly interesting in view of the very low levels of

Facts and fictions 51

Table 2.9 *Attitudes towards home ownership*

	Accrington	Consett	Cheltenham	All respondents
Sample number	200	200	203	603
	%	%	%	%
(a) People who are successful in life become home owners:				
Strongly agree/ tend to agree	63	66	64	65
Neither agree/ disagree	9	5	7	7
Strongly disagree/ tend to disagree	23	27	28	26
No opinion	4	2	–	2
(b) People naturally prefer to own their own homes:				
Strongly agree/ tend to agree	80	82	78	80
Neither agree/ disagree	5	4	7	6
Strongly disagree/ tend to disagree	12	14	14	13
No opinion	3	1	1	2
(c) People who own their homes get too many tax benefits:				
Strongly agree/ tend to agree	8	7	8	8
Neither agree/ disagree	7	4	8	6
Strongly disagree/ tend to disagree	68	81	70	72
No opinion	17	9	14	13

Source: Forrest and Murie (1986). Data from survey of households, carried out as part of ESRC funded research, Urban Change and the Restructuring of Housing Provision.

house price inflation . . . It is clear that many buyers had no conception of the long-term relative decline in value to which their dwellings are subject. In part this must be because in general house prices have risen – even if relative values have fallen. In addition, there is a strong ideological bias in our society in favour of holding such a belief. (p. 56)

Whilst the material and social circumstances of home owners are highly varied, the strength of the ideology is seen in the remarkable uniformity of attitudes and beliefs. In a recent survey of households

52 *Home ownership*

in three contrasting towns (Accrington, Cheltenham and Consett), women in both council housing and home ownership and in 'good' and 'bad' areas were asked a series of questions about home ownership. In Table 2.9 the responses to some of these questions are given in summary form. It is clear that people have strong opinions that being a home owner is part of being 'successful' (it does not follow, of course, that people believe that being a home owner signifies or guarantees success!); that there is strong support for the view that there is a natural desire for home ownership; and that virtually no connection is made between the desire for home ownership and mortgage interest tax relief as a subsidy. Further elaboration of these figures would show that responses to these questions vary only marginally between council tenants and owners. If anything, it is home owners who are rather more sceptical of the first two propositions than tenants. Council tenants, however, are rather more inclined to the view that home owners benefit from tax relief – but only a small minority believe that.

A demand-led tenure?

There is a final element to the discussion of preference. Evidence on preferences for home ownership is sometimes used to explain why home ownership has grown. The picture developed is of a demand-driven tenure – demand-driven in its expansion (rather than pricing within it). However, this is clearly not the whole story and is misleading. There is an important way in which home ownership has developed and changed, not because of consumer-led demand, but because of decisions by institutional investors and supply-side agencies. The earliest major contributions to this debate involved analysis of the process of building and development and argued that how much housing was built, what was built, where, and at what price is best explained by financial and organizational aspects of the building industry and related organizations (see e.g. Merrett, 1979; Ball, 1983). While some of this perspective was sometimes linked with a wider dismissal of home ownership, this is not grounds for rejecting the importance of supply-side factors. Since these early contributions, other contributions have referred to changes in land policy and to the impact of increased competition in the housing finance industry (Rydin, 1986; Barrett and Healey, 1985; Boddy, 1989). Perhaps the most accessible arguments, however, relate to sitting tenant purchase and tenure transfers. These have been major contributors to the growth of home ownership. Hamnett and Randolph (1988), in their study of flat breakup in London, emphasize institutional decisions relating to investment and profit taking. Sales to sitting tenants or with

Facts and fictions 53

vacant possession are not led by tenant demand for ownership. Randolph's (1987) study of sitting tenants buying houses from private landlords presents a similar picture of tenants responding to changes on the supply side. A final example relates to council house purchasers. Broadly, the evidence shows that council house purchasers tend to be more affluent tenants in a position to buy elsewhere in the market, but having preferred to stay in their house and rent rather than move to buy (Murie, 1975; Forrest and Murie, 1988a). It is not council tenants who dislike their council house who buy. Nor do decisions to buy merely reflect attitudes to ownership. Applications and completions of sales fluctuate in relation to changes in rents, discounts, house prices and, recently, uncertainties about the form of landlord. In general, council house purchasers make rational decisions that are not predicated simply on attitudes to ownership and are not simply investment strategies. The uptake of council house purchase does not reflect the working out of a detached attitude to home ownership. It reflects the terms and conditions of state policy towards home ownership and council housing as well as a range of household considerations. What is apparent is the importance of supply-side and policy decisions in influencing demand and their independent effect on the growth of home ownership, alongside demand.

Concluding remarks

This chapter has emphasized that home ownership conveys a series of overlapping and generally positive images. And those images are fuelled daily by the popular press, politicians, organizations, professions and others whose material interests are tied closely to its continued expansion. Ownership is presented as democratic, egalitarian and redistributive. It is a home, not a house. It offers higher status, higher quality, privacy and security. It offers real money gains and a nest egg for the future to be passed on to children or others. It is the domain of family building and family contentment. It offers social and spatial mobility. It is inherently conservative. It offers individual freedom of expression. It is the backbone of middle-class Britain.

These images are questionable because they are typically generalized and moreover they are subject to change. This is not to suggest that they are a pure figment of collective imaginations. Like all images, they are part fact and part fiction. The reality of home ownership is that it is a tenure that varies enormously – spatially, historically and between different groups. In that sense, we need to begin to break home ownership down into its component parts; to distinguish, for example, between outright ownership and mortgaged ownership, between new buyers and established buyers, between freeholders and leaseholders, and between those on low incomes and those with high incomes. Furthermore, differences within home ownership are growing. The stock is ageing and condition is more varied than in the past, the variety of households entering the sector has increased, with more lower-income households and those in marginal economic positions. Problems of arrears have grown and the tenure no longer represents security for all households who live (or have lived) in it. Variations in property value have increased and the experience of home ownership varies regionally and locally.

3 Home ownership: a silent revolution?

This chapter reviews the history of home ownership and, in particular, some of the characteristics of this tenure that have acquired the status of 'truisms'. In this latter respect, three specific issues are referred to: first, the view that home ownership has been an overarching and innate desire of the mass of the British population and that this is evidenced by a history of individual struggle and self-help; second, that home ownership has been pre-eminently a middle-class concern; finally, that the meaning of ownership has been unchanged. These issues are central to the many debates on home ownership and worthy of close examination. Until recently the *history* of home ownership has been largely neglected by academics. Consequently, much of what is available has been written by partisan interests such as the building societies, which have generally promoted the rise of home ownership. That uncritical view of history is repeated by many, and some of the academic commentary offered has tended to take an opposite (and equally uncritical) view of home ownership as entrapment and social bulwark against revolution. Beyond quoting eminent politicians asserting the importance of ownership as social control, little hard evidence is offered for this claim. Neither approach can be regarded as adequate.

The typical commentary on ownership makes the point that in 1910 fewer than 10 per cent of households were estimated to be home owners and that this had increased to some 66 per cent in 1990. The period in between is assumed to mark out a period of steady progress in the rise of home ownership, while the period prior to 1910 is one of frustrated ambition. But how realistic is that 'account'?

There are a number of difficulties to confront when seeking to establish the rise of home ownership. Prior to 1961, tenure was not even recorded in the decennial Census of Population – an indicator of its low importance as an issue prior to that time. A whole variety of surveys and other evidence can be referred to but, unfortunately, what coverage there is varies considerably in

56 *Home ownership*

scope, unit of assessment and accuracy, and only a very incomplete record is possible. What figures can be assembled are almost inevitably aggregate and they give little sense of the wide variations that existed and continue to exist across the country. Such figures provide only the first step in the process of assessing the development of home ownership and problems of interpretation remain. There is a tendency to look at nineteenth-century and early twentieth-century data with late twentieth-century perceptions of capital gains and investment, rapid price inflation and a period in which housing has performed well in relation to many other investments.

The growth of home ownership

It is easiest to begin by looking at the national data for the twentieth century. Table 3.1 is an updated version of data provided by Boddy (1980) and has been compiled from a variety of sources including Butler and Sloman (1975). This document makes no reference to the sources of the data cited though, as we will indicate later, they are perhaps less authoritative than might be the case. The table has been updated to 1988. The figure cited by Boddy for the tenure of households in 1910 is very much a a'guesstimate', with a wider band of 8–15 per cent based upon an assessment of pre-1914 housing owned individually in 1938 being suggested by Butler and Sloman (Cleary, 1965, pp. 184–5). As Swenarton and Taylor (1985) argue, there is no adequate foundation in data of the two supposed bases for this figure: one refers to output, not to the housing stock, and the other depends on a good deal of guesswork and unfortunately is miscalculated (p. 376). They conclude that the national level of owner occupation prior to the First World War is still unknown.

The supposed maximum of 10 per cent is used as the base to assess the growth of home ownership. However, as an examination of local area data reveals, high levels of home ownership were achieved in some areas even before 1918 – though clearly there were massive variations. Evidence is fragmentary. Discussing the situation over the period 1870–1914, Offer comments (1981, pp. 119–20):

> House-ownership was an aspiration of well paid workers in regular employment. Apparently one fifth of the workers in Kenricks, a Birmingham hardware firm, were freeholders in the 1850s; a few of the skilled legal copiers interviewed for Charles Booth's survey in London were house owners. West Yorkshire

Table 3.1 *Housing tenure in Great Britain, 1914–1988 (percentage of all dwellings)*

Year	Home owner	Public rented[1]	Private rented[2]		Other[3]
1914	10.0	1.0	80.0		9.0
1938	25.0	10.0	56.0		9.0
1945	26.0	12.0	54.0		8.0
1951	29.0	18.0	45.0		8.0
1956	34.0	23.0	36.0		7.0
1960	42.0	27.0	26.0		6.0
1961	43.0	27.0	25.0		6.0
1962	44.0	27.0	24.0		5.0
1963	44.6	28.0	22.0		5.4
1964	45.6	28.1	20.9		5.4
1965	46.5	28.2	19.9		5.4
1966	47.1	28.7	18.8		5.4
1967	47.9	29.2	17.7		5.3
1968	48.8	29.5	16.6		5.3
1969	49.4	30.0	15.8		5.2
1970	50.0	30.4	14.9		5.1
1971	50.5	30.6		18.8	
1972	51.5	30.5		18.0	
1973	52.3	30.5		17.2	
1974	52.7	30.8		16.5	
1975	53.0	31.3		15.7	
1976	53.7	31.4		14.8	
1977	54.1	31.7		14.2	
1978	54.7	31.7		13.7	
1979	55.3	31.5		13.1	
1980	56.2	31.2		12.7	
1981	57.1	30.6	10.1		2.1
1982	58.6	29.5	9.6		2.2
1983	59.9	28.6	9.2		2.3
1984	60.9	27.9	8.7		2.4
1985	62.0	27.3	8.3		2.5
1986	63.1	26.6	7.9		2.4
1987	64.1	25.9	7.5		2.5
1988	65.4	24.9	7.1		2.5

Notes:
[1] Local authorities and new towns, and other public bodies.
[2] Figures from 1981 include rented from private owners and other tenures.
[3] Includes housing associations. Figures from 1981 housing associations only.

Sources: Boddy (1980) and *Housing and Construction Statistics* (HMSO).

58 *Home ownership*

and Tyneside, where the building society movement was better developed, appear to have had a higher proportion of home ownership. 'In Oldham', said the preamble to the Unionist Housing Bill of 1912, 'out of 33,000 inhabited houses, over 10,000 or about a third, are owned or in the course of being purchased by artisan proprietors.' The South Wales coalfield apparently had a very high incidence of working class home ownership coming up to 60% in some localities, and Cardiff had an overall percentage of 9.6 falling to 7.2 between 1884 and 1914. In York, at the turn of the century 608 working class house owners (occupying almost 6% of working class housing) were headed by 120 widows, 30 spinsters and 58 retired men, and tailed by eight labourers.

The last two items of evidence are drawn from Daunton's work on Cardiff and South Wales and Rowntree in York. Daunton cites estimates of 60 per cent ownership in Tredegar and 'in the case of Rhondda Valleys, Carmarthenshire and the Western portion of Glamorganshire . . . in the neighbourhood of 70%' (Daunton, 1980, p. 146). Pritchard (1976) suggested that no more than 20 per cent of houses in the south-east of Leicester were owner occupied in 1895.

Rose (1980) argues that worker home ownership was most likely to occur in single-industry communities, and she cites her own research on mining communities in Cornwall and the shoe-making areas of Northamptonshire to support this view. There seems little doubt that in such areas workers were able to exercise their preferences and thus escape the generally degrading accommodation available (especially in mining villages). Similarly, in some areas workers made early attempts to organize their own building societies and to fund adequate living environments. They did so both as a reaction to the housing available and as a way of achieving a 'separate sphere' (Rose, 1980). It is no surprise that employees in single-industry communities should make particular efforts to do so since the alternative would often have been to rent from their employer partly because of isolation often associated with such communities and the absence of other providers.

Dennis (1984) provides a useful summary of findings related to home ownership levels in the nineteenth century (Table 3.2). There were substantial variations between and within towns. For instance, Pritchard's (1976) research on Leicester showed some areas with ownership in 1885 at less than 1 per cent of dwellings and other areas with more than 13 per cent. The same was true of Cardiff in 1884, with a variation between 4.5 per cent in one area to 16 per cent in another (Daunton, 1977).

A silent revolution 59

Table 3.2 *Rates of home ownership in selected cities*

Place	Date	Percentage Home owners	Source
Durham City	1850	17.0	Ratebooks, Holt (1979)
Durham City	1880	17.5	Ratebooks, Holt (1979)
Huddersfield Township	1847	10.7	Ratebooks, Springett (1979)
Huddersfield Township	1896	9.3	Ratebooks, Springett (1979)
Leicester	1855	4.0	Ratebooks, Pritchard (1976)
Oldham	1906	8.3	Ratebooks, Bedale (1980)
Cardiff	1884	9.6	Ratebooks, Daunton (1977)
Cardiff	1914	7.2	Ratebooks, Daunton (1977)
Leeds	1839	3.7	Household survey, Leeds Council (1839)
Bristol*	1839	0.2	Household survey, Fripp (1839)
York*	1899	5.9	Household survey, Rowntree (1910)

* Survey restricted to working-class families.

Source: Dennis (1984).

Contemporary comment can be gleaned from a range of official reports and select committees though, as with the academic research cited, it is always fragmentary. For example, Mr Taylor in evidence to the Royal Commission on Friendly and Benefit Societies regarding his own society in Birmingham stated that they had funded 13,000 purchases and 'we have streets more than a mile long in which absolutely every home belongs to working classes' (Royal Commission, 1871, p. 49). More extensive and probably more reliable analysis is available from the Land Enquiry Committee, which reported in 1914. It surveyed some 268 towns in England and Wales and some of its findings are relevant to our concerns here. The report states:

> We next asked whether working men are less inclined now than they were a few years ago to purchase houses for their own occupation. . . . after extensive enquiry we have come to the conclusion that there is no evidence of any such change. (Of 36 correspondents who dealt with this issue) only eight had noticed a decrease in the desire of persons of small means to buy homes for their own occupation while 28 affirmed that this desire had remained or had increased.

60 *Home ownership*

The report cited the towns of Coventry, Bury, Macclesfield, Leeds, Norwich, Clitheroe, Doncaster, Loughborough, Stockport, Crewe and Dalton in Furness as all being places where working-class home ownership was 'common'. By contrast, the evidence from mining districts suggested ownership by miners was rare.

Even in 1910, home ownership levels amongst the working class were well above 10 per cent in some districts. In towns with a strong artisan and skilled working class, home ownership could rise to relatively high levels. While home ownership was desired by some, not least because it broke the employers' control over the home, there was a considerable difference of opinion on the issue of working-class home ownership. The principal concerns seem to have been that the worker will be 'tied to one locality, and if he wishes to change his employment and go to work elsewhere, he may have either to sell his house at a sacrifice, or have to remain in his existing employment against his will' (Reiss, 1919, p. 137).

The evidence for the 1920s and especially the 1930s is better, partly because this was a period of massive expansion in housing provision in general and home ownership in particular. Around 4 million dwellings were constructed in England and Wales during the period 1914–38, and of these approximately half were built for owner occupation. Credit was cheap and the building societies embarked on substantial campaigns to promote ownership, not least through the purchase of formerly private rented dwellings (1.1 million were bought in this period). The government too gave substantial assistance via building subsidies and loans, land registration procedures and mortgage and loan guarantee schemes. The 1923 Housing Act in particular was directed at expanding home ownership. It provided subsidies to builders to erect houses of modest dimensions and allowed local authorities to lend to them for the same purpose. It empowered authorities to guarantee building society advances on small dwellings and to offer their own mortgages. The Act was introduced by Neville Chamberlain, the Minister of Health, who was quite clear that ownership had to be promoted. As he had commented in 1920, 'every spadeful of manure dug in, every fruit tree planted . . . . converted a potential revolutionary into a citizen' (cited in Merrett, 1982, p. 6).

Perhaps the best evidence of the interwar rise of home ownership comes from the Departmental Committee on Valuation for Rates undertaken in 1939 and involving an extensive survey of the housing stock in England and Wales. This, together with a submission to the Committee by the County Borough Valuers' Association, has enabled Swenarton and Taylor (1985) to estimate that 35 per cent of dwellings were owner occupied in 1938. The evidence does suggest substantial variations according to

A silent revolution 61

the valuation of the property. Of the lowest valuation band (dwellings with a gross rental value not exceeding £20 10s), 19 per cent were owner occupied. In contrast, of those in the highest band (exceeding £100) 81.3 per cent were owner occupied. A survey of middle-class households by Massey (1942) showed that, in 1938/9, 46.5 per cent were buying their homes and a further 18 per cent already owned them. Of the local government officers in the survey, 60 per cent were buying their homes and a further 10 per cent were outright owners. Other surveys support this conclusion (e.g. Ministry of Labour, 1940), and Bellman's (1938) analysis of the occupation of mortgagors to the Abbey Road Society in the 1930s showed that advances to wage-earners doubled over the period 1930–36 from £66,000 to £127,000 while those to the salaried rose from £25,000 to £27,000.

Swenarton and Taylor suggest that 'only the elite of the working class could afford home ownership – and even then at the cost of self sacrifice and thrift' (1985, p. 385), but this in no way detracts from the fact that working-class home ownership was strongly established in specific communities and was growing. Table 3.3 from Swenarton and Taylor's analysis of evidence submitted to the rating enquiry shows wide local variation from Nottingham with 14 per cent to Plymouth with 68 per cent. And in larger towns such as Nottingham or Birmingham there were certain districts where levels of working-class home ownership were high (Birmingham had 48,152 owner-occupied houses in 1939).

Other research supports the figures in Table 3.3. In a series of studies of the propensity to save amongst the working population, Madge (1940) suggested that:

> In Blackburn there were 38 per cent of houses owner-occupied in 1935 but there is not a great tendency to buy houses there now. In our Bristol sample 21 per cent of the families were living in their own houses; another 15 per cent were buying their houses.

and in Coventry:

> The secretary of the Coventry Economic Building Society esti-mated that 50 per cent of Coventry households are tenant purchases . . . . Between 1934 and 1938 was the peak period for purchasing houses and during this period it rose steadily until September 1939 when restrictions were introduced.

The war not only brought an end to the boom but also made some regret that they had bought their own homes. Bombs did

62 *Home ownership*

Table 3.3 *Home ownership in 24 towns in 1939*

Town	Number of houses owner occupied	Total number of houses	Percentage home ownership
1 Nottingham	10,425	72,791	14.3
2 Smethwick	2,947	19,167	15.4
3 Manchester	26,159	167,752	15.6
4 Hull	13,509	75,831	17.8
5 Sheffield	24,617	137,072	18.0
6 Merthyr Tydfil	3,503	15,542	22.5
7 Birmingham	48,152	205,061	23.5
8 Wolverhampton	8,964	35,884	25.0
9 Dudley	3,731	14,630	25.5
10 Stoke-on-Trent	16,794	64,860	25.9
11 Grimsby	7,137	22,860	31.2
12 Chester*	2,629	8,146*	32.3*
13 Burnley	8,953	25,496	35.1
14 Great Yarmouth	5,390	15,232	35.4
15 Norwich	6,196	16,819	36.8
16 Coventry	19,500	51,526	37.8
17 Newport (Mon.)	8,088	21,029	38.5
18 Northampton	10,494	25,887	40.5
19 Oxford	9,870	22,299	44.3
20 Exeter	7,460	16,115	46.3
21 Portsmouth	26,438	54,159	48.8
22 Bristol	40,821	79,959	51.1
23 Hastings	6,768	12,472	54.3
24 Plymouth	18,042	26,356	68.5

Note: The figures for Chester are doubtful. The Departmental Committee thought that the figure for the total number of houses shown in the return was a serious understatement and adjusted the figures accordingly; even so, the figure for the total number of houses (8,146) was considerably below what the Committee believed to be the correct figure of c.11,000.

Source: Swenarton and Taylor (1985). Calculated from PRO, HLG 56/155, X/L04169, Ministry of Housing and Local Government, Departmental Committee on Valuation for Rates 1938–40, submission of County Borough Valuers' Associations 1939.

not discriminate between owned and rented property and the compensation process was far from comprehensive or rapid.

As already stated, perhaps surprisingly it was not until the 1961 Census that housing tenure was included in the decennial Census. However, there was an awareness of the growing importance of the tenure. In a 1947 survey of the British household, a series of housing tenure questions were asked. These revealed that 22

A silent revolution

per cent of households in Britain owned their dwellings and 4 per cent were buying them. By economic group (defined by the basic weekly wage rate of the chief wage-earner), the results were as shown in Table 3.4). Group V consisted of 'the better paid managerial and professional workers' and clearly home ownership was well established here. For all other categories (e.g. for Groups III and IV, which included skilled workers, clerical and lower-paid managers/professionals), private renting was the dominant tenure. McCulloch has argued (1989) that Gray's figures are probably an underestimate and questions assumptions that they indicate a fall in levels of home ownership. He questions the view that such a decline arose from an increase in mortgage default and argues that the small decline in building society borrowers could be associated with mortgages being paid off. Apart from problems of sampling, McCulloch argues that Gray's study may have underestimated those buying houses especially because survey respondents may not have distinguished between a mortgage repayment and a rent.

In addition to this period, there is a suggestion that home ownership fell between 1914 and 1918. There is also some suggestion that it may have fallen in the period 1870–1914 in specific towns (Daunton, 1977; Daniels, 1980).

Since 1947 there has been a general rise in the level of home ownership as a result of new building, transfers from private renting and, in recent years, council house sales. Table 3.1 has shown that home ownership became the biggest tenure (in terms of households) in the late 1950s. It passed the 50 per cent mark in 1970 and in the 1970s it also became the most mixed-class tenure. By 1990 it stands at 66 per cent, with growing evidence that in future it is likely to experience lower rates of increase. The Building Societies Association projection of 74.2 per cent by the year 2000

Table 3.4 *Economic group and tenure, 1947 (percentage of all dwellings)*

Group	Owner occupied	Buying	Rented from council	Other rented	Employer
I (up to £3 per week)	14	1	12	71	2
II (£3–£4)	18	2	14	59	7
III (£4–£5.10)	13	2	17	64	4
IV (£5.10–£10)	30	9	13	57	3
V (over £10)	63	3	1	30	3
Total	22	4	13	57	4

Source: Gray (1947)

64 *Home ownership*

would still seem somewhat optimistic, but crucially this depends upon policies adopted towards this and other tenures.

House prices

House price falls may themselves presage a decline in ownership and there have been periods when prices have fallen both absolutely or relatively in respect of general price and inflation trends. Absolute price falls were recorded in 1948 and 1952–54 for the country as a whole, though the data are unreliable. Table 3.5 shows the situation from 1954 to 1986. Falls relative to the retail price index are more common, as the table also shows (e.g. the years 1970, 1974–77, 1980 and 1981), and there has been some recent evidence of specific areas lagging behind general house price trends (see Karn *et al.*, 1985). While it is true that owning a dwelling has normally been a good investment, there have been occasions and/or areas where home ownership would have resulted in substantial financial losses if owners had sold and where the real value of properties did decline. Thus, recent buyers in areas where prices have fallen may actually have to sell their property at a loss if they need to move. If that same area's prices are also moving down when others are moving up, such buyers will of course have even greater difficulties making a move.

A silent revolution?

Broadly speaking, the growth of home ownership has been continuous although its rate of growth has varied. The question then is, how has this been achieved? Has it been, as so many protagonists imply, a revolution characterized by the silence of numerous individual transactions and the earnest endeavours and preferences of millions of individual home owners?

One perspective on the growth of home ownership is provided in Table 3.6. This distinguishes the different flows that have contributed to the growth in England and Wales. In the interwar years, new building was the dominant factor, although purchases from the private rented sector were also a major contributor. In the postwar period, the dominance of contract building for the public sector initially limited the contribution of new building to the growth of home ownership. Tenancy transfers were more important in the period up to 1960 – again mainly transfers from private renting. The period 1960–75 represents the golden age of speculative housebuilding, and new building accounted for some two-thirds of the growth. Finally, in the last period, while the

Table 3.5 *House prices and inflation, 1954–1986*

4th Qtr	Average price £	All properties Index	Annual change %	Retail price index Index	Annual change %
1954	1,990	100	–	100	
1955	2,080	105	+4.5	104	+4.1
1956	2,150	108	+3.4	107	+2.6
1957	2,180	110	+1.4	114	+4.4
1958	2,220	112	+1.9	116	+2.0
1959	2,330	117	+5.0	116	–
1960	2,500	126	+7.3	118	+1.8
1961	2,730	137	+9.2	123	+4.3
1962	2,870	144	+5.1	127	+2.6
1963	3,160	159	+10.1	129	+2.1
1964	3,420	172	+8.2	135	+4.5
1965	3,670	184	+7.3	141	+4.5
1966	3,850	193	+4.9	147	+3.8
1967	4,120	207	+7.0	150	+2.1
1968	4,390	221	+6.6	158	+5.6
1969	4,540	228	+5.5	166	+5.2
1970	4,920	247	+6.3	174	+7.7
1971	5,940	298	+20.7	195	+9.2
1972	8,460	425	+42.4	210	+7.7
1973	9,760	490	+15.4	232	+10.3
1974	10,200	513	+4.5	274	+18.2
1975	11,280	567	+10.6	343	+25.3
1976	12,200	613	+8.2	395	+14.9
1977	13,200	663	+8.2	447	+13.1
1978	16,600	837	+26.2	483	+8.1
1979	21,540	1,082	+29.3	566	+17.3
1980	23,480	1,180	+9.0	653	+15.2
1981	23,740	1,193	+1.1	730	+11.9
1982	25,530	1,283	+7.5	776	+6.2
1983	28,720	1,443	+12.5	815	+5.1
1984	32,810	1,649	+14.2	852	+4.6
1985	36,210	1,820	+10.4	902	+5.9
1986	41,433	2,082	+14.4	933	+3.4

Source: Nationwide Building Society

Table 3.6 *Home ownership in England and Wales: components of change (millions of dwellings)*

	New building	Purchases from other tenures	Demolitions and changes of use	Net change
1914–38	+1.8	+1.1	neg	+2.9
1938–60	+1.3	+1.5	−0.1	+2.7
1960–75	+2.6	+1.1	−0.2	+3.5
1975–88 (est)	+1.7	+1.9	−0.1	+3.5

Source: Department of the Environment (1977) Cmnd 6851, *Housing Policy*, Technical Volume I, Table 1.24 (HMSO, 1977) and estimates from *Housing and Construction Statistics* (HMSO).

annual rate of growth has been higher than in any other period, purchases from other tenures (two-thirds of them from the public sector) have been more important than new building.

These figures illustrate the importance not just of decisions by builders and developers but of those by private and public landlords. Builders' decisions about what to build where and when are influenced by a range of financial and market judgements. Similarly, private landlords' decisions have reflected their view of their best commercial and financial interest rather than responses to tenants' preferences. For public landlords, decisions have also been affected by political judgements and policies laid down by central government. Tenants in these situations are responding to opportunities and choices presented to them by landlords rather than determining the choices available. The flows that have determined the growth of home ownership are important in another way. Fewer than 60 per cent of owner-occupied dwellings came into the tenure as newly built dwellings. And as the tenure has matured, the proportion that is represented by newly built stock has declined. In 1986 in Great Britain there were some 22 million dwellings. Of these, almost 14 million (63 per cent) were owner occupied. Of these, almost 1.5 million (10 per cent) had been built in the previous 10 years. In other periods the picture was very different. Figure 3.1 shows that in 1938 in England and Wales there were 3.7 million owner-occupied dwellings and 49 per cent of them had been built since 1914. Just as strikingly, in 1960 there were 6.4 million owner-occupied dwellings and 17 per cent had been built in the previous 12 years.

Significantly, our measures of the rise of ownership focus upon the individual, with counts of the number of households or dwellings, and aside from occasional outbursts about the inefficiency

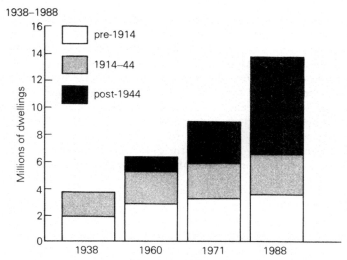

Figure 3.1 Size and age of the owner-occupied stock: England and Wales, 1938–88.
Source: Derived from Department of the Environment (1977) TVI, p. 3 and Department of the Environment, *Housing and Construction Statistics*.

of estate agents and solicitors we get little sense of the range of interests surrounding this tenure, their complex and sometimes conflicting concerns and a historical development that is far from smooth or silent.

The link between the growth of home ownership and the activities of building societies is well established (Boddy, 1980). Other partners in the process, including builders, material producers, estate agents, solicitors, financiers, the DIY and home-furnishing industries and landowners, are important. Each one of these groups controls services or commodities that are consumed within the home ownership process and all have benefited massively from its growth. The rise of home ownership has been a powerful element in the decline of private landlordism, but landlords have benefited from and participated in the growth through selling.

The rise of home ownership has also been associated with electoral and ideological politics. While it would be unwise to suggest that ownership induces conservatism and thus a tendency to vote for the party expressing such views, there can be no doubt that the belief in this link has encouraged the Conservative Party to promote home ownership. It is not possible within the scope of this book to provide a detailed social and political history of this issue. Some accounts refer substantially to this (e.g. Swenarton, 1981; Burnett, 1986; Merrett, 1979; Daunton, 1987). In the remainder of

68 *Home ownership*

this chapter, rather than attempt a lengthy historical examination of these issues, three brief case studies are used to allow some more detailed analysis of aspects of the growth of home ownership. The three case studies are: first, the reform campaigns of the late nineteenth century when mass property ownership assumed some significance; second, the 'homes for heroes' campaigns after the First and Second World Wars when state intervention in housing was strongly supported; and, third, the emergence of mortgage interest tax relief as assistance to home ownership. These case studies provide only selective insights into a complete history, but each touches upon a topic of contemporary relevance.

Property and politics

In nineteenth-century Britain, social standing and political authority were associated with wealth and landed property. While we should not pretend that those linkages do not remain today, they have been weakened by the extension of wealth and property to a broader spectrum of the population. The growth of home ownership has been an important aspect of the process and has itself changed the ownership of wealth and property.

The Reform Act of 1832 extended the franchise (the vote in parliamentary elections) to leaseholders and copy holders of land with an annual value in excess of specified amounts. This change provided the stimulus for the creation of freehold land societies, which aimed to help people acquire land and houses so that they might become voters. These societies had a clear political motive, with their promoters being quite certain that they expected the persons assisted to vote for the party the society was promoting. Over 100 of these societies were formed in the period 1847–57, the three largest being the Birmingham and the National (both Liberal Party) and the Conservative (the Tory Party). Early enthusiasm for this was tempered by the realization that there was no guarantee that the new property owners would vote Liberal or Tory. By the time the 1867 Reform Act extended the franchise to much of the male working class, the land societies had lost importance. By the time of the 1884 Reform Act, they had effectively disappeared as separate entities and had in some cases become building societies. The National lives on today as the Abbey National Building Society, while the land purchase aspect of its activities has become British Land – one of the UK's larger property companies.

The point then is that home ownership was valued by some in the nineteenth century because it related to the franchise and political power. It was apparent to many in the nineteenth and early twentieth centuries that the propertyless made up a much greater

A silent revolution

constituency than the property owners, and after the extensions of the franchise the former group had the potential to exercise great political power. Social reformers of the mid to late nineteenth century were quick to point to this potential and to the dangers of not controlling it. An extension of small property to the masses could assist the protection of large property held by the landed aristocracy and the industrial capitalist. This idea of the ramparts of property began to assume a role in Conservative Party policies in the 1880s, and, as Offer comments, it is the germ of a social process that is still working itself out (Offer, 1981, p. 150).

Leaseholders were an early target. Leases often 'fell in', with considerable unearned increments flowing to the freeholder. Frequently, as in the case of working-class residential property, freeholders let their leasehold properties run down in the last few years before the lease fell in, with consequences for their occupiers. Since it was estimated that there were at least 2 million leaseholders who could be transformed into freeholders and thus become part of the ramparts, Conservative politicians became active in their cause. The Tory, Randolph Churchill, introduced a leasehold enfranchisement bill in March 1884 saying:

> Who was more likely to be a contented citizen, the man who was a freeholder and who was in his property, or the man, who was at the mercy of a colossal landowner. (Cited in Offer, 1981, p. 154)

Lord Salisbury, the Conservative Prime Minister and one of London's wealthiest landowners, could clearly see the logic of the argument, as was indicated by his own speeches and that of his Lord Chancellor, Halsbury, in the debates on the Land Transfer Bill in 1887. Salisbury commented:

> When you talk of the diffusion of property for maintaining the principle of property you mean the diffusion of small quantities among large masses. I entirely concur in that view.

Halsbury went further:

> If there is to be an attack on property it will be resisted with much greater force if it is possible to say that it includes all property, not merely property which has any peculiar privilege, because then it can be said that an attack on property is an attack on property of all kinds. (Offer, 1981, p. 156)

At the same time, Salisbury and many members of his party recognized that such a strategy could erode their own powers and privileges, not least because leasehold enfranchisement would take property from them. Compensation thus became a critical issue, as did the idea of extending the provision of housing, with property being put on the market with low-interest mortgages and subsidized purchase (e.g. via the Small Dwellings Acquisition Act, 1899, and later the 1923 Housing Act). While ownership was central, it was evident from Tory programmes in the early twentieth century that there was also a place for minimum standard public rented housing as a further element of the ramparts strategy.

What this brief example illustrates is the complex intertwining of factors contributing to the growth of home ownership. To those in power it may be a way of retaining power; to those in need it can provide a satisfactory way of being housed. Home ownership and its promotion has multiple causes and consequences and is associated with legal and policy decisions as well as supply and demand factors. Indeed, it may be argued that user demand emerges as a factor at a later stage, only after the tenure form had developed associated with other factors.

Homes for heroes

Home ownership has had a long period of growth to become the dominant tenure in Britain. However, there have been at least two periods when public rental housing has been more prominent than home ownership in housing policy debates. On both occasions, world war provided the social, political and economic context, with governments being plainly aware that better housing should be provided for those returning from military service.

Why and how did this happen? Both the 1914–18 and the 1939–45 world wars involved the mass of the population. 'Pulling together' during wartime resulted in heightened consciousness about the differences between groups and classes and made many more aware of advantage and disadvantage in the UK. Politicians and bureaucrats appreciated this and recognized that, in urging sacrifice, rewards must be offered to those who returned. Thus, for these and other reasons war is associated with change and with the introduction of policies that both reflected national consensus and were intended to go some way to provide better standards and provision than had existed prior to war.

In the First World War, the Land Fit for Heroes Campaign reflected these kinds of tensions, albeit perhaps in heightened form, given the revolutionary tensions that were prevalent in Europe at the time. However, it is apparent that, despite these pressures and even the rent strikes in Glasgow and elsewhere in 1915, the rise of public housing in the period following the First World War was not simply a mechanism to contain revolution. Englander (1983) and Daunton (1987) have both shown how pressures in local housing markets had been intensifying prior to 1914 and these, combined with the need for government to curb inflationary pressures during the war, necessitated the introduction of rent and mortgage increase restrictions. Once imposed under 1915 legislation, these restrictions themselves exacerbated the prewar position where insufficient investment was going into rented housing. But the removal of restrictions would have meant large and instant rent increases because of the scarcity. The only way to tackle this situation was to construct via public initiatives a large number of new dwellings, bring the market back 'into line' and only at that point decontrol the private rental sector.

Thus was born the post First World War public housing drive. The early ambition as laid out by the Coalition government in the 1919 Housing Act was to build 500,000 houses, although by 1921 the programme was abandoned with only 170,000 houses having been built by local authorities. Shortages of finance, materials and labour combined with competition from the private sector and a general government desire to reduce expenditure to curb inflation meant that the prospect of the rapid creation of a substantial public sector fell away. Despite these setbacks, it is evident from the documents of the day that there was widespread acceptance that public sector provision would be a permanent part of the housing scene. The battle really was over how large a part. Through the 1920s and 1930s this battle was played out as governments came and went and policies changed, with the balance of favour swinging from public to private sectors. By the beginning of the Second World War the situation was clear – over 1.3 million public sector dwellings had been built in the interwar period in England and Wales compared to around 2.7 million private sector dwellings, the majority of which were for home owners. Home ownership had emerged as the dominant mechanism for new private housing investment, but a substantial public sector had been created in a 20-year period.

There is no space here to examine why the public sector did not recover sooner from its initial setbacks and go on to rival the private sector. Partly it can be explained by resistance from the local authorities themselves and their reluctance to enter into these kinds of commitments. Partly it can be explained by the instability of the British economy and the fluctuating levels of public expenditure. Partly it can be explained by legal and institutional developments strengthening home ownership and contributing to the emergence of consumer demand for owner-occupied dwellings.

72 *Home ownership*

While consumer demand emerged strongly, it is important to acknowledge that at this stage home ownership was sometimes little different from renting and there were major disputes about the rights of home owners. One notable and prolonged case was that pursued in 1938 by Elsie Borders, a house purchaser who took her building society to court regarding the quality of her house. Her purchase had been made possible by the builders' pool system, which grew up in the 1930s as a way of reducing the deposit necessary to buy a house. Basically, a low deposit was secured by the builder making cash deposits with the society. This collusion led the societies to adopt fairly relaxed attitudes to valuation and it resulted in some very poor-quality new houses coming onto the market. While Elsie Borders and her taxi driver husband Jim lost, their case aroused considerable controversy. As Jackson (1973), Craig (1986) and McCulloch (1990) have shown, the building societies had pushed the case for home ownership very hard – as is evident from early building society advertisements.

On the conclusion of the Second World War a set of circumstances similar to those of 1919 prevailed. The Labour government was concerned to restart house building after the war and local authorities were seen to be best able to achieve this and to channel resources to those in greatest need. Moreover, the public sector stock was to be built at high standards. The government went as far as considering controlling house prices to restrict speculative gains being made due to the shortage of property. In the event they did not proceed.

Financial stringencies, brought about under the Marshall Aid Plan to revive European economies, forced Labour to cut back on its initial targets and standards and in 1951 the Conservatives were returned to power. The Tories retained a strong commitment to the public sector but enhanced the role of the private sector. Standards were cut further and quantity became far more important than quality. The new government set a target of 300,000 houses a year (in total from both sectors). Early on, the public sector made the major contribution, but by the late 1950s the private sector had crept ahead (e.g. in 1959, 129,402 public sector dwellings were built in the UK, compared to 153,166 private sector). Having said that, in the 10 years from 1945, under both Labour and Conservative governments, the public sector doubled in size.

This brief account shows that during the period of growth of home ownership there have been periods, under both Labour and Conservative governments, when the public sector has been strongly promoted. It has been recognized as a sector that is capable of being planned and that can meet needs rapidly and effectively. The widespread criticisms of that sector today are being made in

A silent revolution

73

a different situation and outside of the context in which it was created – a point we might remember, not least with respect to home ownership!

Propping up the property-owning democracy: the case of tax relief

Apart from periodic arrangements encouraging builders to construct houses and building societies to keep their interest rates down, there are two particular subsidies to home owners that are long running (and contentious) – the absence of a capital gains tax (CGT) on the profits arising from individual home ownership and the allowance of tax relief on mortgage interest payments. Mortgage interest tax relief (MITR) has been the target of numerous criticisms and is widely acknowledged to have been an important element in the expansion of home ownership.

Mortgage interest tax relief has unremarkable origins. The income tax system set up in 1803 allowed borrowers to repay the interest on loans net of tax. In 1925/6 the Conservative government allowed a special arrangement to be created whereby building societies received the interest on loans without the deduction of the tax. The borrower was then allowed to set those interest charges against his or her income for tax purposes. This procedure was given legislative force in 1951 and consolidated in the Income Tax Act 1952 by the same party.

In 1963 the balancing factor in the equation – taxation on the imputed rental income of owning your own dwelling (i.e. the extra income, the rent in effect, one 'earns' or 'saves' by owning one's own dwelling) – was abolished. In 1969 tax relief on personal borrowing was limited to mortgages on residences and land in the United Kingdom. In 1974 the Labour government placed a ceiling on mortgage interest relief by specifying the maximum size of mortgage that could attract this subsidy – £25,000 – and restricted this relief to the borrower's main residence. In 1983, the Conservatives raised this to £30,000 and in the run-up to the 1987 budget came close to moving this to £35,000, but did not in the end and it has not been increased since. Indeed, home improvements that were funded via a mortgage up to the £30,000 limit and were eligible for tax relief lost this privilege in the 1988 budget and relief was attached to a dwelling rather than a purchaser – eliminating the double relief possible for joint purchasers.

Mortgage interest tax relief has now assumed considerable importance as a subsidy and a subsidy that is regressive in impact. In 1988 it stood at £4,500 million and was the target of much criticism – with both Labour and Alliance parties indicating that they would modify its use, though neither party intends to abolish it. The debate

74 *Home ownership*

over tax relief has intensified as the amount of revenue forgone has risen. Initially tax relief was relatively unimportant because most people did not pay income tax. However, as incomes have risen and the tax thresholds have been lowered, it has become increasingly significant. It has been estimated that in the late 1930s tax relief amounted to £8–10 million (Holmans, 1987) and this would have been out of a total taxation income (income tax and surtax) of £300–400 million. The value of mortgage interest tax relief has risen sharply since the 1960s as house prices and interest rates have increased and the number of home purchasers has grown. It has also been affected by changes in tax rates. Holmans estimates that, of the increase of £410 million in tax relief/option mortgage subsidy between 1973/4 and 1975/6, £140 million was the consequence of the basic rate of tax being raised from 30 per cent to 35 per cent. Reductions in tax rates in the 1980s have held down the recent rate of growth of this tax relief (see Chapter 5). Mortgage interest tax relief is not unique to the UK nor is interest relief unique to home ownership (landlords get it, as does business). Reaction to the subsidy has bordered on the emotional by those either for or against it. Unsurprisingly, very little systematic research has ever been published on the topic, though it is known the present government has looked closely at the matter. All parties are conscious of the potential impact of major changes in this area and all agree that any change should be phased in to allow households to adjust.

Holmans has commented (p. 465), 'the structure of tax relief and exemptions just grew without being planned'. The problem for government is how to wean the population off this dangerous drug, which besides any other damage has probably pushed up house prices by 5–10 per cent. Regardless of this, it is evident that this subsidy, along with the absence of capital gains, preferential tax treatment for lenders, improvement grants, and supplementary benefits payments to owners, is all part of a system that has done much to support the intrepid English householder alone in his or her castle. Tax relief had no great significance in the beginning, but now a whole set of interests have grown up around it. In an environment where the concern was to make best use of all public subsidy, tax relief would be altered or abolished. As we show later, government will face difficult choices in this area in the years to come. What was a modest act in history has assumed great significance.

Conclusions

The growth of home ownership through this century has been a product of conscious and sustained government policy as well as decisions by investors and individual households. Throughout its history, home ownership has sat within a complex array of market forces and structures. Typically we are regaled with stories about the rise of home ownership through the efforts of motivated and determined individuals who formed the early terminating building societies. Certainly there were groups of working people who did club together in this way, but even in the late eighteenth century and early nineteenth century it was recognized that there was a business to be developed around lending on property (see Ashworth, 1980; Craig, 1987). Since that time, building societies have moved from being local mutual institutions where there was some link between borrowers and depositors to being large national and international financial institutions with money being gathered both wholesale and retail and lent on a variety of securities. Residential property currently remains the main body of business, although even here there are growing doubts about the capacity of the housing market to absorb the volume of funds generated.

Building societies have been part of the preconditions of the growth of home ownership in Britain. Internationally we can see that societies are not an essential or inevitable part of that growth, but here they have played a crucial role. Their localized development helped give each market a very specific character, which really only began to break down in the 1960s. Their lending policies, while earlier giving assistance across a range of property, became increasingly restrictive with an emphasis on new or modern property, and it was only with the concern in the 1970s about lack of lending on pre-1919 property that they substantially re-engaged with this market. The societies have always relied heavily on local networks of agents and this in turn has fed the development of estate agency, mortgage brokerage and solicitors in every locality. For years the domain of the individual entrepreneur, we have recently seen a massive change in this area as large chains of agents have emerged, often owned by banks, building societies and other institutions. What we can see in this is the movement from small localized markets in the nineteenth century to the development of integrated national markets in the late twentieth century.

Transformations in finance and the system of exchange are also apparent in the building industry and in the building materials producer and supply industries. Over time output has become concentrated within a small number of large builders, who in turn rely on a small number of producers and suppliers. The traditional small builder continues as in the past, but their output is low and many now specialize in feeding highly localized sub-markets. As Ball (1983) has indicated, the industry is characterized by inefficiency, undercapitalization and instability.

76 *Home ownership*

It has not changed to the extent that the finance market or estate agency has.

Builders, building societies and estate agents are just three of the elements that go to make up the overall market structure that produces and shapes home ownership. Each industry has its own dynamic and logic, and this does not necessarily mesh with the others. There is, therefore, no smooth-functioning system that 'produces' home ownership nor any blueprint from which its growth is derived. One final illustration of this relates to the importance (referred to earlier) of tenure transfers in the growth of home ownership. Whether these have occurred through sales by local authorities or by private landlords, they initially involve decisions by suppliers and owners.

The transformation of the British housing market and the growth of home ownership over the last 60 years have occured because of investment and disinvestment decisions by builders, landlords and financial institutions. Hamnett and Randolph (1988), in their recent study of large corporate and institutional investors in the purpose-built flat market in London, chart the processes of investment and financial speculation affecting this market and leading to the flat breakup process of the 1970s.

The origins of the middle-class block of flats in London can be traced back to the middle of the nineteenth century. The 1930s flat boom, when large new blocks were erected on the sites of demolished villas or on the edge of London, was associated with the establishment of property investment companies as a major force. Their development was facilitated by borrowing from building societies and they catered for the salaried non-manual household. Hamnett and Randolph emphasize that institutional financial backing was crucial to this development and to the successful breakup operations in the 1970s. At its peak in the mid-1960s the sector catered for over 7 per cent of London's stock of dwellings and 28 per cent of the private rented sector – and its importance was greater in central London. In the period since then, the rationale for ownership has changed from a concern with investment considerations to an emphasis on trading. By the late 1970s no property companies involved in the sector were investment companies. Takeovers, bankruptcies, sales of individual flats, and the emergence of specialist residential property companies investing in the flat market for nothing other than its breakup potential had transformed the market. The large profits made from the breakup of flats by selling individual flats to home owners have become the province of speculative owners only interested in short-term capital gains. Standards of services, maintenance and management are not of importance to these owners and all residents – tenants and leasehold flat purchasers – have been affected. 'An Englishman's home, if it is held on a leasehold, is his landlord's castle' (BSA, 1984, quoted in Hamnett and Randolph, 1988).

The way that key parts of the home ownership market have developed is best understood in terms of financial, economic and taxation changes as well as housing policy developments and dweller control and choice. Issues about making profits, asset stripping, switching investments, interest rates, price inflation and differences between tenanted and vacant possession values are important as well as those about providing shelter. While user decisions and demand are also important elements in growth, it is a false conception to present this as the sole or even the dominant element. And the different influences on growth and different circumstances and conditions under which people become owners have a continuing impact on the nature and experience of home ownership.

4 Property, class and tenure

The home-owner takes a justifiable pride in his property, and is ever conscious of the fact that all he spends in money and labour theron serves but to bind him more closely to the home of his choice. The working-man who is merely a tenant has no real anchorage, no permanent abiding place and in certain circumstances is fair prey for breeders of faction and revolutionaries of every sort and condition. Home-ownership is a civic and national asset. The sense of citizenship is more keenly felt and appreciated, and personal independence opens up many an avenue of wider responsibility and usefulness. (Harold Bellman, 1927 pp. 53–4)

Home ownership gives personal mobility, personal pride, and stimulates the natural instinct of care over, and preservation of, what is one's own. It helps create greater responsibility and stability in society. (Conservative Central Office, 1979 p. 1)

Over half a century separates the above quotations yet the message remains essentially the same. Countless other quotes containing similar ingredients could be found to fill the period between – all stressing that home ownership encourages social stability and pride and reflects natural instincts and that its growth is historically inevitable. The notion that it is a force for social stability is most neatly represented in the powerful slogan of 'a property-owning democracy'. This chapter addresses a series of issues relating to this. It initially discusses historical and other perspectives on property and assesses whether the ownership of housing property has greater significance than other forms of property. It then goes on to outline debates about the importance of divisions in housing consumption and arguments that they have become more important than, and are separate from, social class.

Home ownership and property ownership

Housing as property has a long and complex past. By the mid-nineteenth century house property began to develop as an individual

Property, class and tenure

commodity that was bought and sold and that conveyed social, political and economic meaning and power. As the level of property ownership of all kinds began to increase within the population as a whole so new kinds of property began to be seriously contemplated for the first time. Consumer durables and the housing appropriate for the storage, use and display of these goods became important. The rapid expansion of manufacturing and later machine-based production centred upon existing towns and villages, alongside the enclosure of the countryside and the mechanization of agricultural production, resulted in both a demand for labour in the nascent urban centres and a loss of employment and housing in the countryside. These movements and a rapidly expanding (as well as relocated) population created a substantial demand for housing, which was only partly met through traditional employer provision. Intermediaries of many sort set themselves up in business to meet these housing needs. As traditional patterns of authority and social structure were driven aside by the changes in the distribution and employment of the population, so the whole question of alternative forms of demarcation became important, with housing emerging as a matter of increased significance. Moreover, while the new waged industrial workers were not wealthy, their consumption patterns were of growing importance in the economy and they were increasingly recognized as creating a market that needed to be served. Housing stood out as one important element in that process.

Only in the mid to late twentieth century did mass property ownership in the form of home ownership become a reality. Discussion of the meaning of home ownership and the class relations embedded in it involves analysing a pattern of historic development that even now is changing. Indeed, the title 'home owner' is itself a historically specific creation – drawing together notions of the home (the place of one's dwelling and nurturing) and notions of ownership and private possession. As society has changed and the home has increasingly been seen and projected as a private place distinct from one's home town and the commodity housing that is integral to it, so the individual significance of the home has been enhanced.

Critical responses to the drive for a higher level of home ownership may have accepted too readily that house purchase represents a form of consumption qualitatively distinct from the general norm of privatized consumption. In other words, it is the 'democracy' of property owning that is subjected to scrutiny rather than the notion of 'property owning' itself. But equating home ownership with property ownership involves a specific use of the term 'property' that gives the arguable impression that home owners necessarily have a greater interest than non-owners in a system that perpetuates private property relations. Certainly, those with the bargaining power and the income to compete effectively in the market place for houses, consumer durables, leisure services and so on are better served by a capitalist economy than those who are excluded from prevailing consumption norms. That is, however, rather different from singling out home ownership as a particular form of consumption with real participation rights in the capitalist economy. The argument has moved on from one that emphasized the stabilizing effects of home ownership through debt encumbrance or changes in political consciousness to one that locates home owners as shareholders in the capitalist enterprise. When you buy a refrigerator you are a customer, but when you buy a house you join the cooperative.

From this perspective, the 'man of property' no longer refers exclusively to members of a dominant aristocratic elite. Instead he has become a mass phenomenon. Indeed, almost two-thirds of British households enjoy that privileged position. There may be fewer acres to go round, the structures may be less grand, but the essential features are the same. Home ownership, that central prerequisite for membership of the middle classes, is now open to all. If the working classes still exist, they constitute a few residual pockets of poverty among council tenants.

The above remarks represent a caricature but nevertheless reflect essential beliefs held by a large number of politicians, academics and other commentators. In David Howell's book, *Freedom and capital* (1981), we are told that 'a broad based ownership class' is a prerequisite if we are to have 'the means to cope with the real changes in our society in a politically balanced way' (p. 16). More strongly he asserts that 'societies without a strong and influential middle layer of property conscious people crumble into lawlessness or drift into tyranny' (p. 19). In *The new acquisitive society* (Zweig, 1976), the foreword by Vaizey states:

> Among the characteristics . . . . which are bringing working class consciousness to an end are the enormous increase in home ownership which has marked the last 30 years . . . . (p. 7).

This process, commonly referred to as 'embourgeoisement', has been the subject of considerable research and commentary (see, for example, Goldthorpe and Lockwood, 1968). Whilst the populist analyses of the 1960s by writers such as Packard (1960) have been superseded by weightier theorizations, there is general agreement that something is happening to the working classes. Exactly what, however, is subject to considerable ambiguity and debate.

For example, reference to the end of working-class consciousness begs the question of whether objective class and positions remain unchanged despite the fact that the ideological cement of false consciousness has hardened. Indeed, depending upon initial definitions of class, it is possible to argue that the working classes have all but disappeared or, alternatively, that professions such as teaching are increasingly proletarianized. And some analysts have argued that proletarianization and embourgeoisement are part of the same process.

> This is something which escapes [the bourgeois economist]. For him the rise in the culturally determined subsistence minimum can only mean that 'we are all middle class'. He cannot understand that devaluation of labour power – and, at the limit, proletarianisation – on the one hand and a rise in the subsistence minimum on the other can not only co-exist but are actually part of one and the same development process. (Carchedi, 1975, p. 62)

Regardless of theoretical or political perspectives, there are shared assumptions regarding the uniqueness of housing and it is in this context that the notion of housing class has been seriously and extensively debated (see, for example, Rex and Moore, 1967; Haddon, 1970; Saunders, 1978). The Left have tended to approach the analysis of the extension of home ownership with views that this does indeed undermine revolutionary action, but argue that it is only a concessionary stake in the system and basic social structures remain intact. The Right accept the first half of the equation but argue that the expected political docility accrues from the stake in the system being real rather than illusory.

In common usage, property generally means things, and things possessed by individuals. Clothes, furniture, cars, houses, are all things we might possess that might be our individual property. Yet this concept of property is historically specific and relates to the development of a market economy and the 'commodity fetishism' of capitalism. As McPherson (1978) makes clear, certainly until the late seventeenth century the concept of property referred to rights rather than things.

> The change in common usage, to treating property as the things themselves, came with the spread of the full capitalist market economy from the seventeenth century on, and the replacement of the old limited rights in land and other valuable things by virtually unlimited rights. As rights in land became more absolute and parcels of land became more freely marketable

82   *Home ownership*

> commodities, it became natural to think of the land itself as
> the property. And as aggregations of commercial and industrial
> capital, operating in increasingly free markets and themselves
> freely marketable, overtook in bulk the older kinds of moveable
> wealth based on charters and monopolies, the capital itself,
> whether in money or in the form of actual plant, could easily
> be thought of as the property. The more freely and pervasively
> the market operated, the more this was so. It appeared to be the
> things themselves, not just rights in them, that were exchanged
> in the market. (McPherson, 1978, p. 7)

In contemporary usage, we also tend to assume that property must
be private. Yet, as McPherson illustrates, there are three kinds of
property – common, private and state – and all are the rights of persons, natural (individuals) or artificial (organizations/institutions).
Unlike private or state property, however, common property
is always a right of the natural individual. Indeed, McPherson
emphasizes that 'common property turns out to be the most
unadulterated kind of property' (p. 6). Flowing from this are a
number of consequences for the discussion of home ownership.
First, the notion of home ownership as property ownership (in
the sense of individualized purchase) derives from a contemporary
version of the meaning of 'property'. In this version, property is
equated with things or possessions. Thus, individually owned,
the house is simply one possession among many (albeit often
the largest and most valuable), which for any household might
also include car, furniture and other consumer durables. In other
words, if this meaning is adopted there is no qualitative difference
between a house and any other possession. Secondly, if we accept
that property refers to rights and not things and rights conferred
on the individual by the state, then property rights are conferred
on both tenants and home owners – the former are common, the
latter are private. Thirdly, and again to paraphrase McPherson, the
contemporary notion of the property-owning democracy rests on
a narrow concept of property as a right to exclude others. It might
be argued that true democracy requires a paradigm of property that
is a right not to be excluded. Fourthly, to return to our man of
property, his property constituted rights to receive a revenue from
his estate and other assets. Property conferred social and economic
power. Feudal property was superseded by capitalist property –
the right to appropriate the unpaid labour of others.

In what sense then are contemporary house purchasers becoming
property owners? They purchase the rights to exclude others from
the use of the specific possession – the house. So also does the
purchaser of the car. Landlords are property owners in the sense

Property, class and tenure 83

that they derive a revenue from the rights of use to a set of premises. But what revenue does the home owner receive from property?

The extension of home ownership has become for many social policy analysts and politicians the major means by which a real redistribution of wealth can be achieved. In 1979 Michael Heseltine claimed that: 'in a way and on a scale that was quite unpredictable, ownership of property has brought financial gain of immense value to millions of our citizens' (*House of Commons Debates*, 15 May 1979, col. 80). The value of this process in achieving a more egalitarian social structure has also been emphasized by reformers such as Frank Field (1975). In wealth statistics, wealth in the form of owner-occupied housing is increasingly evident. Atkinson and Harrison (1978) explain the decline in the share of all wealth held by the top wealth owners in terms of the spread of 'popular wealth' – the value of owner-occupied housing, plus the value of consumer durables. But how far is the redistribution merely cosmetic? If house purchase really provides a stake in the system, then the apparent redistribution of wealth should reflect a redistribution of economic and social power. But we must differentiate between different forms of wealth – wealth in the form of capital, which confers social power, and wealth in the form of consumption goods. As Luria (1976) notes: 'only a part of total wealth takes the social form of capital and it is only this part which has implications for the distribution of social power' (p. 267). If we accept this distinction, then the spread of home ownership serves to conceal a continuing concentration of social power rather than contributing towards greater equality. (These issues are returned to in Chapter 6.)

The point is that the equation, property = things = wealth, distorts analyses of home ownership. The property-owning democracy implies a greater distribution of commodities, the enhancement of consumption power (which may reflect the lowering of the value of living labour rather than a rise in real incomes), a democracy strictly limited to the sphere of consumption. A nation of home owners would not necessarily mean anything in terms of the distribution of property rights in the production of social wealth or in the exercise of social power. Indeed, even the supposed benefits of home ownership in the sphere of consumption are liable to be highly unevenly distributed and to enhance rather than undermine the existing class or status structure. This is not to suggest that the spheres of production and consumption can in any sense be seen as separate. Pratt (1986) has correctly pointed to the ways in which housing tenure interconnects with occupational histories. And research on contrasting groups of home owners has shown the complex interplay between housing histories and the exigencies of particular occupations (see Forrest and Murie, 1987, 1989a). However, whilst housing experiences and housing tenure may enhance or inhibit occupational choices and careers, the concentration of power and influence remains oligarchic and fundamentally unaffected by the spread of home ownership. Universal home ownership would not necessarily have more profound implications for the social structure of a capitalist society than universal car ownership. Both developments would indeed have important impacts on, say, the structuring of space and patterns of consumption, but neither need have any implications for democratic participation. Indeed, in the UK there is ample evidence that the postwar growth of home ownership (and particularly its growth under Thatcherism) has been paralleled by an erosion of participative democracy (see, for example, Hillyard and Percy-Smith, 1988).

It is almost axiomatic to suggest that housing is different from any other commodity. It physical size, its durability, its cost, its fixed location, its necessity, its political importance, are all factors that differentiate housing from other consumption goods. We are led to believe that the purchase of a dwelling is a qualitatively difference experience. Yet this is highly questionable in a number of ways. Before embarking on analyses that accept *a priori* that housing is unique, the qualities it shares with other commodities should be examined. For example, there is nothing unique about scarcity in a market economy. Those same processes that create a 'housing question' also create a 'transport question' and an 'education question'. Indeed – given historical changes in acceptable minimum standards – they would also create a 'dishwasher question' if the possession of such a commodity was sufficiently politically charged to warrant such a label. In other words, it is market processes that create scarcity. There is nothing inherent in the nature of the dwelling that is unique. While it can be politically and economically damaging and socially destabilizing to have large numbers of persons homeless or living in squalid conditions, it is not necessarily so dysfunctional as to produce a political response.

Similarly, the trend towards mortgaged house purchase can be set in the context of the sophistication of credit-based consumption and the growth of financial institutions. The early building clubs and building societies set up in predominantly working-class areas in the eighteenth and nineteenth centuries had more modest aims and means than the institutions of mass home ownership that now dominate the financial landscape (see, for example, Chapman and Bartlett, 1971). Whilst housing is undoubtedly the most costly purchase in the lifetime of most households, this is a quantitative rather than a qualitative difference. It is at one end of the cost continuum. There are a large number of expensive 'necessities' that often require credit finance for their acquisition. House purchase is part of this process of debt-encumbered privatized consumption. Whilst the need to maintain mortgage payments undoubtedly has a high priority for most households, it is quite another thing to argue that the purchase of housing changes consciousness in a way that the private acquisition of other commodities does not. We may sacrifice the automatic washing machine before we abandon the car; and we may abandon the car before we get into mortgage arrears. But the notion that mortgage payments have a politically stabilizing influence and make people more committed to job security has little to do with any mystical qualities inherent in the acquisition of a dwelling. Credit-based consumption generally will have this effect. The need for shelter and the need to retain a private domain of social relations are highly valued regardless of tenure (see, for example, Marshall *et al.*, 1988, pp. 215–16). The social fabric of capitalism may increasingly be supported by the transmission of ideology through home, family and school. Consumerism may indeed have displaced conflict over the nature of the labour process. But there would seem to be little empirical evidence to support the view that house purchase is necessarily the pivotal factor in this process.

Consumption sector cleavages and the primacy of class

Debates about housing class have moved on since the early contributions of Rex and Moore (1976), Haddon (1970), Pahl (1970) and Saunders (1977). The real shift in focus in the debate was associated with discussion of consumption cleavages and consumption sectors. Saunders' doubts about the use of the term 'housing class' led him to adopt a framework of consumption sectors rather than try to reformulate class. Dunleavy has outlined this approach in the following terms:

> The concept of sector is a means of characterising and grouping together non-class or 'immediate' social interests distributed in systematic ways by economic, political and ideological structures. Basically, sectors are lines of vertical division in a society, such that certain common interests are shared between social classes in the same sector, while within a social class, sectoral differences reflect a measure of conflict of interests. (Dunleavy, 1979, p. 419)

Saunders (1986a) identified the emergence of consumption sector cleavages as a challenge to nineteenth-century conceptions of class and inequality as phenomena of the organization of production alone. This was not because of some blindness of nineteenth-century writers but because these consumption sector cleavages did not exist in the nineteenth-century. Current levels of accumulation and inheritance associated with housing were inconceivable even 70 years ago. And consumption sectors 'have only arisen in the period of advanced capitalism in which the state has intervened directly both in the organisation of production and consumption. They are products . . . . of the use of state power in civil society and as such they have only appeared in the period since Marx and Weber were writing' (p. 156).

This approach remains the basis for the most plausible current contributions. It does not seek to rewrite class as such, but identifies an additional source of alignments and interests. It could be that such alignments and interests could be read off from class, would be directly determined by class, and so would deepen and strengthen class differences rather than cut across or confuse them. The proponents of consumption sector cleavages, however, have tended to assert their independent and cross-cutting effect.

The challenge to the consumption cleavage position has been best expressed recently by Preteceille (1986). This does not attempt to argue that occupational class directly determines consumption differences. Instead, it asserts the primacy of class. Preteceille claims that the separation between work processes and consumption is a material, economic and ideological reality of capitalist societies but is not necessarily an absolute separation and varies from one city and country to another. Collective consumption is not a separate activity and has more than vague and general connections with the rest of people's lives and particularly their lives at work. State intervention in the provision of consumption goods and services can and does generate new inequalities and divisions over and above those generated through the class system. But class position structures access to consumption (e.g. size and security of income) and different consumers may derive different benefits and costs from state provision according to their class. Class determination does not mean that consumption practices should be the same for, or specific to, particular occupational class groups. Rather the position of each individual in the actual work process has major consequences for life outside work. The critique of the mechanistic and functionalist view of the reproduction of the labour force does not have to lead to the loosening of the links between collective consumption and economic processes.

Preteceille argues that it is not only present relations that tend to organize life, but also the past ones of individuals and of their parents and relatives. Furthermore, determinations between work and consumption processes work both ways. To consider

Property, *class and tenure*

consumption differences as mere reflections or direct consequences of class situation is a gross oversimplification. There are important differences in consumption conditions of the members of each class, but some consumption processes are particularly active components of the (re)production of class differences. None of the wide range of differences in consumption is independent from class relations but rather is produced by a specific set of social processes that are structured by and express in different ways capitalist relations of production. And the basic source of diversity in needs lies in the situation of those groups in the production process, the division of labour and related power structures.

Thus, to return to 'housing classes', they may be regarded as a source of social difference but they relate to position in the work process and are most clearly understood in relation to it. A specific analysis of the processes converging to produce consumption difference indicates the primacy of class relations.

Saunders (1986a) has responded to this position. He states that notwithstanding their internal fragmentation it may still be the case that consumption sectors share certain fundamental interests. Other differences between home owners cannot undermine their common and fundamental interest in maintaining domestic property values, reducing mortgage interest rates, increasing state subsidies through tax relief or grants, and so on. Saunders argues that recognition of the significance of class in affecting access to consumption does not necessarily indicate the primacy of class location. Class is often a poor guide to a household's consumption location, for certain forms of private consumption (most crucially private housing) are commonly purchased in many capitalist societies by large sections of the population, including many working-class families. The key factors structuring access to forms of consumption may have less to do with class *per se* than with whether or not people are engaged in formal employment of any kind and whether households can draw upon more than one income. Seen in this way, class divisions may turn out to have less significance than divisions between employed and unemployed, or between single- and multiple-earner households. Saunders argues that more significant than this is the fact that consumption may generate effects that far outweigh those associated with class location. Ownership of housing is the key factor here. With over 60 per cent of households in the owner-occupied sector in Britain (and an even higher proportion in some other countries), a majority of the population are in a position to accumulate such capital gains as may accrue through the housing market. Inheritance associated with housing, loans secured through housing collateral, access to favourable locations with positive externalities, and release of current income from the need to secure

88 *Home ownership*

capital sums in old age, all suggest that consumption location may be every bit as important as class location in determining life chances.

Saunders' argument moves on from accumulation to assert the importance of ownership of housing in opening up the possibility for some degree of autonomous self-expression. He claims that people do seem to achieve a real and deep satisfaction from the ability to express their own identities through reproducing their own immediate surroundings in which they enjoy an exclusive right of ownership. While Saunders acknowledges constraints and qualifications that need to be taken into account, he insists that 'It is this sense of meaningful experience which people may derive from different modes of consumption which has been lacking hitherto in the debate over consumption sectors' (p. 159), and,

> It remains crucial to an analysis of consumption–sector cleavages that we understand the association which undoubtedly exists for many people between individualised consumption and personal autonomy. (p. 160)

In this way the debate in Britain has moved from housing class to consumption sectors and from examination of the role of council housing to home ownership. Home ownership is now the only growing major tenure in Britain and the inflation of house prices involves real gains associated with housing. The recent house price increases in London and the South East may have delivered larger gains than are available through wages and salaries obtained through work. Housing and housing tenure position are the key examples of sectoral differences within social classes – differences that it is suggested involve a measure of conflict of interest. It is suggested that home owners have common interests irrespective of class and separate from non–owners in the same class. These interests relate to two elements – accumulation of wealth and the real and deep satisfaction and ability to express identity through exclusive rights of ownership. Both these issues are central to the chapters that follow and will be pursued in greater detail (see also, Murie, 1986). In the remainder of this chapter we merely raise some preliminary doubts regarding the assertion of common interests among home owners and the longer-term significance of tenurial divisions.

Differentiation among home owners

To what extent then is it realistic to talk about shared material interests among home owners? Many are seriously indebted, whilst others own outright. Some will experience massive house price

Property, class and tenure   89

increases; some may experience losses. Some will inherit the parental home; some may be first-generation owners. Some will occupy a £1 million house in an exclusive part of London; others a decaying Victorian terrace in inner Liverpool. Our image of home ownership as a tenure that confers status and relative affluence derives from a time when those positional advantages were enjoyed by only a minority. And that minority were, by and large, relatively advantaged in terms of class background and their position in the labour market. Indeed, as Hirsch (1977) has pointed out, positional goods (in this case, high-status, owner-occupied dwellings) can *only* be acquired by a minority.

> Thus the extension of middle-class objectives has outdistanced middle-class opportunities. The excess demand on middle class life-styles reinforces the underlying inflationary thrust. To the extent that the demands for private consumption underlying the collective wage claims take the form of positional goods in restricted absolute supply – for education that provides better access to the more sought after jobs, for housing in the more sought after locations – such demands are doomed to eventual non-fulfilment. (Hirsch, 1977, p. 173)

But old images die hard. Most people would associate housing deprivation with renting. Owner occupation solves housing problems; it does not create them. Yet if housing is allocated through the market, there is an inevitable hierarchy of housing conditions and opportunities. It is likely that those who derive real advantage from the operation of the housing market experience their housing privileges alongside other material advantages. Housing position may reflect and enhance class position, rather than transform it. As home ownership expands, the market is becoming more stratified and more segmented. Half the households in Britain may be labelled as home owners, but some buy at the cheapest supermarket and others frequent the chic boutiques.

> the housing market functions to create a growing differentiation amongst owner occupiers. This growing differentiation means that wealth accrues to some, more rapidly than it does to others. The evidence further suggests that this process of accumulation transfers wealth to those who already have substantial assets, thus reinforcing rather than reducing existing social inequalities. (Thorns, 1981, p. 28)

What this begins to suggest is that the processes currently underway in the British housing market (including the large-scale privatization of public sector dwellings) will amplify income and class differentials in housing.

Recent commentaries have identified that, while the divisions between owners and renters have indeed become more marked, the downgrading of the public housing sector has been accompanied by the marginalization of a large group of low-income owners (see, for example, Forrest and Murie, 1988a; Karn et al., 1985). This latter group may derive few material advantages from house purchase and may be relatively disadvantaged when compared with some public tenants. Furthermore, in the light of the sale of publicly owned dwellings, it is likely that as the better former public sector dwellings filter through the market they will not be appropriated by the least affluent house buyers. Those less affluent households who would have derived real housing advantage in the public sector may be forced to buy a rundown dwelling in need of considerable investment. The rate at which such a property will appreciate in value is uncertain and cannot be taken for granted. Past arguments that home ownership is benefiting a whole class in society at the expense of another (e.g. Pahl, 1975) now require considerable qualification. Home ownership may be a game all can play, but the chances of winning are skewed heavily in certain directions. The contrast between the middle-class professional couple setting out in the early years of their house purchase career and the late-middle-aged steelworker buying a council house with a redundancy payment may be very great, and for some the stake in the system may be very limited.

There is so much variation within home ownership that it is difficult to see how the notion of tenure (any tenure) as an autonomous undifferentiated status group can stand up to scrutiny. Whilst the concept of a housing class seems to constitute no more than an alternative form of labelling to the more standard category of tenure, Weberian notions of class as status groups in the sphere of consumption are useful in so far as they reassert the need for detailed analyses of forms and styles of consumption. Any attempt, however, to equate tenure with status group throws up differentiating factors that appear at least as significant as the similarities. Part of the problem lies in the essentially static nature of the concept. In this sense, Haddon's critique of Rex and Moore remains as pertinent as ever. We require a new set of categories that can link Marxist class categories with developments in consumption patterns as well as take account of the life cycle. Housing position reflects and modifies consumption position, but it is not a determining factor. We need to begin to capture a sense of process and dynamism, of differing consumption trajectories, to understand status differentiations. The forces and interests that supposedly bind together home owners

Property, class and tenure 91

only seem to make sense when posed in opposition to council or private tenants. Yet there is sufficient evidence from published statistics and studies to indicate that seeing any of those tenures as homogeneous is also highly problematic.

Changing meanings and associations

The belief that movement through the home ownership hierarchy is possible for everyone is still nurtured implicitly and explicitly by those whose interests are closely tied economically and politically to a higher level of home ownership. In the last decade in particular, the hard sell has been enhanced by arguments relating to the investment potential of dwellings and the benefits of inheritance for the next generation: arguments growing out of the extraordinary levels of house price inflation in the late 1960s, early 1970s and late 1980s. There is now greater emphasis on the accumulative potential of house purchase, particularly when council tenants are being persuaded of the benefits of buying the dwellings they occupy. This emphasis on exchange value is hardly surprising given that in other ways (for example, space, standards and location) those in the best council houses may be better off than some home owners.

As we saw in Chapter 3, the emphasis in the 1920s and 1930s was very different. The growth of tertiary employment involved a new group keen to escape the urban areas for the suburban–rural ideal. Cheaper house prices, lower interest rates and higher mortgage advances combined with steadier incomes for the new white-collar employees and skilled manual workers to facilitate the move to the suburbs. The possibilities for this suburban expansion had been created by the growth of the rail network prior to the First World War, a process well documented by Jackson (1973). What emerges from his account and others (e.g. Pawley, 1978; Burnett, 1978) is the combination of factors that encouraged the expansion of owner occupation. Far from being a conspiracy by a dominant elite to undermine the revolutionary fervour of the masses, a series of economic, social and legislative changes coalesced to create a favourable climate for the expansion of home ownership. The political and ideological impact of mass individualized home ownership had been articulated by various commentators. However, present-day champions of the cause, including the building societies and the Conservative Party, were by no means unequivocal in their support until well into the twentieth century. Indeed, Pawley (1978) suggests that the 1957 Rent Act marked the final turning point for the Conservatives away from the support of private landlordism to the acceptance of home ownership as the 'normal' tenure for the masses.

The move to a new suburban home in the early 1930s was likely to be perceived as an end in itself rather than as a means to accumulation or further social mobility. The promised land of the upper middle classes, the rural idyll within easy reach of the urban nucleus, was at last available to those lower down the status hierarchy. The fact that those being emulated had long since moved on was neither here nor there. The images being conveyed seem hardly credible today, but for those leaving a lifetime of inner city residence it was more plausible. Jackson provides some amusing examples of the overenthusiasm of some builders in their representation of the suburbs. Would-be purchasers of semis in West Molesey, Hampstead, were told they could take advantage of the flat roof to 'take meals in the open' or even 'sleep al fresco' (from Jackson, 1973, p. 139). Fairly humble dwellings were described as 'mansions' or 'country residences'. This emphasis on a healthy environment and new-found class affluence was combined with various other gimmicks and offers such as firework displays, free season tickets, free furnishings, groceries or landscaping. It should be remembered that, unlike the dominant contemporary experience, the early 1930s saw house prices falling and building society deposits outstripping borrowers. The pressure to sell was much greater and the potential market relatively untapped.

If 'suburbia' was already a pejorative term for some prior to the Second World War, for the new owners it represented a real improvement in their housing circumstances. Their emphasis was on the quality of the dwelling and its environs, and the fact that it was owned rather than rented was less important. Whilst purchasers were keen to preserve their new exclusivity, their defence was an expression of class snobbery rather than a concern with resale values.

But suburban home ownership was only one aspect of the gradual shift in tenure that began in the early part of this century. Inner urban home ownership was also increasing but under different circumstances. Stewart (1981) conveys very different images of the shift from private renting to home ownership in her account of the process in Saltley, Birmingham:

> The shift to owner occupation was spearheaded by this new wave of entrepreneurs in touch with the market and with sources of finance. They made their major impact after 1931 when owner occupation was expanding rapidly in the newly built areas. Their method was to buy these blocks of houses then split them up by way of underlease and sell to the sitting tenants or new owner occupiers when the tenant died or left. They absorbed the

Property, class and tenure 93

occupier's capacity to pay increased housing costs by pushing up the price of each house. (Stewart, 1981, p. 13)

The group of new home owners emerging from this process became owners without moving to a new environment or new dwelling. They were skilled workers in the local factories buying leasehold mainly because of the advantages this gave to the landlord as a way round rent control and as a means to a greater return on investment.

The progressive transfer of privately rented dwellings to sitting tenants has continued throughout the century and we are now witnessing a similar process in the public sector. For individuals and households who enter home ownership in this way, the experience of changing tenure is mild by comparison with those who combine a changed tenure status with a changed location. Indeed, for the sitting tenant purchaser there may be little to experience apart from the received messages concerning possible capital gains and financial security.

In contrast, Crossick (1977) illustrates the more complex relationships between changes in the labour process, suburban development, status differentiation and home centredness among the emerging lower middle classes at the turn of the century. Those seeking to escape the residential and work environment of the working classes had a strong individualistic and competitive ideology, with collectivism being the characteristic of a lower social order. According to Crossick, the assertion of status and the very marked home centredness of this group reflected a vulnerability, a fear of being dragged down from their tentative grasp on the next rung of the social ladder. For this group, the suburban home, owned or rented, took on particular meanings in specific historical circumstances.

Rose (1980) develops this theme further in her discussion of the historical significance of working–class home ownership. In her view, the development of early forms of home ownership among certain sections of the working classes reflected a 'commonsense' politics, with struggles around basic production and social relations becoming subordinated to conflicts over wages and the distribution of the social product. The political terrain became what Rose terms the 'subjective limits of the possible', a struggle to achieve enhanced satisfaction in the sphere of consumption and family life as compensation for alienation in the workplace. Rose emphasizes the important consequences of this process in terms of the separation of home and workplace, the fragmentation of everyday life and the atomization of working–class demands and the different meanings and experiences of males and females in relation to the home.

As industrial capitalism developed, women became the 'ideal wives' in the 'ideal home' progressively relegated and isolated as 'physical and emotional supports to the men who had to present themselves for work under capitalist relations of exploitation the following morning'. Rose's arguments are particularly important because studies of suburbanization and home ownership have generally been highly male oriented. A central theme has been the home as a retreat from the alienating demands of the workplace, the haven in a heartless world (Lasch, 1977) for exploited males. It is only very recently that increasing attention is being paid to the changing historical position of women within and outside the home environment (see, for example, Burman, 1979).

Whilst greater attention should be given to patriarchal relations in discussions of housing issues, it is also clear that class position alters the experiences of the home for males and females. In contemporary times, for example, the childless middle-class couple pursuing parallel careers may have a much lower degree of home centredness than the standard nuclear family or the working-class household where both adult members are out of paid employment. For the latter, the home may become a prison rather than an escape and home ownership an even more complete form of confinement.

Home ownership then is a category that must be 'unpacked' historically in terms of class or status group and by gender. It is not an isolated, autonomous experience. Home ownership formed part of a very different set of experiences in its development. It has never meant the same thing for all people. Households that entered home ownership before the war are now outright owners. Some may have bought as sitting private tenants and may still be occupying decaying inner city terraces. Former council tenants encouraged by substantial discounts to purchase as sitting tenants are in a variety of locations with different tenure mixes. Others, such as single-person owners, those whose history involves divorce or late marriage, and more idiosyncratic household structures such as the multiple mortgaged collective are also home owners. Home owners are a highly differentiated group occupying a wide range of positions in the hierarchy of housing opportunities and conditions. And it is by no means a hierarchy where promotion is guaranteed.

Concluding comments

This chapter has shown that meanings, attitudes and material interests within home ownership are highly varied. Any set of analytical categories and discussion of the significance of this tenure must

Property, class and tenure

accommodate such variations. The need to escape a preoccupation with tenure and to develop historically sensitive concepts relating to key differences in housing consumption constitutes part of the research agenda for the next decade. Whilst it would be wrong to deny that the most disadvantaged households are likely to be found in the private or public rented sectors, it would be equally erroneous to suggest that the social distance between the less affluent owners and tenants in general is as great as some tenure analyses would have us believe.

There is growing evidence and analysis of differentiation within tenures, and of differences in meanings attached to tenure over time and spatially. None of the major categories is homogeneous. Not all council housing comprises stigmatized estates and run-down or badly designed flats and maisonettes. Similarly, not all owner-occupied properties are well-maintained, detached villas in leafy desirable suburbs. In some areas it is owner occupation that includes the less desirable, residual stock of dwellings taken up by those who are marginalized economically and politically. In other areas it is parts of the council stock that fulfil this role. The slower rate of house price inflation in the northern regions of England and in Scotland compared with Greater London and the south of England relates to affluence and economic buoyancy. It results in a situation where the package of benefits associated with home ownership and the perceptions of that tenure are very different. It seems likely that this partly explains regional differences in preferences for home ownership.

Furthermore, the images of attitude to dwelling associated with ownership are not generally sustained. Saunders identifies possibilities for the extension of personal autonomy outside the formal workplace and with the possibility for some degree of autonomous self-expression through a world of objects created or modified through our own labour as linked to ownership rather than as existing in all tenures.

Three considerations can be offered in response to this. First, not all owners are likely to identify the same advantages of ownership. Second, the opportunities for autonomy and self-expression are likely to reflect the wider life experience and to be a product of work, family and community situation as well as housing. Third it is evident that, just as some owners do not respond to ownership in the way implied, so many tenants do invest time and effort in rented accommodation and do not find that lack of ownership prevents autonomous self-expression. There may be differences in the degree of alienation and powerlessness associated with different tenures, and households may express themselves in different ways in different tenures. (Perhaps in council housing it is internal decoration rather than external display – see, for example, Holme, 1985.) What is difficult to sustain is a view that such attributes are exclusive to tenures or derive from ownership rather than life experience and attitudes that may often coincide with tenure status.

The debate about consumption sector cleavages and attitudes to the home is referred to again in Chapter 6, which focuses on issues of wealth and accumulation, and Chapter 7. In these chapters, as in this, it is argued that to focus on tenure and on home ownership as a key division in society is unjustified. In concluding this chapter it is relevant to refer to three other sources of doubt about the primacy of ownership.

First the demand to own and the returns made from ownership are strongly influenced by policy. The growing demand for home ownership in Britain has been influenced by significant and increasing financial and ideological support. The discussion about the interests generated by ownership refers to a set of historically specific circumstances rather than necessary attributes of the tenure. These are, in particular, that house prices have risen faster than the rate of inflation and housing investment has provided greater returns than other forms of investment; that mortgage interest rates have been lower than inflation rates; and that tax relief and fiscal arrangements have privileged the housing sector relative to other forms of investment. Changes in policy, in rates of inflation, in interest rates and in other factors influence the nature and extent of the gains to be made from different parts of the home ownership sector. Changes in policy towards other tenures and the desirability of those tenures are also relevant.

Secondly, as home ownership grows, it is less determined by new building, more dependent on second-hand sales and chains of sales, and becomes more unstable and liable to rapid fluctuations in price and market collapse. So the variation in the owner-occupied market will become more marked and the primacy of ownership will become more doubtful.

Thirdly, the underlying trends in the British market – commodification, privatization and marginalization within each tenure – involve a reassertion of the connection between housing and income and wealth. As home ownership approaches a 70 per cent share of the housing market, the problems of disrepair, repossession, eviction, flitting and homelessness are more apparent. The growth phase of home ownership in the period of transition in which the form of private housing provision has changed from rentier landlordism to individual home ownership is likely to have had different characteristics than a later phase. In the growth phase, home ownership was associated with the younger employed, in a

Property, class and tenure

growing full employment economy with an expanding welfare service net. In a later phase, recession, restructuring and declining welfare provision mean that home ownership and home owners have a much more mixed experience. The sector is increasingly dependent on grants and state subsidy. The more vulnerable owners are less likely to be able to sustain ownership status. The quality of housing that people are in and the rate of accumulation involved will increasingly reflect income and wealth. Both housing and economic trends suggest that inequalities deriving from consumption in housing will become more closely associated with occupational class. The excitement over the extent to which consumption cleavages in housing cross-cut occupational class should be tempered by a recognition that we have been looking at a system in transition and that at the end of transition there is likely to be a better fit between occupational class and housing class. In this situation also it may be that we should be looking for new key social divisions in relation to the impact of recession and restructuring, to marginalization and the position of those who are not in employment or in the growth sectors of the economy and to differences in relation to region, gender and race as well as class, rather than to housing classes conceived in terms of housing tenures. This is not to understate or underestimate the significance of home ownership in people's lives or to forget the chronic exclusion experienced by many non-owners. But to draw the principal social divide between tenures and to ignore the major social divisions within home ownership, or to regard other processes as less important in the shaping of people's lives and material interests, is to overstate the case.

5 The fragmented market

Would you pay £35,000 for a converted broom cupboard? Somebody did. In fact, they paid £36,500. National media reported in 1988 that such a property was on the market. The room was 12 ft by 7 ft 6 in and it had a bathroom of 1 1/2 sq. ft. It did have a window and, most significantly, it was opposite Harrods. A beach hut offered for sale by a Bournemouth estate agent attracted similar media attention. For £12,000 (possibly up to £15,000) the buyer would get a 7 ft x 7 ft hut with no amenities and no electricity. By way of contrast an estate agent in Burnley was reported as saying 'We have 20 to 30 starter homes at £12,000 on our books' (*The Times*, 9 August 1988, p. 1). Such examples are presented as the operation of the market taken to lunatic extremes – yet it is quite consistent with the more general and accepted state of the housing market in London and the South East, where a modest terraced house may be priced at £80,000 or more. Indeed, in Kensington and Chelsea (the location of the converted broom cupboard) in 1988 the average house price was £136,500, and first-time buyers paid, on average, £125,000 to enter the market and put down a deposit of some £32,000 (London Research Centre, 1988). Access is dependent on high household incomes, typically from two earners, and the servicing of a heavy debt. The average income of borrowers in Greater London was over £21,000 in 1988 and the average advance was nearly £50,000 (Building Societies Association, 1988).

Contrast this with the situation in the north of England where a modest detached house would not have been substantially more expensive in 1986 than the converted broom cupboard (Nationwide Building Society, 1986). A recent analysis by Nationwide Anglia ranks highest and lowest prices for three-bedroomed semis. Whilst a prospective buyer in Haringey in north London would have to pay over £113,000, in Llanelli in Wales £20,000 would secure a similar property (Nationwide Anglia, 1988).

House prices are periodically big news. In 1986 a consultant's report had a section headed 'TWO NATIONS – House Prices Divide the Country' (Reward Regional Surveys, 1986). A Nationwide Building Society report showed a further widening of the 'North–South divide'. House prices in London, on average, were

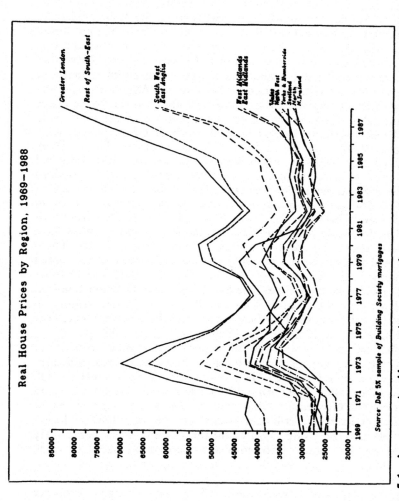

Figure 5.1 Average regional house prices expressed as a percentage of average house prices in the South East (excluding Greater London) (1969–89).

Source: Derived from Council of Mortgage Lenders (1989) *Housing Finance*.

100   *Home ownership*

23 per cent higher than in the previous year. This was over ten times the increase in Northern Ireland and nearly eight times the increase in the north of England and Scotland (Nationwide Building Society, 1987). As the house price boom continued through 1988, the pattern of inflation moved outward from the South East to East Anglia, the South West and then to the West Midlands. Moreover, it was evident that there were pockets of high house price inflation within relatively depressed regions or cities and that differentials can be as great within as between regions. Nevertheless, the overall pattern retains a strong north–south dimension. Of over 460 districts analysed by Nationwide Anglia, those in the South East of England took the first 86 places in the house prices league table. Conversely, those at the bottom of the table were in Wales, Northern Ireland or well north of Luton (Nationwide Anglia, 1988). And an analysis of house prices by Lloyds Bank showed that 'the four regions in the South and East have had real average increases of 3% since 1969 (slightly more in London) while every other region has fallen below the national average of 2.2%. The gaps in house price levels which already existed in 1969 mainly between the South East and other regions have thus widened considerably, but East Anglia and the South West have moved above the national average' (Lloyds Bank, 1988). These regional differentials are strongly evident in the price of residential building land. For example, between October 1986 and October 1987 residential land prices rose by 52.5 per cent in Outer London, 41.1 per cent in the South West and 39 per cent in East Anglia. In contrast, prices in the Northern region rose by a mere 9.6 per cent and in Wales by 10.8 per cent (Valuation Office, 1987, p. 19).

National daily newspapers have published regular accounts of this widening gap in property values and house price inflation. The *Observer* referred to 'The boom that divides a nation' (30 November 1986). The *Financial Times* described 'The great housing barrier' (27 November 1986) and the *Daily Telegraph* talked of 'Differentials wider still and wider' (10 January 1987). Homelessness may be rising rapidly and the housing stock pervasively dacaying, but house price movement are more likely to catch the attention of the middle-class readership of the quality newspapers.

In the slump of 1989/90 the headlines have changed. Property prices are regularly reported but the figures refer to price falls and the anecdotes are about losers and those trapped in high mortgaged, unsaleable properties. Although the relative rates of house price inflation have evened out across the country, absolute differentials remain profound. As Figure 5.1 illustrates, whilst regional house price differentials have narrowed somewhat in 1989 as the housing market went into recession, a longer term perspective indicates a widening gap between 'north' and 'south'.

Contrasts in house prices both within and between localities are the most visible and obvious expression of a highly differentiated market. Assumptions are made nevertheless that the various price strata connect in some meaningful way. If the owner-occupied market is represented as a ladder, it is assumed that the rungs are on the same ladder, with the promise, if not the possibility, of progression from the bottom to the top. There may be winners and losers, but this is presented as a matter of luck and of housing market acumen, rather than as a product of the odds being systematically biased in favour of some of the expense of others.

Chapter 2 discussed the general socioeconomic profile of home owners. This chapter explores in more detail the divisions within home ownership. In the past, issues of mobility, subsidy and inequality in housing have tended to polarize the positions of owners and tenants. But the owner-occupied market is itself historically, socially and spatially fragmented and no particular tenure is immune from more deeply embedded social and economic processes. Thus problems supposedly confined to the rental tenures, such as unemployment, physical decay and arrears, are now emerging within home ownership. Whilst house price profiles describe a highly segmented market, relationships are considerably more complicated than an observed association between income and price. Rather than conceptualize the owner-occupied market as a price/income continuum, it is more appropriately viewed as a layering of historical accretions, which has drawn in different groups at different times under different conditions. And contemporary housing market changes, state policies and changes in the labour market produce a wide variety of experiences and aspirations among home owners. In the final section of this chapter some of these points are illustrated through case studies of the housing histories of home owners in two contrasting segments of the market.

Fraying at the edges?

The growth of home ownership has been both socially and spatially uneven. The areas with the highest levels of home ownership are to be found in the north as well as the south of England. In some cases they are the predictable middle-class enclaves of suburban affluence nestling along the south coast. But some of the highest levels of home ownership are to be found in the declining industrial areas of North West England and it is predominantly working-class

102 *Home ownership*

home ownership with a long history. It is widely assumed that there is a necessary relationship between rising affluence and rising levels of owner occupation. As was shown earlier, however, such a hypothesis holds neither nationally nor internationally. Within Britain, a high or rising level of home ownership may be the product of economic decline and relative poverty rather than growth and affluence. In the interwar years, factory owners sold off substantial numbers of company houses to their workers as a way of generating additional cash and relieving themselves of increasingly burdensome housing responsibilities. Disposals of thiss kind in areas with low house prices enabled substantial numbers of working-class households to become home owners. And later phases of disposals in the 1950s and 1960s by private landlords had a similar effect. This has contributed to a situation where in some areas there are now tracts of low-value, owner-occupied Victorian terraces requiring substantial maintenance and repair – and the owners are typically elderly or on low incomes. Whilst national analyses of trends between 1961 and 1981 indicate a progressive filtering down of home ownership through the social structure and increasing dilution as it reaches the lower socioeconomic group (Hamnett, 1984), relationships between tenure, income and class are more complicated at the local level.

The image of suburban affluence, of rapidly escalating property values, of a tenure superior in every way to council housing, derives then from a partial view of the reality of home ownership. Recent correctives to this view have tended to express the heterogeneous and fragmented nature of the owner-occupied market in terms of the consequences of drawing in lower-income households at a time of economic recession and high unemployment. Home ownership, it seems, is fraying at the edges. Faced with declining rental opportunities, many lower-income households have little choice but to take out a mortgage. They may then find themselves financially over-committed, occupying a property in need of substantial investment and perhaps at an inappropriate stage in the family life cycle. Describing some of the areas of inner city home ownership in Liverpool and Birmingham, Karn *et al.* (1985) suggest that:

> Britain could even experience the same wholesale abandonment or dereliction of owner occupied housing as found in inner areas of US cities, especially if prices begin to fall in absolute as well as relative terms in response to increasing fabric deterioration and the inability to raise a mortgage or find a buyer. (p. 128)

Whilst Britain appears to be far from this situation at present, the reputation and image of home ownership are affected by the

The fragmented market 103

increase in mortgage arrears and repossession cases (Doling *et el.*, 1986). The number of homeless households accepted by local authorities in England whose homelessness resulted principally from mortgage arrears or default was 2,000 in 1979. By 1987 this had risen to 10,500. As a percentage of all homelessness acceptances by local authorities, this represented an increase from 4 per cent to 9 per cent. In Wales, where a higher proportion of households are owner occupiers, the comparable increase was from 7.2 per cent in 1979 to 15 per cent in 1987 (*Hansard*, 27 June 1988). Whilst it would be misguided to overestimate the scale of the problem, representing as it does a small proportion of home owners with a mortgage, it is nevertheless an issue of increasing prominence with potentially damaging political and fiscal implications. A shrinking public sector is thus facing increasing demands from displaced home owners. And the cost of mortgage interest payments to people who had been unemployed for up to six months was around £61 million in 1983 (*Hansard*, 12 June 1986). It is perhaps a sign of the times when 'one of the UK's most innovative and successful' consumer financial services groups advertises for a Mortgage Arrears Manager (advert in national daily).

Whilst a focus on marginal home owners is understandable, such a limited perspective on heterogeneity within the tenure tends to convey a message that within any locality the vast majority of owners enjoy equally a set of advantageous circumstances, and difficulties and contrasting experiences are confined to a peripheral minority. This is not necessarily the case. To return to an example from the North West of England, Hyndburn has a housing stock that is 80 per cent owner occupied. At a local level it is nearer than most to the property-owning democracy. What does it look like? In 1987, an unimproved Victorian terraced house could still be purchased for around £4,000 and a similar property fully improved would be unlikely to be valued at more than £15,000. It is also of extremely low quality by contemporary standards. In 1984, approximately 40 per cent of the private housing stock was unfit, substandard or in need of major repair. Some 3,000–4,000 private sector dwellings lacked basic amenities and a further 3,000 were in need of renovation. Every year a further 150–300 dwellings fall into disrepair. Vacancies are concentrated in the private rather than the public sector. Some 10 per cent of dwellings with rateable values below £75 are empty. The Borough's Housing Investment Programme of 1986/7 stated:

> At current levels of activity the Authority is dealing with about 130 properties per annum by clearance and 300 per annum by renovation . . . . it will be 35 years (2020 AD) at least before

every owner occupier can enjoy amenities that are considered in a national context to be basic necessities in a property free of major defects. (Borough of Hyndburn, 1985)

Moreover, a significant number of owner–occupied properties lack front or back gardens, thus limiting the scope for improvement and extension. This means that many properties are inappropriate for the social consumption norms of the late twentieth century. As a report by the Borough Planning Officer noted:

> Between 50% and 60% of the Borough's dwellings are 'two up two down' terraces. Despite falling household sizes . . . . these properties are increasingly likely to suffer from social obsolescence. Demand for these properties is likely to fall with increases in the ownership of cars and consumer durables, particularly fridges, freezers, washing machines and tumble dryers. The ability to accommodate consumer durables by kitchen extensions is likely to be limited because of the lack of space around these properties. (Borough of Hyndburn, 1982)

Whilst there have been low costs of access to home ownership, both households and the local authority have faced the escalating costs of decay and social obsolescence. In neither case have the resources been available to deal with the problems on any scale. Ironically, therefore, the problems of home ownership in Hyndburn derive from the general low value of properties and low demand (and the implications of this situation for the economics of investment in improvement) rather than the price barriers confronting those on low incomes.

In this context the relationships between council housing and home ownership can be reversed. In terms of space and amenity standards, council tenants are relatively privileged. It is the council houses that are good–quality, three–bedroomed, semi–detached with gardens. And much of the demand for council housing is from elderly home owners. For example, among medical or ordinary older applicants for council housing, some two–thirds are home owners (June 1987 figures). And if one looks at allocation to sheltered housing schemes, a similar proportion come from the owner–occupied sector (Means, 1988). This point has been illustrated further in Chapter 4. As Means comments, there are in Hyndburn at least a number of elderly home owners who appear oblivious to the fact that owner occupation is always the preferred tenure (p. 15). In Hyndburn, therefore, the experiences of a large number of home owners and not just of a marginal group are very different from idealized assumptions.

The fragmented market 105

Indeed, the particular housing problems of the area were the subject of a parliamentary debate in 1984. The local MP Ken Hargreaves described the situation as follows:

> The main thrust of the Government's housing policy has been to promote owner occupation by extending its availability to lower income groups. There are, however, a small number of areas in the country where high levels of owner occupation have already been achieved due to the self-reliance and independence of the inhabitants and the way in which they have resisted the onslaught of municipal socialism in housing. They take pride in owning their own home and therefore in these areas the problem is not to promote owner occupation but to retain it.

He continued:

> Government action is needed to prove to these people that there is a long-term future for low income owner occupation. Unless some way is found to provide additional help in Hyndburn, it will be 30 years before all our owner occupied households can enjoy basic amenities in properties free from major defects.

In reply, Sir George Young, the Parliamentary Under Secretary of State for the Environment, acknowledged the great contrast between this description of home ownership and the more dominant southern perception. '"Low cost homes" in such an area, has a different meaning from the usual one. For someone like myself as a London member used to London prices, the sort of figures that I have just been quoting seem remarkable' (*Hansard*, 12 November 1984).

The fragmented and dislocated nature of the home ownership market can be seen, therefore, in the different routes in and different levels of demand and the implications of this for property values and access. And particular modes of access may have specific consequences in later periods. It is clear, for example, that shifts in mortgage interest rates, building costs and house price movements can affect the housing market trajectories of different groups. Access for working-class households has in many instances been facilitated by discounting of market prices. The withdrawal of industrial capital from housing provision and disinvestment by petit bourgeois and large institutional landlords enabled low-cost and often low-quality entry often for lower-income households (see, for example, Hamnett and Randolph, 1988). The pressure to draw the more attractive assets in the public sector into home ownership has expanded as it has become evident that the building industry

Home ownership

is unable to provide new housing for low income groups without substantial state subsidy or drastic reductions in space and amenity standards. In the drive to extend home ownership government has introduced an increasing variety of low cost schemes such as homesteading, equity sharing and improvement for sale (for a detailed discussion see Forrest, Lansley, and Murie, 1984). They have, however, made only a small contribution to the growth of the tenure. By far the most significant new layer of home ownership has been added through the privatization of council housing.

Between 1979 and 1989, over 1 million council tenants have entered home ownership without changing dwelling and at significantly less than the market price. The social and spatial pattern of this process is well documented (see for example, Dunn, Forrest and Murie, 1987: Forrest and Murie, 1988a). What is less clear is the way in which council house purchase will affect the housing market trajectories of former tenants. A significant number have bought an accumulating asset enabling them to realize or reinvest a capital gain on resale. The equity stored and ultimately realized will depend upon a number of factors: principally the size of the original discount, the specific nature and location of the dwelling and house price movements in the locality. In some cases, particularly in London, substantial gains will be realized. For example, a tenant qualifying for a 60 per cent discount on a dwelling valued at £50,000 (which is low for council houses in London) would have paid £20,000. Given current house price trends in London, it could be worth £100,000 after five years. This would offer on resale the possibility of trading up, substantial equity withdrawal and/or an attractively located dwelling on retirement. Even if the house price increases of former council dwellings remain significantly less than for similar dwellings on the private market, a valuable asset will have been acquired. And not all council dwellings were purpose built. Many were acquired by local authorities for renovation and are indistinguishable from other privately owned properties. Moreover, they are not located on large council estates.

By contrast, the housing future is rather less optimistic for a tenant purchasing a less popular house or flat on a large estate in an area of low housing demand. The resale value could be extremely low. Indeed, the combined effect of rising rents, rising discounts and falling interest rates is producing a situation where for some tenants day-to-day housing costs can be reduced by house purchase. Predictably, rental costs and purchase costs are least divergent in areas of economic decline. But purchasing (say) a high-rise flat on a peripheral estate in Liverpool under these conditions may have little to do with tenure preference and offer limited prospects of social or spatial mobility. For public sector

The fragmented market

107

tenants who do not qualify for full housing benefit and whose rents are moving nearer market rents, the move into owner occupation may be more of a coping strategy to reduce housing costs. In such circumstances, the move from tenant to owner-occupation status could more thoroughly entrap the household. A newspaper feature on 'Winners and losers in the great council house sales bonanza' (the *Observer*, 22 June 1986) contrasted two purchasers – one in London, the other in Birmingham. The tenant in London who had purchased his dwelling for £30,000 had it valued four months later for £67,000. The tenant in Birmingham paid £4,000 for a house with structural defects that had proved unsaleable for £15,000 six years later (see also Platt, 1986).

The rising number of repossession cases was referred to in Chapter 2. Mortgage default and mounting arrears are evident in all areas and are by no means restricted to those who purchase council houses. Indeed, given the generous discount on offer and the low discounted prices, council house purchasers are less vulnerable to arrears and repossession than those low-income purchasers paying the full market price involving a mortgage representing a greater multiple of income. By March 1985, however, almost 12 per cent of Right to Buy loans were at least one month in arrears. While the proportion in serious arrears was less than 3 per cent, this indicated a worrying trend among relatively recent borrowers. And there was a geography to this development. In areas where the housing market was relatively buoyant such as Inner and Outer London, the proportion of borrowers at least one month in arrears was around 8 per cent. In South and West Yorkshire, however, the figures were 18 per cent and 20 per cent respectively (Association of Metropolitan Authorities, 1986). It may be that higher house prices in London restrict council house purchase to those on higher incomes and in more secure employment. Alternatively, the ability to sell up or borrow on the property is easier in areas of high demand. But:

> the problem may be less easily solved especially in areas where property prices are stagnant and on estates or in blocks of flats where sales have failed to 'take off'.
>
> Local authorities may have to adopt new strategies for dealing with mortgage arrears in such circumstances if they want to avoid the danger of having a high level of abandonment and repossessions.
>
> (Association of Metropolitan Authorities, 1986, p. 24)

The privatization of council housing has generated a significant increase in the level of home ownership, but movement between

108 *Home ownership*

the two main tenures is not all one way. Failed owners are increasingly accommodated by local authorities. Not only has the council stock borne the burden of the further extension of home ownership, its dwindling resources have to accommodate the casualties of the recession and the victims of rising mortgage interest rates. As the most valuable physical assets of the public sector are absorbed by the private market, the social housing sector has developed an increasingly residual status.

Segmented markets, differential subsidies

Price differentials, contrasting routes and circumstances of entry, and the increase in disrepair and inequality all contribute to a view of heterogeneity and fragmentation in the owner-occupied market. Differentiation is not, however, limited to a distinction between the majority of home owners who are faring well or very well and a minority of failed or struggling purchasers, but cuts across the market as a whole. The product itself is becoming increasingly differentiated through more sophisticated market segmentation in the building industry. Whilst we remain a long way from the fragmented nature of the US housing market, we are certainly moving in that direction (for some discussion of this, see Ball *et al.*, 1988). Demographic changes, increased market penetration affecting particular groups and developments in the speculative housebuilding industry have combined to generate a greater range of new dwellings targeted at specific kinds of potential buyers. For example, a report by the consultants Laing and Cruickshank in 1982 commented:

> The single parent and single person households are projected to be one third of the total number of private households by 1986, a product of both a rising divorce rate, and an increased preference for those leaving home to buy rather than rent. This is a market which has not traditionally been well served by new housing, both price and unit design being obstacles. However, the house building industry is working much harder now at providing the type of unit wanted and, at different ends of the spectrum, Barratt's Studio Solos for the young and McCarthy and Stone's serviced retirement homes are achieving success on a large scale. When will we see service accommodation for single mothers? (p. 13)

The report continued:

The fragmented market

the make-up of the market is changing faster than its size: there is a large backlog still to be tapped (ie living in rented accommodation) and growth to come. The three main areas of growth look to be young singles of both sexes, single parent females in their thirties and women of post retirement age living on their own. (p. 13)

In the early 1980s the emphasis was on enabling younger, first-time purchasers to gain access to the bottom of the housing market. The construction of starter homes of varying size and quality increased. The general shift in new production was from semi-detached to terraced properties. In 1982, one architect observed that 'new dwellings are now smaller than at any time since the First World War' (Levitt, 1982). And a manager of Wimpey Homes stated that:

In the 1960s the typical first time buyer's house was a three-bedroom semi-detached of some 1000 ft. super . . . . Today a home suitable for the first time buyer will have a floor area of 450–500/ft. super. It will normally have one or two bedrooms and will usually be terraced. (Stonehouse, 1981, p. 128)

In the mid-1980s, adverse publicity, low profit margins and difficulties of selling pushed the volume housebuilders and smaller regionally based companies into lower-risk parts of the market. In the later 1980s, with the boom in house prices, housebuilders shifted their attention to the higher-risk but high-profit, higher-price parts of the market. New building was aimed at either higher-income households or more affluent elderly people.

The disposal of vacant flats and houses by local authorities opened up further opportunities for the building industry in the 1980s. A combination of ideological predilection and a squeeze on finance has encouraged a number of local authorities to sell off properties to private developers for refurbishment and sale. In some cases this has provided low-cost homes for new entrants to the owner-occupied market. For example, Barratt's paid Salford City Council £50,000 for 208 flats in five four-storey blocks. After refurbishment, and over £200,000 of grant aid from central government, it produced 170 flats selling at between £14,350 and £20,000 in 1953 (Usher, 1987). In other cases the transformation has been more dramatic in terms of both the market served and the nature of the refurbishment. This has been most evident in the London housing market where difficult-to-let council-owned tower blocks have become high-status residences for young professionals. One illustrative example is Moravian Tower, a 1969 red-brick high-rise

110 *Home ownership*

block in Kensington and Chelsea, which at the time of writing was having £6 million invested in it by Ideal Homes. The result will be one-, two- and three-bedroomed flats selling for between £100,000 and £400,000. Hanging gardens planted on every third floor will be set behind a glazed atrium. Elsewhere, a former block of Metropolitan Police flats was advertised as 'the elegance of regency style in the Heart of Westminster' and on sale for upwards of £165,000. It is interesting also to note the name changes that often accompany these transfers from the public to the private sector. The St John's Estate became Battersea Village. The Ordsall Flats in Salford became Regent Park. The Stinesdale Estate became Pennine Meadows. Lost are the labels that convey the bureaucratic and impersonal to be replaced by new images of rural idylls and small-scale communities.

Another source of division within the home ownership market relates to the value of mortgage interest tax relief for owners in different income bands. Until recently, discussion of fairness or equity in the housing market focused on comparisons between owners and tenants. For example, the Housing Policy Review of 1977 paid considerably greater attention to comparing average subsidies for council tenants and owners with a mortgage than it did to assessing differential subsidy within the owner–occupied sector. It did, however, acknowledge that 'As tax relief is obtained, in effect, at the marginal rate of income tax paid by any mortgage, those with high incomes will obtain a higher rate of tax relief on the same amount of mortgage interest' (Department of the Environment, 1977, TV III, p. 5).

Since 1977, policy changes and the continuing residualization of council housing have made inter-tenure comparisons of subsidy rather a pointless exercise. The general fiscal squeeze and the reduction of Exchequer subsidy to public sector housing has increased pressure for the reform of tax expenditures associated with housing. The greatest attention has been paid to mortgage interest tax relief (MITR), although this should not be taken in isolation. In 1979/80 the value of MITR was £1,639 million; in 1990 it is estimated to be £7,000 million. There is now at least some acceptance across the political spectrum that the value of MITR should be included in the housing expenditure calculus. And it is uncontroversial that higher–earning households paying above the standard rate of tax and occupying higher-priced dwellings benefit disproportionately. The extent of these disparities within home ownership is illustrated in Table 5.1. In 1988/9, for mort-gaged owners with a total annual income of less than £5,000, the average value of MITR mortgage interest tax relief was £300 per annum. At the other extreme, those households with incomes

The fragmented market

Table 5.1 *Value of mortgage interest tax relief for different income groups, 1988/9*

Range of total income	Numbers receiving MITR	%	Average value of relief per mortgager	Total cost	% of total cost
(£)	('000s)		£	£m.	%
Up to 5,000	690	8	300	210	5
5,001–7,500	470	5	360	170	4
7,501–10,000	830	10	400	330	8
10,001–12,500	1,210	14	450	550	13
12,501–15,000	1,230	14	480	590	14
15,001–17,500	1,020	12	490	510	12
17,501–20,000	870	10	490	430	10
20,001–25,000	1,110	13	510	570	13
25,001–30,000	470	6	630	300	7
30,001–40,000	440	5	780	340	8
40,001–50,000	120	1	900	110	3
Over 50,000	140	2	1,020	140	3
TOTAL	8,600	100		4,250	100

Source: Hansard, 25 July 1988, vol. 138, no. 195, cols 100–102.

in excess of £50,000 gained £1,020 per annum in MITR. The average value of MITR was £490 per annum and was concentrated among those households with incomes of between £10,000 and £25,000. In the overall distribution the affluent home owner gained most and the poorest gained least. Those owners with incomes up to £10,000 accounted for 23 per cent of all mortgages but they shared only 17 per cent of the total value of MITR. Conversely, mortgagors with incomes in excess of £30,000 represented 8 per cent of households involved but accounted for around 14 per cent of the total cost of mortgage interest MITR. As Kelly (1986) put it: 'A home owner earning over £30,000 is likely to receive three times as much help with housing costs as a home owner earning £9,000 or a tenant earning £5,200' (p. 13).

The total estimated cost of higher-rate tax relief on mortgage interest in 1988/9 is some £300 million. These figures, however, take no account of behavioural changes that might flow from the restriction of relief to a maximum £30,000 per dwelling rather than as previously to individual mortgagors. Two-earner couples account for more than half of all tax units qualifying for MITR at the higher rate. It should also be noted that, whilst there has

112 *Home ownership*

been a longstanding campaign by various social policy analysts to restrict relief to the basic rate of tax, the measures in the 1988 budget somewhat sidestepped this debate by abolishing tax rates above 40 per cent. This measure effectively reduced the overall cost of MITR (as does any reduction in tax rates) whilst delivering substantial increases in disposable income to higher earners. If tax rates continue to be reduced, the value of MITR and its importance in decisions relating to home ownership will be affected. The overall tax expenditure bill could, however, continue to rise as the proportion of owners with mortgages qualifying for the full £30,000 relief increases – and if interest rates increase or remain high.

Spatial mobility and occupational subsidies

Mortgage interest tax relief could be represented as an inverted pyramid. Outright owners, low-income owners with very small mortgages, those fully below tax thresholds, and those occupying low-value dwellings (perhaps in need of repair and maintenance) benefit least. This much is uncontroversial. What tends to be left out of the analysis, however, are the various employment-related subsidies that add a further layer of subsidy and assistance at the top of the income structure. Evidence of those forms of housing assistance is patchy. Whilst considerable comment has been made about the company welfare state in more general discussion of the various fringe benefits available to particular groups (see Field, 1981; Green *et al.*, 1984), there has been little systematic discussion of employer-related assistance in the housing sphere.

The most obvious sectoral advantages accrue to those working in banking, insurance and finance through their access to low-interest loans. After a probationary period, all employees who work in many financial institutions become eligible for beneficial loans. Green *et al.* (1984), for example, state that 'House purchase loans, when available, are generally fairly open to all types of employees. But they are confined largely to the financial sector, where the proportion of manual workers is relative small' (p. 23). However, as with mortgage interest tax relief, those in the higher echelons derive the greatest benefit. The value of loans for top managers ranged between £11,000 and £20,000. The proportion of managers and top executives receiving such loans was estimated at between 4.7 per cent and 8.2 per cent for each of the years 1973 to 1983 and was highest in 1983:

The amounts borrowed are normally related to income, so managers and executives benefit most in absolute terms. In the

The fragmented market

113

mid 1970s the implied amount of subsidy could be substantial, between about 6% and 10% in terms of gross salary for those top managers receiving house loans. (Green *et al.*, 1984, p. 23)

Whilst it is not possible to provide an exact figure for the number of employees involved, a conservative estimate would suggest a figure of about 800,000 receiving some form of benefit – about 3 per cent of the employed population (*Employment Gazette*, November 1986). This may not appear a significant number, but beneficial loans represent a major hidden subsidy and, unlike low-interest loans for other purposes, they are currently exempt from tax. Moreover, they have grown in importance with the expansion of the financial sector and the growth of home ownership. Their value has increased with house price inflation and higher real interest rates, particularly in the case of employees on very low fixed rates. So both the value and the volume of this form of assistance have increased in recent years.

Sectoral advantage in the form of beneficial loans has other dimensions. It is likely to have a geography in the sense that employees in the financial sector are more numerous in certain localities. For example, the proportion of the employed population in the financial sector in the Greater London area is 19 per cent, and in the South East 13 per cent. This compares with 7 per cent in Yorkshire and Humberside and 6 per cent in the North (*Employment Gazette*, November 1986). And there could be highly localized effects in smaller towns where above-average numbers of people work in insurance or finance. There will also be pockets of advantage in some northern towns such as Halifax or Bradford where a building society is one of the major employers. In other words, not everyone is competing on the same terms, and when interest rates are increased there is a segment of the labour market that is effectively shielded from the impact. It should be noted that in this context this is a tied benefit. If an employee leaves the financial sector, he or she is likely to lose access to cheap mortgage finance. In many households it may well be the female second earner in the household who is affected in this way and those in relatively junior positions.

Sectoral benefits, therefore, are not necessarily associated with high status or male employment. This is not the case with various other allowances. There is an increasingly privileged core of workers with strong bargaining power who move in an exclusive circuit where their housing mobility, housing standards and general lifestyles are protected and enhanced through employer-related benefits. Typically they are in senior, high-status jobs in the financial sector or multinationals and typically they will be white, male graduates. The costs and problems of relocating such employees are now a prominent concern of the Confederation of British Industry (CBI), which has set up an Employee Relocation Council. Recent reports by specialist relocation consultants have highlighted housing costs as an increasingly important factor inhibiting employee mobility (see, for example, Merrill Lynch, 1986; Black Horse Relocation, 1986). A CBI study of company housing needs in the South East found that over 60 per cent of firms contacted thought that the housing market was interfering with their recruitment and retention efforts in a major way. The high purchase price of housing was ranked as the most serious problem (Confederation of British Industry, 1988). Some 10 per cent of companies estimated the annual cost to the company of help with employees' housing costs to be in excess of £100,000. A study of recruitment difficulties among firms in mid-Berkshire concluded that 'the main difficulties are related to the recruitment from lower cost housing areas of professional and managerial staff who are already owner occupiers' (Parsons, 1987, p. 32).

How far the mobility of this group is impeded by house price differentials will depend on specific personnel policies and will vary between firms and between sectors. But the evident concern with house price movements and crude north–south divisions is less about the impact on unemployment levels than about the financial burden borne by firms and by individuals in higher-status jobs requiring high mobility.

Arguably, therefore, sharp divisions may be emerging between those with highly localized housing and job histories and a group of increasingly mobile core workers who move from positions of job strength within internal labour markets (Salt and Flowerdew, 1986; Craig *et al.*, 1985). To some extent, therefore, there is a housing market division that corresponds to the familiar distinction between primary and secondary labour markets. Whilst such a bifurcation of the labour market is generally recognized as requiring considerable refinement and qualification (see Gleave and Sellens, 1984), such a conception usefully 'captures the essence of the structure' (Weeks, 1980, p. 557). Past research established strong interconnections between employment in the secondary labour market, low geographic mobility and the public housing sector (Gleave and Palmer, 1979). Recession, economic restructuring and tenure restructuring (principally through council house sales, minimal public sector building and the progressive penetration of home ownership down the income structure) indicate the need for a reappraisal of these relationships. In general terms, the rental tenures increasingly accommodate the economically inactive and redundant, and labour market divisions may now be of more relevance in explaining contrasting trajectories and mobility patterns *within* home ownership. Those in the strongest labour market positions, with saleable and marketable skills in the growth sectors of the economy, move in national, indeed international, housing markets. An early nomadic existence around branch plants and subsidiaries culminates in the career objective of a senior post in a headquarters that is typically located in London or the South East. They occupy sub-sectors of housing markets, often up-market new housing developments offering easy access and disposal, which are connected to similar sub-sectors in other towns rather than to the local housing market. To facilitate and encourage residential and job mobility, and to compensate for the social and financial disruptions associated with such moves, companies increasingly provide generous subsidies.

These subsidies are associated particularly with movement from low- to higher-priced areas for housing, and they cover removal expenses, legal fees, bridging finance, grants for new fixtures and fittings, free rented accommodation during search times for the next dwelling and allowances and low-interest loans for school fees (see, for example, Merrill Lynch, 1986). For instance, of the 121 companies in the CBI survey in the South East that regarded the housing market as interfering in a serious way with their company operations, almost all provided payment for direct removal costs of existing staff who were transferring to the area. Over 90 per cent paid for short-term accommodation in 'digs' or hotels and 46 per cent provided financial assistance in the form of cheap mortgages or excess mortgage interest allowance. These measures applied to professional and managerial staff, with fewer (though still a substantial number) firms offering similar help to manual, technical and clerical employees (CBI, 1988). Generous assistance with increased mortgage costs may also be a significant element, and it is this extensive pattern of benefits that distinguishes this group from employees in the banking and financial sector. In some cases, increased mortgage allowances are limited to moves to the London area, but this is not always so. The volume and extent of such subsidies and allowances have not been thoroughly investigated (but see Johnson *et al.*, 1974; Salt, 1985), but it is evident that many households simply could not contemplate moving to high cost areas without generous financial assistance. Refusal or reluctance to move could seriously jeopardize career prospects and an unassisted move would necessitate a significant drop in living standards. The prospect of a final move to the London area necessitates maintaining maximum investment in housing if eventual promotion to a senior post

116   *Home ownership*

is not to be accompanied by a reduction in housing space and quality.

The incidence and range of forms of assistance available to relocating executives is well illustrated in the survey of the 151 companies included in PA's Top Management Renumeration Service. As reported in an IDS report (1988), senior executives were offered extensive help in relocating. Almost all existing executives moving within their companies had expenses such as legal fees, stamp duty, estate agent commission and other removal costs paid for by their company. And as Table 5.2 shows, a significant proportion had access to more substantial subsidy such as special loans for house purchase or guarantees against losses on the sale of their existing dwelling. The subsidies available to newly recruited executives were marginally less generous but still substantial compared to the costs incurred by the majority of moving home owners.

Not all moves are moves to London and the South East. Prohibitive commercial and residential costs have been a major factor in encouraging decentralization from the core of London to the outer periphery and Britain's 'sunbelt' – a zone of relative affluence and economic growth stretching along the M4 motorway from London to Bristol. Employees invited to and choosing to move with a relocating company benefit doubly from employer-related housing assistance and lower house prices. An example is provided by London Life Association, a major financial institution, which

Table 5.2 *Relocation allowances for new and existing executives*

	Existing executive %	New executive %
Meet all travelling expenses	98	92
Reimburse physical removal costs	98	97
Pay for preliminary visit	90	79
Pay disturbance allowance	90	70
Meet temporary accommodation costs	97	92
Reimburse extra school expenses	21	7
Company loan for house purchase	21	13
Guarantee loan from building society	26	19
Pay estate agent commission	90	78
Pay legal fees for house sale/purchase	98	90
Pay stamp duty on new purchase	92	83
Pay proportion of any loss on sale	35	5
Other, unspecified financial aid	36	29

Source: IDS Top Pay Unit (1988) Executive Mobility Research File 8.

moved its head office activities from in and around London to Bristol. To facilitate the move the company allowed 10 days' paid holiday for house hunting, paid all legal and removal costs, offered more generous car purchase loans and even bought 10 furnished flats in one of the more attractive parts of Bristol and rented these off to staff as a temporary staging post. Before moving to Bristol, 79 per cent of the households that moved had been home owners. This proportion rose to 98 per cent after (or soon after) relocation. Moreover, more than a third of the relocated households were able to maintain or enhance their housing standards whilst extracting significant amounts of equity from the proceeds of the sale of their previous dwellings (average £5,400) (City of Bristol Planning department, 1985). There was also some evidence of a shortage of suitable, high-value, high-status accommodation. These sorts of moves may be contributing towards increasing polarization of housing markets and residential areas in places like Bristol. Whereas house prices in one area may be determined by essentially local factors, in others the relocation of employees from higher-priced areas (combined with retirement migration) may fuel excessive house price inflation in certain sub-sectors and create widening price divisions between those areas where demand is essentially local and those used by affluent in-migrants. The expectation would be that, in the future, retirement migration among owner occupiers in London and the South East could be a significant aspect of housing demand in rural and other areas offering attractive environments. It may also lead to a gradual shift in supply and demand, reducing regional house price differentials. Overall economic trends still indicate, however, a shift in economic activity towards the South and East. There are also suggestions that 'should the Channel Tunnel be completed the pull to the south will probably strengthen' (Morrell, 1986).

If these economic patterns continue, increasing contrasts are likely between housing circumstances in areas of growth and decline, between rich and poor in all localities and between the factors inhibiting and enhancing the mobility of different groups in the population. These contrasts are most apparent when the housing circumstances of middle-class professionals in the growth sectors are compared with marginalized groups in the rental sectors and in the low-value, low-quality sub-sectors of owner occupation. There are, however, strata of middle-class and working-class owner occupiers whose subsidies are limited to mortgage interest tax relief and whose ability to move and enhance their housing conditions is determined largely by the vicissitudes of the housing market. Within this group, housing histories are increasingly differentiated by where they have taken place. Take the position

118 *Home ownership*

of the average earner who bought a modest dwelling in London 20 years ago. Whether or not they have moved house, they will be sitting on a valuable and fast-accumulating asset. The value of the dwelling may be some 10 times annual salary. On retirement they could move and maintain their housing standards whilst realizing a substantial capital gain. The majority of owners elsewhere are likely to have more modest prospects. A report by Nationwide Building Society indicated that, on average, home owners in Greater London enjoyed an annual rate of return on their dwelling of some 18 per cent between 1975 and 1985. This compared with 11 per cent in the West Midlands or 12 per cent in Yorkshire and Humberside (Nationwide Building Society, 1986). And this imbalance in housing costs and rates of accumulation is reflected in the spatial distribution of the revenue costs of tax relief on mortgage interest (see Chapter 2).

Even for those in relatively well-paid professional employment, the prospects of a better job in a higher housing cost area would have to be balanced against a significant and inevitable fall in living standards. The optimum housing position is to be in a multiple-earning household with one or more members in professional or managerial employment and with a long housing history in London or the South East and in a company offering generous relocation allowances or moving between companies offering such allowances on recruitment. This is evident from a recent survey of new house sales in Surrey, in the Greater London area. Trend data indicate that in-migration from outside the Greater London area has declined. Almost half of all mover households had principal earners in professional or managerial employment and a similar proportion had more than one earner. Only 6 per cent of moves originated from outside the county and these were predominantly work-related moves by people in high-status, well-paid employment (Surrey County Council, Planning Department, 1986). In other words, those who moved into new owner-occupied housing in Surrey either from within the county or from outside tended to have optimum household structures and to be in jobs more likely to offer the sorts of mobility privileges referred to earlier. It would appear that home ownership in the South of England (and sub-sectors within other localities) is becoming a closed shop, an increasingly exclusive club with escalating new membership costs. Whether this is a temporary state of affairs or whether it indicates a developing structural fission in the owner-occupied market in the UK remains to be seen. Some commentators are, however, beginning to speculate that current house price divisions may be more permanent. Among other factors contributing to higher house prices in the South are the increasing concentration of the

The housing histories of home owners

Fragmentation and segmentation within home ownership are perhaps best illustrated through an examination of actual housing experiences. If, for example, we took contrasting areas of a city and two groups of home owners in roughly comparable age cohorts, we could look at the key factors that differentiate their housing histories. Some exploratory research of this kind was carried out in Bristol in 1985 (for a more detailed description of the research methodology, see Forrest and Murie, 1985).

The two localities chosen were strikingly different – visually and in terms of local prices. In one area, house prices averaged £20,000, whereas in the other prices ranged from £80,000 to £140,000, which at that time represented the top end of the owner-occupied market in Bristol.

The wealthy area is Clifton Heath, a leafy wooded suburban area of Bristol. Two of the roads are of large detached houses in large gardens (a third of an acre or more). Most of the houses were built between the wars, many to high standards by a respected local builder. These are large houses with large rooms and five or more bedrooms. Most had been modernized to include new kitchens and two or more bathrooms and WCs. Most, however, retained some original features including wooden panelling on walls, original fireplaces and wooden parquet flooring. Clifton Heath also included a group of newly built properties on a site with development still taking place. These were executive dwellings marketed at £80,000 or more. The whole area was regarded as one of the highest-status residential areas in Bristol.

In contrast, the working-class area is a dense cluster of terraced housing developed at the turn of the century, some of which was built above old mine workings. It is a stable affluent working-class district close to the city centre and the old Wills tobacco factory, which provided relatively well-paid jobs until its recent closure. These are houses with small rear gardens and very short front garden paths. They were built without internal bathrooms or toilets, although these have mostly been added by rebuilding rear extensions. Rooms are small, although in some cases two rooms have been knocked through into one. Some of the dwellings are built on steeply sloping land with steps up or down from street

120 Home ownership

level to front doors or with changes of level within the dwelling – notably between the body of the house and the rear extension.

The two areas conformed in many respects to the descriptions of such areas contained in the literature. Eastminster was not a gentrified or abandoned district. Many residents had lived most of their lives in the area and it was common for them to have relatives living in the immediate neighbourhood. It was generally regarded as a close-knit community with strong kin and friendship links. The majority of those interviewed were 'locals' who had lived in or near the area throughout their lives or had left it for relatively short periods only, during the war or for jobs. This applied equally to males and females. One of the respondents had spent her whole life (66 years) in the same dwelling and her husband had lived in only one other dwelling, some two streets away. One woman offered the following description of the locality:

> 'It's friendly and many people have relatives around here. Many people in this street, their families grow up and marry and buy houses just round the corner. There's quite a lot of that situation around here.'

And a male living nearby elaborated:

> 'The people who moved in next door have parents who live round the corner. He's got about five or six brothers who live round here. She's got three or four brothers and sisters. They're all in this local area. They all live within five or six streets. We actually counted one night that 15 people came up those steps from round here, just came round to visit them. People are in and out of that house all the time because, well they can almost speak to one another over the garden walls. And they're not the only family like that. Take the history of this house. We are only the second owners of this house. The original owners died. Their son lives three doors up so the people brought up in this house they only just live up the road still now. That's quite common round here.'

In contrast, those in Clifton Heath were not locals, had rarely been born in the neighbourhood, or indeed in Bristol, and had moved around the country usually in connection with their own or their parent's jobs. They were unlikely to have relatives or friends living nearby or in Bristol and the locality was rarely regarded as either close-knit or a community. There was a strong sense of social isolation, which was particularly evident among working males and less so among women with children and outside paid

The fragmented market 121

employment for whom school and related activities provided some contact with neighbours. But even here, catchment area changes had encouraged more private schooling, so that the links between school and locality were tenuous and diverse. The males tended to refer to colleagues and acquaintances rather than friends:

> 'I don't have any . . . . I had one great friend who then emigrated to Canada when I was about 26 and he was really my only friend. I have acquaintances and associates. That's one of the disadvantages of this sort of career.'

And social isolation through work was compounded through the form and layout of their residences and the use of and dependency on (usually) two cars. As one retiring executive remarked: 'the only thing that connects these houses is the sewers and a touch of income. Everybody comes and goes in cars.' Another commented that he had not seen his neighbours since Christmas (this was in June). And one couple told the (apocryphal?) story of neighbours they had met who said:

> '. . . . their daughter had just got married to somebody she had met at a northern university and it transpired that they'd both lived in this road and they'd both lived here all their lives and their parents had lived here all their lives. One at the top of the road and one at the bottom and they did not know one another. They had met by chance at university and finished up getting married. That's how close-knit this community is!'

For some this was a positive feature of the area – high-priced privacy. Others, however, bemoaned the lack of neighbourliness. There was also a difference between patterns of contact in the older-established affluent streets and the new executive development. In the latter, neighbours had been brought together in adversity when unwelcome changes were made to the layout and density of the development. Property values were threatened and a residents' association had been formed to combat the higher densities and buildings proposed:

> 'I would say that events over the last year have created a close-knit community . . . . I think it's fair to say that if this hadn't arisen, if we hadn't had these communal problems, I'm not sure that we would know our neighbours.'

For another couple nearby, buying on a new estate formed part of a strategy for coping with frequent and disruptive job moves and loss of friends:

Home ownership

. . . . if you buy a new house on an estate everybody's in the same boat and it doesn't matter whether they've moved a quarter of a mile or 200 miles they are to some degree in a new area, in some degree strange to it and therefore you tend to get usually a community spirit within the estate and it's easier to make friends that way.

Surprisingly, perhaps, the problems of home ownership, of discontentment with design, quality, price and values were not to be found in Eastminster but in the new executive development in Clifton Heath where people were paying £80,000 or £90,000 for the locality rather than the dwelling and for a school catchment area which had subsequently been changed.

One couple in Eastminster had always been owner occupiers, and their parents had in both cases been home owners. But this was unusual. Typically, parents had been in rented or tied accommodation and only three couples had bought houses at marriage. Older persons in the area had experienced a marked improvement in their housing conditions during their lives. Their most common tenure experience in childhood and as adults (prior to ownership) was of privately rented or tied accommodation. For most of the couples interviewed their current house was the only one they had owned and only two couples had ever owned more than one other dwelling. None had had second homes or 'investment' properties. The majority of those who had married had lived in only two or fewer dwellings since marriage. With the exception of a professional soldier who subsequently entered the civil service and two younger single persons in white-collar jobs, those living in the 'working-class' area were in jobs with no career or promotion prospects. Job histories included experience of redundancy and 'deskilling' as well as early retirement through ill health.

It was relatively common among those in Clifton Heath for the parental home to have been owner occupied. There was, however, a considerable experience of tied housing and private renting. None of those in the wealthy area moved into their own home as home owners prior to marriage. And not all became home owners on marriage. Indeed, an early start in home ownership was not a common feature of this group. Nor was it the case that these households had been involved in a whole series of moves 'climbing the housing ladder'. For one household their present dwelling was the only one ever owned and six others had only ever bought two dwellings. Clifton Heath did, however, include some households with a long experience of buying and selling and of a significant escalation in the value of the dwellings purchased.

The fragmented market 123

Some households had bought a sequence of six dwellings. In each of these cases the principal wage-earner was a business executive benefiting from considerable assistance with the costs of moving home. The various forms of employer-related assistance referred to earlier emerged as a significant feature of the housing histories of the affluent owners and one of the major factors differentiating their housing histories from those in Eastminster. The difficulties of attracting senior staff to the high-priced South East had generated a range of complex schemes designed to subsidize the costs of moving. But such schemes were clearly not limited to removal expenses or to moves to London. One executive described the scheme in his company as follows:

'The total amount the company would subsidise you was £25,000. We had a mortgage of £5,000 from the previous two and we therefore had £20,000 to play with. As I said, initially the allowance was for four years and you got a lump sum on the anniversary of moving into your new house. The company then changed that to pay it on a monthly basis on your salary slip. They also increased the period from four years to seven years but for the fifth and sixth year it is at a reduced rate so we then had an allowance of £5,000 for a four year period, the fifth year it was reduced by a third and the sixth year it was reduced by a third, so the seventh year it disappeared. That was to ease the pain of losing it. So the total amount you could have was £25,000, therefore we had £20,000 to go. We had our house on the market in . . . . for £43,000 but we were actually looking for properties up to £63,000 and we saw various properties. The only one that was within this range was this bungalow that we bought. So we didn't use all the allowance up. Now also the company then changed its policy with regard to expenses and started to give you two allowances, one was 20% of your salary for carpets and curtains which was non-taxable; there is a tax cut-off point, if you are entitled to £2,000 and you can only have £1,400 tax free, then for the other £600 they would give you £900, as you would lose the tax allowance. In addition to that one, they give another allowance which was 15% of your basic salary which was totally taxable and that was for the intangible costs of moving. Your 20% one was for carpets, curtains and everything else, the other one was for the intangible items like disturbance, moving into a new area and also it would pay any school uniforms as a separate item because we had kids who were then going into different schools and of course, depending on what schools the kids were in, the school uniforms could come to quite a bit.'

124 *Home ownership*

Generally, those in Clifton Heath were more likely than those in Eastminster to have moved house as children, prior to marriage, after marriage before becoming owner occupiers, and as owner occupiers. The most striking difference was their greater rate of movement since marriage and as owner occupiers. A major element in this difference was job history. In the wealthy area, all of the households had embarked upon executive or professional careers or had a family business. The history of their housing moves was largely a history of job changes that required movement between cities.

What was striking about the contrasting housing histories of the two groups was the importance of employment factors in the shaping of their housing experiences. Factors such as parental tenure, age at marriage, when children were born, and early or late entry to owner occupation did not emerge as key differentiating features. The major contrast was between those owners whose housing histories had been shaped by the distinctive nature of employment as business executives, salaried professionals and officers in the armed forces, in contrast to those whose skills rendered them easily substitutable as homogenized labour.

There was also a wide range of attitudes towards home ownership. Few people had coherent images of the range of tenures on offer. People offered views of housing tenure reflecting their own experience as adults and children. For some, this was exclusively an experience of home ownership. For others, the reference point for attitudes to tenure was tied accommodation or private renting. Very few 'affluent' owners had experiences of council housing. And for some, renting was associated with higher costs or tied housing with very regular and disruptive movement. In this sense, attitudes towards, and the meanings attached to, home ownership can only be made sense of in the light of past experience and cannot be assumed to reflect some commonly held values and aspirations.

Concluding comments

This chapter began by describing some of the obvious ways in which the owner–occupied market is fragmented and differentiated. House price divisions, contrasts in terms of dwelling type and conditions, and the problems of marginal home owners are, however, essentially epiphenomena reflecting more deep-seated processes of differentiation. What has been suggested is that key differences relate to the nature of the labour market. But this should not be conceptualized simply in terms of disparities in direct income and thus purchasing power in the housing market. Particular

The fragmented market 125

forms of employment shape housing histories in specific ways. In some cases, owner-occupied areas operate as short-term staging posts for nomadic business executives and professionals. In other areas, home ownership has emerged almost incidentally within a world of work and social and kinship networks that remain deeply embedded in the locality. Different groups of home owners are playing by different rules. Some receive substantial state subsidies; others very little. For some, promotion and progress in job terms automatically involve moving house. Some receive substantial occupational assistance in the form of low-interest loans or mobility allowances and grants. Others have employment histories that do not involve moves away from the area of birth and signally lack any occupational benefits.

The owner-occupied market is not simply fragmented through the direct and indirect purchasing power of different groups. There is not one housing ladder with a competitive scramble fuelled by a common set of motivations and values. Rather there are different ladders, which rarely touch or overlap. Some housing experiences do not involve more than one rung and some involve leaping to a higher rung without using those below. It is also inaccurate to assume that people necessarily evaluate their housing histories in terms of a series of escalating exchange values. In this context it is appropriate to conclude this chapter with the reflections of one household:

'We started with an unfurnished flat, a furnished flat, a detached house, a semi-detached and now we've got a terraced one so I suppose you could well say we had gone backwards really. But that's not how we see it. Each one had its different good points. The terraced house is a lot warmer than the detached. The detached house was on a nice new estate but this is much sounder built.'

As was discussed in the last chapter, studies of housing market behaviour are often preoccupied with aspects of investment and the relative merits of owning or renting. The questions asked and the way they are framed can produce responses that provide a very limited view of people's housing experiences and aspirations. They can generate a picture of a highly unified market where the experience and meaning of housing (regardless of tenure) are set apart from the social, spatial and family context in which those housing changes have occurred. Massive transformation in forms of housing provision have in many ways occurred against a background of continuity and stability. There is a danger of attributing too great a social impact to tenure change and the growth of home ownership. As home ownership has grown, the fragmentation and differentiation that have emerged have reflected pre-existing variations in local class structures, housing stocks, labour markets and cultural differences. Equally, however, progressive market penetration and segmentation within the housing market are likely to produce a product tailored much more closely to the effective demands of particular groups in particular places.

6 Wealth: realizing the dream

Earlier chapters in this book have presented a variety of perspectives on the nature and growth of home ownership in Britain. In this chapter attention is focused on wealth and accumulation as a key element in the social and spatial inequalities associated with the privatization of housing. A considerable volume of literature details the situations and problems of particular sections of the population (the elderly, marginal owners, the homeless) and the conditions that characterize particular localities (inner cities, stress areas). However, the processes, and especially the housing processes, that contribute to these problems and conditions are not always spelled out. Much of the literature is concerned only with descriptions of housing situations and conditions. Other studies that emphasize access, equity, the effects of public policy or institutional and financial constraints tend to start with the identification and examination of disadvantaged groups. This may involve assumptions about a cycle of deprivation (and households that bring deprivation upon themselves) or about the relationship between the position of disadvantaged groups of households and institutional, bureaucratic practice or broader economic and structural change. In either case, the accounts of the process involved are often either implicit or limited to those aspects that are unavoidably included. Thus the discussion of council tenants in difficult-to-let housing or of elderly owner occupiers in delapidated housing is likely to contain very different details, reflecting the different situations of the households involved and the particular bureaucratic and institutional contacts experienced in each case. Such emphasis and such accounts are valuable and necessary. However, there is a need also to identify broader processes that affect all households and to represent these processes other than through descriptions of formal institutional and financial arrangements.

A broader view of processes is desirable to correct two contrasting tendencies. One is to regard housing inequalities and differences as simple reflections of other inequalities (in class or employment or occupation or income). The second is to imply that housing and housing processes form a separate world unaffected by other

128   *Home ownership*

social relationships and determined by independent housing policy and housing finance rules and constraints.

The housing literature tends to be regarded (quite rightly) as being concerned with detailed accounts of housing and has very little to say to those who are concerned more broadly with social inequality and differences in life chances. Housing research tends to focus on the role of housing in meeting the need for shelter; on housing shortage and house condition; on homelessness; on where housing needs are met most satisfactorily and through what process. But the housing market can be presented as an important determinant of life chance. Where people live can be a critical influence on access to other services that vary dramatically in quality (schools, health services, leisure facilities). Housing is not only a source of shelter but is increasingly important as a source and store of wealth. A different framework for discussion of housing issues is needed if the role of the housing market as a determinant of life chances is of principal interest rather than the operation of particular institutions or policies.

The need for a different framework for discussion of housing issues is apparent when recent political and policy discussion is looked at. The Thatcher government since 1979 has consciously moved away from the academic/technical concerns that have presented housing issues in terms of the language of need and equity. The competition between the major parties to be seen as the party of home ownership had already involved a dramatic diversion of resourrces away from concern with housing production and equalizing access to adequate housing towards subsidizing consumption through individual ownership with little regard for equity. However, since 1979 the extension of individual ownership has become the dominant policy objective. And the terms in which this has been justified involve little reference to need and stress (Murie, 1985). The Conservative Party Manifesto of 1979 made no reference to homelessness, housing stress or housing need, but emphasized the extension of home ownership, especially through the sale of council houses, as an end in itself. Subsequent government statements involved reference to making a reality of a property-owning democracy and giving 'more of our people that freedom and mobility and that prospect of handing something on to their children and grandchildren'. In contrast, when pressed about the calculations (including housing and demographic forecasts) used to inform housing investment and expenditure plans, the Secretary of State for the Environment consistently denied that public expenditure decisions were based on calculations of what was needed. In a situation of crude housing surplus, housing policy ceased to be about projections of need (which was seen as

Realizing the dream 129

a moving target) and became concerned with goals about public expenditure and the promotion of market processes, incentives, choices, self-help and redistribution of wealth. Rather than being based on a redistributive welfare state approach, housing policy was intended to 'create a climate in which those who are able can prosper, choose their own priorities and seek the rewards and satisfaction that relate to themselves, their families and their communities' (*Hansard*, 15 May 1979, cols 79–80). Under such an approach, the housing market is an arena for expression of different choices, and an appropriate area for investment and accumulation, and not merely a mechanism for meeting the need for shelter. In these ways the key themes in political discussion of housing are not adequately embraced by traditional academic and research frameworks.

The themes suggested by political debate also grow out of discussion of commodification and privatization. As was outlined in Chapter 1, the environment in which home ownership and the housing market are being reshaped in the 1980s and 1990s is one in which housing transactions are increasingly carried out through market processes and the development of competitive mortgage markets. Exchange agencies and an active second-hand housing market are key features of this. Market relationships have penetrated further and determine a wider range of housing activities and decisions than in the past.

The historical change in the commodity form of housing (commodification) has been associated with the reorganization of housing production and consumption and with changing opportunities for the yields from private housing investment. In this way an account of commodification of housing is not an account of legislative and policy change but involves consideration of housing production and investment in the context of other changes in the economy and society. In particular it involves a consideration of housing alongside alternative areas for private investment. In a similar way, a focus on the social impact of the growth of individual ownership of housing involves more than the reproduction of the statistics of tenure and the characteristics of home owners and their homes. The development of competitive and complex market arrangements raises more questions about what individualized ownership provides in wider social and political terms. This involves addressing differences in the experience of home ownership as well as differences between owners and non–owners. The analysis of processes of production and consumption in housing cannot be based on abstract notions of housing service but must acknowledge that dwellings are commodities that are bought and sold, appreciate in value and

130 *Home ownership*

yield capital gains. As commodification of housing in consumption has increased, so these features of housing become more apparent sources of social differences. However, decisions about housing production and investment are not isolated housing decisions. They are related to broader processes that affect investment in the built form generally and that affect individual and family and corporate decisions about wealth and investment. These in particular involve relationships with incomes, employment, housing costs, interest rates, other demands and preferences concerning the use of resources (including those associated with change in the family cycle). The impact on life chances of the way the housing market has developed relates to what is happening in these other areas of social and economic life and to the relationship between them and housing. Housing processes and the housing market feed back opportunities and constraints relating, for example, to resources for consumption, access to credit, access to jobs and other resources.

Discussion of the differential experience of housing and of its impact on life chances must focus on capital accumulation and capital gain; trading up and mobility, spatial, life cycle and tenurial differences; and on housing wealth in relation to class and political power. The accumulation and transfer of wealth through housing processes includes references to the differential significance of housing wealth for different households, whether inherited wealth through housing is used for housing purposes and the importance of transfers from one generation who are home owners to the next generation. It also concerns the use of wealth accumulated through housing, or through the inheritance of housing, for other purposes, e.g. education, health, increased consumption of other consumer durables.

Housing in the distribution of wealth

The significance of housing as a source and store of wealth has become more marked in Britain in recent year. The fullest and most up-to-date statistics on the distribution of wealth provide ample evidence of the importance of the growth of individual ownership and the capital appreciation of owner-occupied dwellings. The reports provided by the Royal Commission on the Distribution of Income and Wealth in 1977 provide the fullest evidence on housing and wealth. In these it was estimated that the percentage of gross personal wealth accounted for by dwellings increased between 1960 and 1975 from 19 per cent to 39 per cent. The estimated value of dwellings as a percentage of all net wealth rose

Realizing the dream 131

in the same period from 17 per cent to 37 per cent. This increase was due to a major growth in owner occupation combined with substantial increases in the values of dwellings relative to those of other assets. Some of this increase reflects problems with the Inland Revenue data used. The number of wealth owners with dwellings is under-recorded, as is the gross value of dwellings. It is also important to bear in mind that 1974 and 1975 figures are affected by the very rapid house price increase of 1970–74 (124 per cent). The estimates provided by the Inland Revenue are stated to be subject to a fairly wide margin of error and are in some respects incomplete. The deficiencies of detailed figures affect year-by-year changes and these cannot be regarded as indicating a trend. However, the figures since 1974 are of some interest. Residential building (freehold and leasehold) accounted for 42 per cent of the net wealth of individuals in 1974 and the annual figures thereafter, up to 1984, are as follows: 43, 41, 40, 41, 43, 47, 44, 43, 42, 41 per cent. There is little evidence in these figures of any substantial growth especially as the level of home ownership grew between 1974 and 1984 from 50 per cent to 59 per cent.

Furthermore, there are good reasons to doubt whether the environment has remained so favourable for the growth of housing in wealth. An analysis in 1985 (Building Societies Association, 1985) noted that housing had grown steadily as a proportion of wealth held as physical assets (from 60 per cent in 1957 to 71 per cent in 1983). Until 1980 the proportion of net wealth invested in physical assets grew strongly, but after that date the trend changed. Prior to 1980, high inflation and negative real interest rates encouraged individuals to favour physical assets, especially housing, which could be expected to maintain or increase value. The increase in house prices and government policy further encouraged housing investment. However, the environment affecting such decisions had changed significantly since 1980:

> The rate of inflation has fallen and positive real rates of interest have again become available on many financial assets. Moreover, regulatory changes have meant that housing has lost its special attractions. The mortgage interest tax relief limit has been raised only marginally compared to the increase in house prices while new financial assets (particularly index linked gilts and national savings certificates) have become available that offer the same inflation-protecting benefits as housing but without the transaction and maintenance costs. In addition the virtual abolition of capital gains tax has removed housing's special position in this respect.

132

Home ownership

This source goes on to note that between 1980 and 1983 the value of dwellings owned by the personal sector rose by 32 per cent compared to increases in the value of holdings of ordinary shares of 55 per cent and government stock of 53 per cent. However, caution about drawing conclusions from this is strongly expressed. Two further developments also need to be taken into account. First, the transfer of over 1 million council dwellings (1979–87) is unlikely to be reflected in figures built up from evidence about capital holdings at death (estate-based calculations). Secondly, the major house price inflation of 1986–88 and, more importantly (depending on the rate of recovery), the collapse in the value of stocks and shares in 1987 will have increased the value (and share) of housing assets relative to other important forms of wealth holding. On balance these latter effects are likely to have increased the importance of housing in wealth up to 1989 and reduced it since then.

The importance of housing in wealth does not just reflect a growth of owner occupation (or a decline in private renting), but also depends on the movement of house prices relative to retail prices and to the value of other assets. Bearing in mind the reservations with these data, it does seem likely that, as a result of the impact of house price movements and of the economic recession on the value of other assets, the importance of housing assets in wealth increased after 1978 and 1986, and decreased since 1989.

The Royal Commission's 1977 report provided basic evidence of a redistribution of wealth through the growth of owner occupation and decline of private landlordism. However, this redistribution does not indicate a general equalization. Relatively few large wealth holders have a major proportion of their assets in the form of dwellings. Consequently, the increase in the value of houses compared with other assets has meant that the gap in wealth between home owners with few other assets and those with substantial other assets has narrowed. At the same time, the gap between home owners and households with few assets of any kind, and not including a house, has widened. Thus, under the influence of inflation, home owners have largely moved out of the categories of households with least net wealth, and dwellings represent an increasing proportion of wealth in the middle and higher ranges of wealth holdings. Persons in the bottom range of wealth owners (less than £5,000) have below-average holdings of dwellings and land. For those in the middle range (£5,000–20,000), dwellings account for more than 50 per cent of assets. In view of the dominance of house property in the assets of households with assets valued at between £5,000 and £50,000, it is evident that few households that do not own dwellings can accumulate wealth on a scale comparable with the home owner. Figure 6.1 uses Inland Revenue data to provide an update of these figures and conveys the same general message of the overwhelming importance of housing wealth among those in the middle range, and its reduced significance for top wealth holders, whose wealth is mainly held in stocks, shares and land. Furthermore, there is an evident difference between the higher wealth holders and those in the bottom group. These data also neglect those with little or no wealth.

There are a number of dimensions to this question. Housing market changes, and particularly those relating to the structure of housing finance, have reduced inequalities in wealth in certain areas. This is certainly true of the decline of the private rented sector, the breakup of property portfolios held by landlords, and the relative improvement in the position of the dwelling owner compared with the owner of other assets. Housing trends have led to a reduction in wealth inequalities but only up to a point where the existence of non-owners of dwellings and the increasing inequality between tenants and owners of dwellings is reached. While the growth of direct public provision of housing has been a major factor in the decline of private renting, a situation has been maintained where tenants have no claim on the wealth stored in the dwellings they occupy. Assistance in accumulating wealth is in fact only available to those who can buy. Those who must rent in the public and private sectors are unable to benefit from these policies in terms of wealth accumulation.

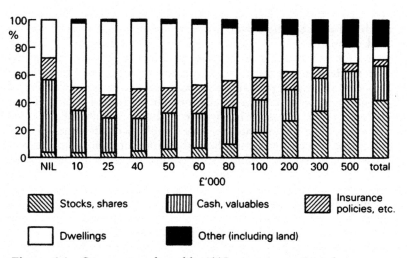

Figure 6.1 Gross personal wealth, 1985: asset composition by range.
Source: Board of Inland Revenue (1987)

134   *Home ownership*

Descriptive data of this type are easily marshalled to support a view that accumulation through housing processes is substantial and has been increasing. They contribute to arguments that changes in the ownership of dwellings have had a considerable impact on social inequality and have either reduced class inequalities or introduced interests and conflicts of interest that complicate class relations. They can be mobilized to indicate a reduction in inequality or in the importance of class in society or a redrawing of social divisions along housing tenure lines. Home owners in contrast to tenants are able to make real capital gains from their own house. As a result owners have a source of income in addition to the job market and have real interests around this.

The analysis of housing in statistics on wealth initially demonstrates the importance of housing in wealth. However, such an analysis as it stands begs a considerable number of questions. Initially, and most obviously, it is important whether or not the definition of wealth is one that relates to real accumulation, which extends and enhances life chances or is a source of social and economic power and which places the home owner in a different social situation with different interests than say the tenant or the owner of other highly priced commodities.

Definitions and statistics

Some general cautionary remarks are appropriate at this stage. The principal source of data on wealth holdings is capital holdings at death collated by the Inland Revenue. Patterns of overall wealth holding in the population as a whole are extrapolated from the estates left in any one year. A major problem with this estate multiplier method is that the present situation is to a great extent being projected from past patterns. For example, the image we derive of housing and wealth from recent mortality patterns will be more likely to reflect the social structure of home ownership, say, 30 years ago. Housing inheritance, for example, will vary qualitatively and quantitatively, reflecting both the different cohorts in the past growth of home ownership and current differences in the relative values of different assets. Some cohorts may contain, for example, disproportionately large numbers of households that bought as sitting private tenants. In other (subsequent) periods council house purchasers may figure more prominently. And there may be strong regional variations. All this cautions against erecting too simplistic a model of future housing inheritance from the present position.

It is also important to acknowledge that the history of the development of home ownership is highly uneven, and different

Realizing the dream 135

regions and towns have varied histories of tenure change. In some areas, working-class home ownership has been well established for half a century. In other cases, the growth of home ownership as a mass tenure is a relatively recent phenomenon and council housing remains the dominant tenure for those on lower incomes (certainly prior to the Right to Buy for council tenants). What this means is that home ownership will have a geography of maturation and the pattern of property inheritance may be highly varied over time and space. This will be further complicated by variations in regional house price inflation – an issue that has been particularly prominent since 1985.

Leaving aside the problems of data availability, the Royal Commission on the Distribution of Income and Wealth in 1977 adopted a conventional distinction between marketed assets and rights that have a capital value. They concluded that no single definition of personal wealth was ideal in all circumstances, that the concept of personal wealth cannot be reduced to a single definitive statement, and that different definitions will be appropriate for different purposes. For those concerned with the distribution of immediate command over resources, personal wealth may best be defined in terms of the ownership of marketable assets only, while for those concerned with the distribution of economic welfare generally the definition may be extended to cover the value of some non-marketable assets.

The Royal Commission made some calculation of the effects on the distribution of wealth of adopting different concepts of wealth. For example, by including the right to a state pension, wealth appears to be spread more equally. The relevance of this to the housing debate is that the argument advanced for including the right to a pension in the concept of wealth – on the grounds that the entitlement provides a secure source of future income in essentially the same way as does the interest on some forms of saving – has been argued to apply to other entitlements, including the right to a cheap council house (*sic*). This is a key issue in addressing accumulation through housing. If entitlement to flows of income through subsidy for council housing (or owner occupation) are represented as wealth, then housing processes become more significant determinants of the value of gross personal wealth. Complications arise especially concerning measuring the value of entitlements. Rent pooling, historic cost accounting and subsidy withdrawal have all been features of council housing that complicate any measurement of the capital value of entitlements. However, these are technical objections and the more fundamental concern relates back to adopting a definition that will indicate differences in immediate command over resources that could be

136 *Home ownership*

constituted in a variety of forms and switched between them rather than a flow of income over time. Except in so far as, say, council tenants could 'sell' their tenancy entitlements for cash, there is no sense in which the capital value of the use of a council house can be realized or the tenant can shift the form in which wealth is held. While access to non-marketed assets constitutes a real capital value, it does not constitute accumulation that can be legally realized, or transferred into other forms of wealth, or borrowed against.

The process that enables individuals to accumulate wealth (through housing) that can be realized and transferred is almost exclusively the prerogative of owners of dwellings, including both landlords and owner occupiers. But do all home owners own a realizable and transferrable asset? A home owner with a new 100 per cent mortgage does not; an owner whose property is depreciating in value or has a market value of less than the outstanding debt may not. Furthermore, it is strongly and reasonably argued that sale or transfer for many home owners is conditional upon the purchase of another dwelling. These home owners could not realize the value of their asset and reinvest it in some other form of capital holding.

These are all issues that must be addressed if the nature and extent to which housing processes facilitate accumulation is to be placed in a realistic perspective. Attempts to quantify wealth – such as those of the Royal Commission – have not gone far enough to address these issues to provide a satisfactory picture of accumulation through housing. Although profound problems remain with the sources of data, some response to key issues is possible.

Rates of accumulation

Housing has played, and does play, a major role in wealth accumulation. The importance of this reflects not just a growth in home ownership but also the movement of house prices relative to other prices and to the value of other assets. Reference has already been made to discussion of whether housing kept pace with other assets in the early 1980s. Nevertheless, it is generally accepted that, compared with other types of asset, home ownership has performed well over a long period of time – partly because of tax arrangements. The comparisons presented by the Royal Commission on the Distribution of Income and Wealth and reproduced elsewhere (Murie and Forrest, 1980b, Murie 1983) establish this favourable comparison. More recent contributions (Nationwide Building Society, 1986; Nationwide Anglia 1989) have calculated rates of return in different ways, but still demonstrate attractive rates of return over a long period.

Realizing the dream   137

More recently, discussion of rates of return has been used in a different context. Saunders and Harris (1988) have sought to analyse rates of return for individual home owners in order to counteract resistance to the notion that home owners are making money. It is not clear that discussion of rates of return in this context is the appropriate way to achieve this purpose. This is principally because high rates of return do not mean high absolute returns. It is also because the method of calculating rates of return is not straightforward.

Saunders and Harris claim that calculations of rates of return that do not distinguish between returns on borrowed cash and the buyer's own resources are misleading. Rates of return, they argue, have to be calculated on the rate of capital appreciation as a percentage of the original deposit rather than as a percentage of the entire purchase price. There is a logic to this approach; however, it neglects the fact that the rate of return calculated in this way does not derive only from the deposit. It occurs only because of an accompanying loan. The key to rate of return is likely to be related to the comparison between rates of inflation and the rate of interest charged on this loan. The calculation around deposit rather than this real rate of interest produces an idiosyncratic pattern of rates of return, which says little about similarities or differencies in experience and throws a smokescreen across the debate. Perhaps the clearest example of this is that the method of calculating rates of return produces infinite returns where 100 per cent of the purchase price was borrowed. Saunders and Harris acknowledge this, and deal with it by leaving these cases out.

Their evidence is drawn from interviews with 522 householders in 450 different houses in Slough, Derby and Burnley in the buoyant market conditions of the mid 1980s. Their calculation of total capital gain is based on current value less mortgage debt less original deposit. It ignores transaction costs, repair and maintenance, and other expenditures. It also ignores the opportunity for accumulation forgone by paying mortgage payments. This is justified on the grounds that owners would have to pay at least as much in rents as they pay in mortgage payments if they chose to invest their cash in some other way. But this is an oversimplification. First, it is based on an assumption of non-mobility. This has a greater significance for home owners who consequently benefit from historic costings, which in many cases are periodically revised and updated on moving. Rents, on the other hand – in public and private sectors – are not tied to historic costs in the same way. Secondly, the profile of costs for owners and tenants is different even where they amount to similar sums over a lifetime. Home owners' costs are front loaded and in real terms decline over

138 *Home ownership*

time (especially if they do not move house or remortgage). In contrast, rents will often be lower initially but increase over time. This profile of payments is of some importance as it implies that a tenant with the same income would have more cash to invest elsewhere in the early years. The discounted value of their 'investment' opportunity is logically greater than that applying to owners at a later stage. For all of these reasons Saunders and Harris's calculations of rates of return are misleading. They ignore the implications of the case that does not fit and they fail to make reasonable assumptions about transaction costs, mobility and the historic-cost basis and the implications of the profile of payments for the rate of return attributable to ownership.

Saunders and Harris's approach is based on arithmetic calculations of percentage rates of return rather than the volume of wealth involved. If the debate is concerned with patterns of inequality of wealth holding, this seems inappropriate. A high return on a very small investment does not narrow the absolute gap with a moderate or small return on a very large investment. It is in terms of rate of return that Saunders and Harris deny social class differences and attempt to refute that patterns of accumulation through house ownership will tend to reflect (but not be determined solely by) differences in income and lifetime earnings.

Reference to absolute gains may be more relevant than rate of return. Saunders and Harris acknowledge this in discussing differences in absolute gains between regions and localities. They also acknowledge that their method of calculating rates of return means that by far the biggest single determinant of rates of return and total capital gains is the time that has elapsed since the original purchase. Their figures are further distorted by the way in which they treat discounts on council house sales. Rather than treating the initial value of these as a grant or gift or as part of the cash deposit laid down by tenants (an entitlement earned on the basis of tenancy), discounts are treated as part of the rate of return associated with an initial deposit (except of course where 100 per cent mortgages were involved, when the method collapses). Nevertheless, Saunders and Harris refer to their own and other data to assert that relative returns on investment in Christchurch, New Zealand, appear remarkably uniform, although absolute gains varied (Pratt, 1986); that rates of increase were actually highest in low-priced areas of Glasgow, although absolute gains were highest in high-price areas (Munro and Maclennan, 1987); and that owners of the cheapest housing secured a higher rate of return on capital investment although they made lower absolute gains (their own data). This seems a very tenuous basis on which to dismiss the view that differentials in wealth accumulation through

Realizing the dream 139

home ownership mean that the operation of the housing market exacerbates inequalities arising out of differential returns in the labour market; and to assert that proportionate wage and salary differentials may actually be reduced as a result of differential rates of gain from private house ownership. If absolute gains rather than contentious calculations of rates of return are given pride of place in the analysis, it is hard to see how their conclusions would hold.

All this is not to deny accumulation associated with housing but to caution against overstating and generalizing. Rates of return are probably better represented by the calculations made by the Nationwide Building Society (1986), which take into account mobility and transaction costs. These identify different rates of return depending on mobility and refer to regional variations rather than individuals and to imputed rental values. Their figures range from 13 per cent to 25 per cent, compared with Saunders and Harris's extreme for nominal rates of infinity, mean (excluding infinity and those who bought outright at first purchase) of 62 per cent and median of 26 per cent. Part of Saunders and Harris's concern is to correct what they see as a deep resistance in the academic literature to the notion that home owners are making money from their housing. If there is such a general resistance it should be challenged. It is not best challenged through overstating rates of return or generalizing about 'two thirds of the population sharing in the benefits of rapid capital accumulation' and 'that home ownership has come to represent the equivalent to a certificate of entitlement to share in the fruits of economic growth' and 'is quite literally a stake in the system'. In Saunders and Harris's own terms, owners in Burnley whose property has a current value of less than £5,000 will rarely have benefited from 'rapid capital accumulation' and certainly have not made absolute gains comparable with other households, including tenants. Their experience of the benefits of ownership is widely different from that of some other owners. Moreover, it seems likely that if Saunders and Harris had carried out their survey in the very different housing market conditions obtaining in 1989 they would have had a very different picture – not least in terms of rates of return. This aspect is returned to later in this book. Emphasizing variation and caution about calculating rates of return is not to resist the notion that a key feature of home ownership is accumulation, but is to resist the temptation to respond to one untenable position by asserting another untenable position built on categorical statements about a segmented and differentiated system.

Saunders and Harris's contribution to the debate relates to other issues in this chapter. They identify a number of 'fallacious' arguments about gains associated with housing: that they are not

140 *Home ownership*

realizable; that only affluent owners make gains; and that owners are indifferent to investment potential. All of these contentions are stated and rejected in terms of home ownership as a whole. The arguments presented in this book suggest that it should not be expected that home ownership involves necessary relationships. Such arguments are fallacious, whichever opposite contention they defend. The rate of gain varies between regions and according to time period. In some cases gains are not real – some properties are sold at less than they were purchased for and more are sold at a smaller amount in real terms. Discussion of how far returns are realizable, of differential accumulation and of the influence of investment on decisions is available elsewhere (Murie, 1983; Forrest and Murie, 1988b) and in the remainder of this chapter.

It is also undeniable that some home owners are in arrears, are repossessed, fail to maintain properties and are desperate to move to renting. In most cases, these are small sectors of the whole tenure. While they will tend to have low incomes they are only some of those with low incomes and other factors are involved.

In general, however, Saunders and Harris's zealous rejection of flawed assertions leads them to present a picture of home ownership that fails to reflect the volume of empirical data about variations in the tenure. While they are right to reject overstatements and produce empirical data that challenge them, they are wrong to represent these overstatements as the accepted view. And refuting such overstatements does not justify the creation of a new hyperbolic chimera or carefully avoiding more cautious and qualified perspectives on home ownership that are at least as compatible with the empirical data to which they refer.

Realizable wealth

Starting from a view that what it is necessary to identify is the extent to which housing processes provide opportunities to make money gains that can be realized and transferred, three propositions can be put forward as the basis for modification of the picture presented:

1. That money gains are not made by all owners but are realizable where owners trade down or are in a position to trade down in the housing market.
2. That where owners do move but do not trade down, in some cases there is substantial 'leakage'.
3. That where owners do not move, in some cases the appreciation of the value of the asset is such that they move into a

position where they *could* trade down (especially to a smaller house) or *do* realize some of the capital value through borrowing on the security of the dwelling. This represents a realization of capital that is not available to non-owners.

These kinds of considerations would suggest that the realizable wealth associated with home ownership is overstated by conventional statistics of wealth, which refer to total asset value. However, realizable wealth is more significant than is indicated by leakage associated with moving house or increasing borrowing. It may be argued that in many cases this realizable wealth is not realized during the lifetime of the home owner, but this is to impose an alternative concept of wealth that becomes a denial of the notion of wealth itself. None the less, it is in this context that the inheritance of wealth through house property becomes important.

There is a growing body of evidence on marginal and failed owners. In some parts of the owner-occupied market, processes of obsolescence and house price changes leave owners with a diminishing asset value net of the debt involved. In some cases, the mortgage debt exceeds market value. In these cases there is no realizable money gain. In other cases, the realization of money gain is problematic because there is nowhere to 'trade down' to. Supply and access restrictions may prevent a move to rented property being a mechanism for realizing money gains. Evidence of mortgage failure and repossession, negative real rates of accumulation and wide regional and local disparities in rates of house price increase are the most immediate challenge to any view that all owners are in the same position in relation to accumulation (see, for example, Moreton and Tate, 1986; Munro and Maclennan, 1987; Doling *et al*, 1986; Karn *et al* 1985; Ford, 1988).

In contrast to this, there is increasing evidence on issues of credit and leakage associated with home ownership. Remortgaging of houses in order to finance the purchase of consumer durables has been associated with the 1972–3 house price boom in Britain. The boom of the late 1980s no doubt involved the same process. Christopher Johnson, writing in February 1984, stated:

> Once upon a time people used to recoil from the idea of getting into debt, as they thought of the sad fate of Dickens' Mr Micawber or Mr Dorrit languishing in debtors' prisons, like his own father. Now it has come to be regarded as financially naive, if not downright unpatriotic, not to borrow as much as possible. The current British recovery, after all, has been based on consumer spending increases directly attributable to the surge

142 *Home ownership*

both in consumer credit and in home mortgages, which finance consumer spending indirectly. (p. 1)

Johnson refers to the difference between the saving ratio (the proportion of personal disposable income after tax that is saved) in the personal and in household sector. The personal sector saving ratio had been boosted mainly through undistributed profits by unincorporated businesses. In contrast, the household sector saving ratio in 1971 and 1983 was estimated to be zero. The household saving ratio falls where there is a surge in household borrowing (as in 1971–3 and 1981–3). Johnson comments:

> Home mortgages have risen from 72 per cent to 82 per cent of all household debt since 1970, ... with a growth rate of 17 per cent a year, a fraction more than the rate of growth of total debt. Tax relief on all personal interest is a feature of the US financial system, but during the 1970s it was in force in the UK only for the two years from 1972–74, after which it was phased out by the Labour Government. Since then tax relief has been limited to mortgage interest. It is thus not surprising that households borrow as much as possible for house purchase and home improvements; what is perhaps surprising is that the higher effective interest rates on consumer credit and other personal borrowing – higher in nominal terms than mortgage rates and without tax relief – have virtually no deterrent effect on the demand, which is often associated with impulse purchasing decisions. (p. 1–2)

Turnbull (1984) comments similarly:

> One of the most interesting features of the British economy in recent years has been the surprising strength of consumer spending. Despite sharply rising unemployment and falling real incomes, real consumers' expenditure moved ahead in both 1981 and 1982. In 1983 there was a gain of over 3% . . . . the boom of mortgage credit has been a pivotal factor behind the buoyancy of expenditure. (p. 3)

He gones on to state that since 1980 the growth in mortgage lending has far outstripped the personal sector's housing investment:

> Funds have not, therefore, been directed solely towards the acquisition of additional and better housing. Instead, a large proportion of mortgage credit has been associated with increased debt on the existing owner occupied housing stock. Mortgage funds have therefore circulated within the personal sector,

Realizing the dream 143

thereby becoming available for consumption purposes via a process known as 'equity withdrawal'. (p.3)

The conventional view (expressed by Turnbull) is that this more rapid growth in mortgage lending is not accounted for by direct lending for consumer expenditure. Rather, it is associated with decisions not to reinvest the full proceeds from the sale of a previous dwelling. Equity withdrawal has been rising appreciably since 1980 and is associated with the increasing percentage of purchase price funded by a mortgage. According to Ball (1986), in 1980 only 46 per cent of purchase price on average was funded by a mortgage and this had risen to 59 per cent in 1984. First-time buyers are also borrowing a larger proportion of purchase price. These figures relate both to what is realizable wealth and to actual realization through equity withdrawal.

While actual realization has been growing, the extent to which home ownership represents debt rather than ownership has grown for those with mortgages. Two side issues should be noted here. First, where equity withdrawal is associated with moving house, transaction costs are involved. These are considerable and affect the real rate of leakage and the real investment on which a return is being made. One recent comment on the effect of transaction costs associated with moving states:

The average borrower who purchased a house 15 years ago and has stayed put will have enjoyed a net rate of return of 17%. A person who first bought at the same time but who moved to a larger house every five years will . . . . have paid out an additional £4,677 in transaction costs and reduced the net return to 15%. (Nationwide Building Society, 1986)

Secondly, rates of house price increase vary considerably by region and locality. The boom in house prices in Greater London and the South East (see Chapter 2) has focused attention on the widening gap in prices between these and other areas in the country. All of the dimensions of accumulation referred to in this section, from leakage to potential realizable wealth, are likely to be experienced differentially for owners between regions. Those in regions with slower rates of house price inflation have fewer opportunities for these gains or for accumulation in general.

Household debt has risen significantly. However, it remains low in relation to income when comparison is made with the USA. What is important is the extent to which this increasing indebtedness is associated with increased levels of home ownership, increased borrowing by individuals to facilitate home purchase or improvement, or increased use of the home as a source of credit that is spent in areas other than housing. To the extent that the last of these aspects is involved, home owners are realizing the wealth they have accumulated through housing and converting it into disposable income. They may be doing this in order to cope with other problems or in pursuit of various other strategies.

The General Household Survey (GHS) 1982 provides evidence of the extent to which owner occupiers made use of a form of credit that was not available to households in rented accommodation (OPCS, 1983a). This involves data on home owners with loans raised on the security of their homes for purposes other than the purchase of their current accommodation (e.g. topping up or bridging loans). The loans referred to include those for purposes such as the improvement or extension of the borrower's property, the purchase of a second home, the purchase of consumer goods or financing a business. The GHS shows that in the years 1980, 1981 and 1982, 4 per cent, 5 per cent and 4 per cent respectively of owner occupiers in Great Britain had such loans. Households currently buying their accommodation with a mortgage were nearly twice as likely as outright owners to have used this form of credit. The majority of these households (60 per cent in 1982) had raised loans to improve or extend their current homes, and a substantial minority had used the money to finance business ventures (19 per cent in 1982). Owner occupiers who had loans on the security of their homes were more likely than owner occupiers as a whole to be young, to be in small or large family households, to have higher income, to be in managerial or skilled manual occupations and to be economically active. When comparison with mortgagors is made, those who are more likely to raise such loans are those aged 30–44, professional, employers and managers and junior non-manual workers. This evidence can be referred to in the context of discussion of leakage. It indicates use of home ownership status and a tendency for more affluent owners to make the greatest use of this. Financial institutions also use home ownership status as a test of eligibility. Where loans have been raised for house improvements or any other reason, some leakage may be involved.

The problems of estimating the extent of capital leakage are considerable. A cautious calculation by Kemeny and Thomas (1984) suggested that 0.6–1.0 per cent of the total value of personal sector dwellings is realized each year. This includes (but is likely to underestimate) the leakage of capital released to last-time sellers. The Bank of England estimated in 1985 that 'net cash withdrawal' from the private housing market totalled £7.2 billion in 1984 and was equivalent to 3 per cent of total consumer spending.

Not all of this is spending on consumption and some goes into savings. A more recent estimate by Holman (1986) suggests that inheritance accounted for about 40 per cent of the leakage from home ownership between 1982 and 1984 compared with 32 per cent withdrawn by moving owners who took a larger mortgage than they required, and 5 per cent who sold and moved into a cheaper house bought without a mortgage. In their estimate, Lowe and Watson (1989) suggest a higher cash figure for inheritance (£3.8 billion in 1984) and a substantially higher figure for equity withdrawal generally (£12.5 billion). This is partly because Lowe and Watson attempt a more comprehensive definition, including sales of rented dwellings (where cash passes to landlords for other uses), remortgaging and increasing the mortgage advance to house price ratio (thereby releasing savings for other uses). But even on a narrower definition, total equity withdrawal was £9.7 billion in 1984. The discussion of capital leakage is normally linked with questions of distortion of the savings market (and impact on finance to productive industry) and distortions of the housing market (and the need to reform housing finance to reduce subsidies to consumption and discourage capital leakage). The extent of leakage is a consequence of the fiscal arrangements associated with owner occupation and would be modified by changes in these arrangements. However, in terms of the discussion in this chapter, capital leakage associated with remortgaging is a manifest realization of housing wealth. Leaving aside issues of inheritance and realization affecting beneficiaries, the potential extent of realization of wealth held in housing is considerably greater. In terms of a distinction between measures of asset holding and measures of realizable wealth, this is significant. The whole picture, as Lowe and Watson have remarked, contradicts views expressed by Kemeny (1981) and Ball (1983) that equity gains through home ownership are not realizable and do not accrue to anyone.

Inheritance

The analysis of leakage includes that associated with last-time sellers. While this may include persons moving out of home ownership for various reasons, it will include sales following transfers of ownership through inheritance. The issue of inheritance is an important one in the discussion of accumulation as it offers the most tangible realization and transfer of an asset.

Harbury and Hitchens (1979) have argued that 'inheritance is the major determinant of wealth inequality'. Townsend (1979) refers to 'the considerable importance of the inheritance of land and

146 *Home ownership*

property . . . . in explaining substantial assets'. (p.346) Given that housing is an important element in asset building, it is inevitably a major determinant, through inheritance, of wealth inequality. The Royal Commission on the Distribution of Income and Wealth provided some evidence on this in 1977. Irrespective of property left in estates, members of the immediate family are the major beneficiaries. This is especially true in the ranges where housing is proportionally likely to be most important. On average, some 50 per cent of disposable estate bequeathed to relatives passes within the same generation and 46 per cent to the second generation. As the average age at death is 74 years for men and 79 for women, most inheritances are received by persons who are already in middle or old age and only the descendants of the very wealthy are likely to inherit at an early age.

An individual may be able to take advantage of expectations before an inheritance is actually received, for example by accumulating debts to be repaid at a later date. Thus an inheritance is not necessarily an unexpected windfall and the opportunities of the eventual recipient may have been enhanced beforehand.

While bequests to members of the third and fourth generation are of relatively minor importance, they are more important in the largest estates. In small estates, transfers to spouses and children account for the bulk of disposable property, whereas in the largest estates the greater absolute size of the property to be distributed allows the immediate claims of spouses and children to be met while still leaving sizeable sums to be bequeathed to other beneficiaries, including members of the third generation. In the largest estates there is also a greater incentive for 'generation skipping' as a means of reducing the impact of estate duty on the transfer of wealth.

These aspects are relevant to housing in two ways. First, housing assets form part of the estates concerned and are an element in the inequality generated. Secondly, the beneficiaries may invest inherited wealth in housing. Arguably this is less probable among older beneficiaries, and the available research evidence on this is discussed below. Where such an invest- ment does result, clearly beneficiaries of owner occupiers are more likely to be able to trade up or compete favourably with non-beneficiaries than are the beneficiaries of tenants. As housing is an investment as well as a consumption good, competi- tion for housing will be affected by wealth as well as income.

The more direct housing consequences of inheritance have been speculated upon elsewhere (Murie and Forrest, 1980b; Forrest and Murie, 1989b) and a number of general views can be summarized. First-generation owners whose purchase of housing between the wars marked the first significant growth of owner occupation are

Realizing the dream 147

now ageing outright owners and the numbers of estates containing an element of house property has increased. This is evident from the increasing number of dwellings coming on to the market through the dissolution of elderly households and the increase in the proportion of outright owners where the head of household is aged 60 or over: from 62 per cent in 1972 to 69 per cent in 1984. It is clear that an increasing number of households will become substantial beneficiaries as a result of trends in housing and this could have significant social and economic repercussions.

However, statistics on inheritance reflect the historical pattern of growth of home ownership and who became home owners in the past. The transfer of over 1 million council dwellings between 1979 and 1988 will be reflected in inheritance only in, say, 30 or more years' time. Similarly, evidence that it is the more expensive homes that are being inherited in Glasgow probably reflects the relatively privileged nature of home ownership in Scotland 40 years ago. The importance of housing inheritance will reflect both different stages or cohorts of growth of home ownership and current differences in the relative values of different assets.

Moira Munro's (1988) analysis of the Commissary records held at the Sheriff Court in Glasgow involved reference to the wills of individuals who had died testate in Glasgow in a period of just under six months in 1984. Some 30 per cent of the sample included heritable estates and all but one of these included a dwelling. Estates without any housing component were concentrated at the lowest end in terms of value and 80 per cent were valued at £15,000 or less. In direct contrast, 80 per cent of the estates that included housing wealth were valued at more than £15,000. As with other sources of data, housing declined in relative importance as the total value of estates increased. Munro's analysis is particularly interesting as it refers to gender and marital status and enables transfers to spouses to be seen as temporary or transitional. Transfers by single, widowed or divorced persons (including therefore a surviving spouse) represent the most interesting transfers in terms of intergenerational transfer. The intergenerational element is considerably increased if this approach is adopted: 96 per cent of estates bequeathed by married persons pass to the spouse. If all estates are considered together, irrespective of marital status, 43 per cent pass to a spouse and 34 per cent to the next generation. 'Transitional bequests' obscure the long-term pattern.

The analysis makes clear the typical paths by which estates containing housing wealth are transferred between generations. Within a married couple, the initial transfer of wealth is to the longer-lived spouse, with a relatively small 'leakage' to other family members. On the death of that surviving spouse, most

148   *Home ownership*

of the wealth passes to the following generation – 38 per cent to sons and daughters and 18 per cent to nephews and nieces. Very little goes to the grandchildren and little over a third stays in the same generation or is passed outside the family.

On the death of a single, widowed or divorced person, the wealth is divided, on average, amongst 2.3 people. The amount of inheritance received at this stage is still likely to be substantial, but as the housing wealth is often such a large proportion of the total wealth there would frequently not be sufficient money in the estate to allow any of the inheritors to keep the house. Munro's analysis also shows that, as indicated by the Royal Commission, inheritances are overwhelmingly received in old or middle age. However, the concentration on immediate family is somewhat more marked in Munro's sample, which was mainly of moderate rather than large estates. In light of thee average age of death, it is clear that the following generation, who receive 56 per cent of the estates of the single, widowed and divorced group, are likely to be middle-aged themselves.

Munro concludes that it is probable that much of the wealth that passes from estates with housing wealth will be received by households that have been able to undertake house purchase in their own right, resulting in deeper wealth divisions between those who own houses and those who do not in the longer term.

Hamnett, Harmer and Williams (1989) have recently completed a study of inheritance using a random survey of households in Great Britain. Of 3,298 respondents, 506 or 15 per cent lived in a household where one or more members had received an inheritance of £1,000 or more at some stage. In 302 of these cases, inheritance included residential property. This implies that between 1.91 million and 1.98 million households in Britain contain members who have inherited house property during their lives. Housing inheritance is an important and quite widespread phenomenon. Unfortunately this study, unlike Moira Munro's, does not enable inheritances by a spouse to be distinguished from intergenerational transfers. Consequently the nature of beneficiaries is weighted to an unknown extent towards older home owners. The overwhelming majority of beneficiaries were already home owners at inheritance. The fact that home owners were some six times more likely to have inherited than council tenants reflects differences in parental tenure and social class as well as problems in identifying inheritance by a spouse. The class composition of beneficiaries reflects the class composition of home ownership in the past rather than currently. The cohort of households whose estates were involved were home owners at a stage where home ownership was still more exclusively the preserve of white-collar

Realizing the dream 149

and higher-income families. Given intergenerational continuities in social class, it is not surprising that the beneficiaries were not only likely to be home owners, but also more likely to be from higher social classes. Households classified as professional and managerial (A and B) were four times more likely to inherit than unskilled workers (E). People in the South East were four times more likely to inherit than those in Scotland, three times as likely as those in Yorkshire and twice as likely as those in some other regions. Council tenants and working-class households were more likely to be joint beneficiaries and for this reason, and because the value of the estates involved is smaller, tend to receive smaller inheritances. The regional differences in this followed the pattern already indicated.

Hamnett, Harmer and Williams' study provides the first data on the uses to which inherited property is put. Of the 302 households inheriting at least a share in a property, two-thirds (198) sold the property more or less immediately. Twenty-two per cent (67) decided to live in the property; this group will include most of the spouse inheritors. In a further eight cases the property was lived in by another person. Only 11 beneficiaries let the property for rent, and six of these had sold at the time of interview. Not surprisingly, joint beneficiaries were more likely to have sold the property more or less immediately (79 per cent compared with 44 per cent of sole beneficiaries). Leaving this aside, evidence was provided on the use of money released from property inheritance: 27 per cent of households spent 'most of the money' on property purchase or improvement; 49 per cent on investment in financial assets and particularly in building societies (27 per cent); and 24 per cent on consumption. The impact of housing inheritance clearly does not always, or even principally, feed back into the beneficiaries' housing career. However, leaving aside those properties lived in by the beneficiary or another person, a small group (24) used money released to become owners for the first time; eight others used money to move up-market; four bought a second home; four assisted children or grandchildren to buy; and 30 used money for home improvement. When aggregated up to national level, these figures do not suggest a dramatic impact. Sales by beneficiaries annually contribute towards some 7 per cent of all second-hand property transactions (excluding right to buy purchases); some 4 per cent of all first-time purchases for home ownership; some 1.5 per cent of trading up; and a tiny proportion of improvement. Furthermore, the release of property into private rental is small and dwarfed by the flows of property out of the sector – including sales of inherited rented property. These are important indicators of scale and lead the authors to conclude that the housing market effects are not as great as has been suggested. However for almost 50 per cent of beneficiaries to live in the inherited property or to let others, presumably relatives, live in the (unsold) property, or to use some of the money released for housing is a substantial effect. In addition, the importance of investment in building societies, and even in other financial sectors, implies some feedback into housing.

This evidence generally confirms the existing view that intergenerational inheritance is likely to occur at a stage when beneficiaries are already well into their housing careers. Except in anticipation, inheritance is less likely to affect new households, and, while it may encourage trading up and house price inflation, its overall effect on this is probably limited. Nevertheless, households without the advantage of access to cash through inheritance or loans and gifts associated with ownership are disadvantaged in relation to price (deposit) obstacles on gaining entry to owner occupation and to trading up beyond a limited level. The likelihood of being trapped in the rental sector or at particular points in the owner–occupied sector may increase for households without the (realized or anticipated) benefits of inheritance, or the access to funds associated with ownership by parents or relatives. While inheritance may increase the mobility of existing owners to a limited extent and encourage trading up, it may contribute to reducing mobility and choice for those who lack any equivalent asset – whether they are owners or renters. While these effects exist, they are not large and will often be outweighed by other factors.

The historical development of individualized home ownership means that inheritance associated with this tenure is likely to become of increasing significance in the overall distribution of wealth. However, there are factors that will operate against this growth. Wealth stored in housing may be increasingly drawn on to finance expenditures in old age. Recent work has identified a potentially important leakage associated with equity release schemes. The extent to which equity in owner-occupied housing is capitalized by elderly owners in order to change their accommodation in old age could substantially alter expectations about inheritance. Equity release may be achieved by trading down or by moving into rented housing or some form of residential accommodation. A small but increasing number of elderly owners are taking advantage of mortgage annuity or home reversion schemes to generate additional income in old age without moving house. For more affluent elderly home owners, the building industry is targeting more tailored forms of provision (for example 'Sundowner' developments), which are likely to absorb some of their accumulated housing wealth.

Realizing the dream 151

Private sheltered housing tends to be bought by elderly owners trading down and releasing equity. This process involves some erosion of equity holdings, and increasing service charges are a further source of erosion. While the numbers of such developments are relatively small, the potential market is large and its growth would contribute to a reduction in equity holdings in old age (Fleiss, 1985; G. Williams, 1986). In general, as the home-owning population ages, the construction and financial sectors are adjusting their products and services to profit from the substantial equity stored in dwellings. Little systematic evidence is available at present, but it is clear that substantial numbers of elderly owner occupiers have limited incomes and occupy properties requiring expenditure on repair and maintenance. Releasing some of the equity in their property may be the only available method of enhancing income generally or enabling necessary repairs to be carried out. Inevitably there will be greater pressures on elderly owner occupiers in lower-value, lower-quality properties.

It is also important in this context to identify potential developments in policy. For example, the Griffiths Report (1988) *Community care: agenda for action* identified the possibilities of individuals meeting their own care needs in old age by drawing on savings and in this context referred directly to 'schemes for encouraging owner occupiers to use their equity to provide income which can be used to pay for services in retirement . . . .'. (p.22)

Without going into further detail, it is evident that various pressures are developing that are likely to erode the equity ultimately transferred by elderly home owners. These pressures will vary in form and significance, spatially and socially, but the general implication is that it is that group of ageing outright owners for whom their dwelling is their sole capital asset who will be under greatest pressure to capitalize some or all of their property equity. There are, however, more general processes at work associated with a property and finance market adjusting to the reality of an ageing of the owner-occupied sector, which indicate the need for greater caution in predicting the global amounts that will be transferred to the next generation. There are also direct and indirect pressures related to the privatization of health care, which may also absorb substantial amounts of housing equity prior to death. The general context for discussion of these issues is one in which the period of retirement is becoming longer – people retire from work at a younger age and live to an older age. This phenomenon may contribute to the pressures for equity release.

Some recent research suggests that mortgage annuity schemes have various eligibility constraints that concentrate their use among

152 *Home ownership*

households with moderate incomes living in modestly valued properties in a reasonable state of repair (Leather, 1987). The implication is that, for the more marginal elderly home owners, options may be rather more limited. There will be less equity to release, repairs and maintenance problems will be more pressing and more expensive, and loans on the security of the property may be available only through fringe financiers.

Finally, discussions of housing wealth and inheritance have pointed out important spatial and social differentiation. The value of inheritance associated with housing will reflect regional and other price variations, and the distributional impact will reflect aspects of family size and structure. The pattern of intergenerational transfers will not be the same for all home owners, but will be highly differentiated and may be more likely to accentuate rather than smooth out social divisions.

Wealth and power

The preceding discussion of housing as wealth has raised issues of definition and measurement that are important in identifying the extent and nature of accumulation through housing. But there is another dimension to the concept of wealth which the discussion has neglected. In much of the analysis of wealth and inequalities in wealth the important dimension is not the money value of assets at a particular time but the power and control that is associated with the ownership of assets. As was discussed in Chapter 5, a distinction is made between total wealth and wealth that has implications for the distribution of social power.

Hird and Irvine (1979) state:

It is almost a precondition for producing wealth in our society that one own and control capital. This is also perhaps the main factor determining the distribution of wealth: workers can generally fight for higher wages only while owners and managers make the investment decisions which determine what will be produced, how and where. Capital is thus different from other forms of wealth: shares in an industrial company, for example, will typically grow in value over time, produce a regular dividend, confer legal ownership over part of the company's material assets, and are, moreover, easily marketable when necessary. Other forms of wealth are quite different: consumer goods generally depreciate and have a low second-hand value; the value of houses may in the main appreciate, but they are often difficult to sell, and the owner generally needs to buy

Realizing the dream   153

another as a replacement; pensions provide an entitlement to a future income only for as long as the pensioner lives, are not transferable, and often depreciate in value; and cash, although it confers immediate economic power through its purchasing power, generally depreciates. It is changes in the ownership and control of the means of production that need to be treated as the central criteria in assessing the distribution of wealth, for changes in other forms of wealth are intimately related to these. (p.201-2)

In these terms it is not sufficient to distinguish between whether and to what extent housing assets are marketable or realizable. Rather it is important to distinguish between housing as a category of asset that has a market value and other assets that have a market value but also involve ownership and control of the process of wealth creation. Hird and Irvine refer to this latter category as capital (company securities, listed ordinary shares, land). When this distinction is drawn and applied to the statistical analysis provided by the Royal Commission on the Distribution of Income and Wealth, (chaired by Lord Diamond) they calculate that:

0.1 per cent of the population are shown to own well over a quarter of capital assets; moreover, the top 8.3 per cent own 94.6 per cent of listed ordinary shares and 90.9 per cent of all land (as well as 80.5 per cent of listed UK Government securities). At the other end of the scale, the wealth of the poor is held mainly as household goods, cash, national savings and life policies; in the middle ranges, the main feature of importance seems to be the large holdings of wealth as dwellings and building society deposits. Thus the very rich not only own an inordinate amount of wealth, but they hold it in those forms of assets that carry economic power. By failing to evaluate this central feature in wealth holdings, Diamond's statistical analyses become extremely misleading: the reader might never grasp that the production, reproduction and distribution of wealth are all controlled by a small section of the population. But for critical social scientists, it must be the ownership of capital, not consumer goods, houses, or the right to a pension that forms the central element in assessing the patterns of social inequality. (p.202-3)

They go on to argue that the effective control of other wealth lies with a smaller group of managers rather than with the owners of assets. The direction of such an argument is that wider ownership of wealth or of realizable wealth through housing is a trend that

154   *Home ownership*

does not involve wider ownership of capital or equality in economic power. In that sense it does not imply increasing equality or classlessness and raises doubts about the strength of the common interest involved in home ownership.

Speculation and investment strategies

Discussion of potential rather than actual realization of wealth held in housing relates to discussion of individual housing strategies designed to increase wealth. Farmer and Barrel (1981) have suggested that, for individuals striving to increase their wealth, the structure of housing finance makes speculation in the owner-occupied market attractive. Home owners can make large capital gains not only because of rises in the real prices of houses but also because they are not paying market rates of interest on mortgages. Consequently, some 'entrepreneurs' will see the owner-occupied housing market as a preferable sphere for their enterprise. Where such individuals are job holders, this strategy, unlike some other types of speculation, will not put their income at risk, will not risk bankruptcy and has (in recent years at least) low capital risk. Farmer and Barrel suggest that:

> For a multitude of potential small businessmen, house-ownership has undoubtedly offered a more satisfactory combination of risk and return than they could possibly have got elsewhere. For many, ownership is just one of a number of entrepreneurial ventures, but for some at least it will be the only one. (1981, p.318)

It is the rational entrepreneur who may choose to enjoy some of the fruits of speculation through leakage. Farmer and Barrel suggest a division of owner occupiers into non-movers, plungers (who reborrow as much as possible on moving), and cautious individuals (who borrow more cautiously). By referring to national figures, Farmer and Barrel indicate how different strategies in recent years could yield different gains and losses.

Three comments are relevant to this perspective on strategies to enhance accumulation through housing. First, it highlights awareness of the accumulative capacity of housing – a feature supported by survey evidence, which demonstrates that savings/investment considerations do influence house purchase decisions. Such considerations are often not of primary importance and are elements in a wider set of calculations (Murie, 1983). This issue was more fully discussed in Chapter 4. Secondly, it is apparent that the

Realizing the dream 155

opportunity to enter into successful speculative activity is greater for those with secure and rising incomes elsewhere. The plungers in Farmer and Barrel's discussion are likely to include not only those in safe but 'unproductive' and well-paid public sector jobs but also those in the private sector in professional and salaried occupations. These include private sector housing professionals and those in jobs where preferential borrowing terms and assistance with moving house further enhance the potential rate of return on entrepreneurial activity in housing. Thirdly, it is evident that opportunities to become a home owner entrepreneur depend initially upon the capacity to enter those parts of the market that offer high rates of return, and upon the nature of employment and income growth facilitating movement, and that the actual size of capital accumulation achieved will vary spatially.

The general issue of accumulation through housing is related to a final set of issues about housing choice. The terminology of housing ladders and escalators is associated with home ownership in academic as well as other literature. There is little evidence that dwellings 'filter' down or that households benefit from filtering (Murie *et al*, 1976; Boddy and Gray, 1979). Nevertheless, there is an implication that, because considerable capital gains can be made from housing, and because these can be substantial compared to the income derived from the work process, housing careerists, spiralists or entrepreneurs are at work. These individuals demonstrate a difference of interest and behaviour associated with housing. They have so far identified housing consumption as the route to accumulation that their energies and their political priorities are focused on housing consumption rather than on the workplace. Farmer and Barrel's representation of this group suggests that it is an exotic group with secure jobs rather than a large sector of home owners. Attempts to identify the group in practice suggest they are a minor protected species. Even among those who have moved up and through the owner–occupied market, there is little to suggest that manipulation of the housing world has been a central feature of this movement. But Farmer and Barrel are not alone in attributing priority to investment. Saunders and Harris (1988) have recently stated that 'not only do home owners make real gains out of their housing, but most of them are aware of this and many develop strategies designed to maximise it' (pp.32–3). In this section the intention is to discuss some of the evidence relevant to this. The view that housing investment is a conscious element in most movement decisions by home owners is not in dispute. What is at issue is how important an aspect it is.

The tendency for higher-income home owners to live in higher-value dwellings (especially among those in the process of buying) is

156 *Home ownership*

well established (Royal Commission on the Distribution of Income and Wealth, 1977; Murie, 1983). It is also apparent that households are aware of investment aspects of housing. For example, a household survey carried out in 1975 (British Market Research Bureau, 1977) included a series of open-ended questions about the advantages and disadvantages of different tenures: 27 per cent of home owners identified 'a saving/investment' as an advantage of home ownership, and other advantages (feeling of security, 16 per cent; can use as collateral, 3 per cent; cheaper in the long term, 7 per cent; can leave to children, 5 per cent) are linked to this. In addition, many of the reasons expressed as 'better dwellings' involve a reference to a package of attributes including value and saleability.

This is significant evidence about attitudes that must influence housing decisions. However, conventional housing surveys have not tended to emphasize investment considerations. Such surveys highlight household and family change and formation as reasons for moving. Even among established (continuing) households, a high proportion of moves relate to changes in household size and structure. In addition to this, other housing reasons and job-related reasons are most frequently referred to. For example, evidence from the General Household Survey in 1971 showed that some one-third of professionals, managers and employers who moved house gave job reasons as the main reason for moving. This is almost three times the proportion among semi-skilled and unskilled workers. In contrast, housing reasons were most commonly referred to by lower social class groups. Moves for job-related reasons were more common for home owners than for those in other tenures and accounted for 29 per cent of moves. Housing reasons accounted for 36 per cent of moves (OPCS, 1973). Adjustments to the size of dwelling accounted for over half of these. Interviews with households at the top end of the housing market suggest that they have often progressed through a series of job-related moves, often assisted by the employer and often designed to enable future job-related mobility rather than to maximize accumulation through housing (Forrest and Murie, 1987). There may be others (and civil servants have been suggested) in high-paid secure jobs that do not involve regular relocation whose entrepreneurial energies are left to be exercised in the housing market. But the case is not proven. Indeed, it seems likely that family and educational considerations will be more significant triggers to movement and determinants of where to move than speculation.

A methodological problem pervades all attempts to use survey methods in this context. Many questions about the advantages of owning explicitly or implicitly involve comparisons with renting.

In addition, there are probably more severe problems of bias and *post facto* rationalization in asking why certain actions were taken in the past.

Three elements should be added to this picture. First, while investment considerations may not be so prominent in triggering moves, they may be important in determining which house is selected. Second, it is generally recognized that choice is likely to reflect a range of factors and an attempt to satisfy a number of criteria rather than to be dominated by single factors. Social survey methodology has not been well geared to dealing with this complexity. Third, it is likely that the importance of investment and accumulation factors has increased in recent years and that earlier studies are of less value. As home ownership has expanded, and with the experience of periods of rapid house price inflation and accumulation, there is more discussion and awareness of home ownership gains. And developments in mortgage finance and agency services have made movement and trading up easier.

Evidence on why people move or do not move, on what determines where they move and on preferences and choices does identify an awareness of accumulation but does not support any general assumption of speculative activity. There is little evidence that people pursue housing careers in the sense of planned, long-term trajectories related to maximizing financial gains. Rather the data support a primacy of work process. The immobile home owner is not speculating; few of those who do move move from the bottom to the top of the market and reasons for moving are likely to relate to housing and family; those who do move often and who accumulate through housing moves are often doing so because their job dictates. In the discussion of different interests associated with housing, evidence about speculative movers does not offer a great source of support.

Conclusions

These kinds of considerations relate back to the debate around housing differences and the extent to which the accumulative capacity of home ownership provides a significant cleavage in the interests of persons in the same position in relation to the means of production but in different housing tenures. The significance of accumulation through home ownership is exaggerated if reference is made to the money value of dwellings. Reference should be to realizable wealth. Using this yardstick it is apparent that not all home owners accumulate through housing and that the extent of accumulation is considerably less than is implied if asset values are referred to. The discussion of leakage and inheritance demonstrates that some housing wealth is realized and transferred both within lifetimes and between generations. The potential exists for much greater realization through remortgaging and trading down. Nevertheless, the capacity for accumulation is not in itself a source of economic power. The extent to which it affects the interests and orientations of home owners is very much less than would be the case otherwise. Home owners do have material interests relating to the different ways their dwellings are financed and exchanged, but the extent to which these distort or override other interests, say in the sphere of production, will not be the same for all owners. And generally they are likely to be very much less significant than would be the case if total asset values were realizable or if wealth held in the form of housing provided economic power.

Accumulation through home ownership is not the necessary experience of all home owners and the rate of accumulation varies considerably over time, between different locations and in different parts of the housing market. Some, but not all, of these differences will relate to job history and income. The factors most likely to cut across conventional occupational class differences relate to regional and local variations – to where housing is owned and to patterns of movement between regions – as well as to the number of earners in the household and to family changes.

In relation to housing movement and housing careers the nature of the work process, and the extent to which mobility is a necessary aspect of job career, structures the way that benefits are taken from housing consumption. It has also been argued that the accumulative dimension of home ownership tends to be overstated and is by no means general. The experience of 1989 of high and rising interest rates, declining house prices in some areas and a fall in the number of transactions reinforces the view that some of the assumptions about home ownership relate to contingent rather than necessary factors. These considerations and differentiation within tenures lead to some caution about the over-enthusiastic assertion that new consumption cleavages are more important than traditional class differences. As against this, it is evident that housing processes do introduce real inequalities. Where people own houses, when they own them and for how long affects accumulation. The size of intergenerational transfers also relates to this. There is no doubt that Saunders is correct in asserting that inequalities generated through consumption are of key importance. In so far as these can be explained by employment and work, the connection is often indirect and cannot be read off from general descriptions of occupational class. The assertion of the primacy of class becomes a problem only if it is seen to deny that the

Realizing the dream 159

differences that develop from position in relation to consumption can outweigh the differences associated with the sphere of production. Thus employees in similar occupational categories earning similar amounts and moving house as a result of the requirements of employment will move more or less often, at different times and to different locations. Their housing situation and rate of accumulation are undoubtedly structured by the work process. Their rate of accumulation and their position in relation to consumption, although structured by the same process, will be very different. Rates of gain and the importance of consumption sector gains relative to those directly associated with employment may diverge considerably. What this does not establish is that the political and social attitudes of those who own or those who benefit most from owning are changed by this. This question is taken up in the following chapter.

7 *A tenure in transition*

This book has emphasized the diversity of experience of home ownership between and within localities and over time. This is not to suggest an infinite regression towards highly localized, historically specific case studies of housing provision. But it is designed to emphasize the diversity of conditions that have contributed to the growth of home ownership and the changing nature of the tenure through that growth. In this and the final chapter, we look more closely at the way home ownership has changed and at current features of it. Initially three themes are discussed. These are the nature and extent of financial and other state support for home ownership; the extent to which home ownership changes political attitudes and voting behaviour; and the limitations of crude stereotypes which equate home ownership with privatism and particular attitudes towards the home. The second half of the chapter builds on previous discussion of change and differentiation in home ownership to outline key stages of the transition of home ownership and to comment briefly on new policies affecting the tenure.

The socialization of home ownership

Home ownership tends to be equated with the private sector in contrast to state-subsidized, organized and managed housing. Such a picture is not accurate in the 1990s. This was not always the case. The private housing boom in the 1930s, for example, was fuelled by rapidly rising real incomes, falling building costs, falling house prices and cheap finance. Entry to home ownership was achieved with minimal subsidies on the demand side but through factors operating mainly on the supply of dwellings and resulting in speculative building and sales by private landlords (Stewart, 1981). These circumstances contrast sharply with the present situation. In recent years private housebuilding has fluctuated and has failed to achieve a sustained level of activity. New building in all tenures remains well below previous levels and a growing shortfall is apparent between levels of construction and improvement and

A tenure in transition 161

estimated housing needs. The very high house price inflation of 1987–8 has left real affordability issues affecting access to home ownership. Subsidies to enhance the effective demand for private sector dwellings have continued to grow without generating a similar rate of growth in new building. Private sector housing is increasingly state subsidized.

Our common image of the first-time buyer household is the newly married couple living in a privately rented flat or with parents. Having saved a deposit, they find a house, agree a price, take out a mortgage through their building society and move in when the vendors are able to occupy their newly acquired dwelling elsewhere in the private market. In some cases it may be a newly constructed house or flat and the problem of chains of moves is avoided. But whether it is a new or second-hand dwelling it is seen as a private transaction on the open market, involving private and not state institutions. This image has never been wholly accurate – purchases by sitting tenants from private landlords have been a key route in to home ownership, especially for lower-income households. But the early 1980s saw the development of a range of alternative ways into home ownership designed to encourage its expansion. Some of these developments have resulted in a decline in quality and space standards but, more importantly, they involve more direct state sponsorship. The 'normal' routes to home ownership have been supplemented by schemes such as local authority building for sale, improvement for sale, shared ownership and do-it-yourself shared ownership.

The Housing Act 1980 contained provisions to encourage local authorities to participate in these activities and to act as guarantors for lower-income households seeking building society funds. But the most significant alternative route by far is access to home ownership by virtue of being a council tenant and the opportunities created by the Right to Buy introduced in the Housing Act 1980. Over the first nine years of that policy (1980–9) over 1 million dwellings that were previously council owned became owner occupied. And, most significantly, they have been of greater importance to the numerical growth of home ownership than speculative building. In other words, the continued growth of home ownership has become increasingly dependent on state intervention. This intervention involves major specific extensions of subsidies and other mechanisms to encourage owner occupation. Financial encouragements include tax reliefs on mortgage interest and capital gains, valued at £15.5 billion in 1988/9 (HM Treasury, 1989) and various discounts on price or reductions in cost for purchasers. For example, discounts for shared owners and deferral of interest payments for homesteaders are real subsidies. In 1988/9

162   *Home ownership*

the value of the discount on council home sales was £2,700 million. The average value of discount for a purchaser of a council house was £6,800 in the period October 1980 to December 1982. This could be calculated as a loss to the ratepayer of £1,782 million. The average Exchequer contribution to improvement for sale schemes was £2,214 (Kirkham, 1983, p.18). This proliferation of encouragements to potential owners has represented poor value for money. The objective of drawing into owner occupation groups of households that could not have afforded to buy on the open market has been achieved in some cases, but by and large the schemes have represented a subsidized extension of choice to those already in a position to exercise that choice in the market. Moreover, they have added a new layer of inequities between owners and tenants and amongst owners (Forrest, Lansley and Murie, 1984).

The shift in subsidies towards the consumption of owner-occupied dwellings requires a reassessment of the view that it is the council housing sector that is reliant on public expenditure. There has been a reorientation of state expenditure and state intervention rather than a general withdrawal and cutback. While public provision through council housing and general subsidy to council housing has been cut back, various elements have combined to increase state support of the owner-occupied market. Many of these costs are tax expenditures and are not presented as spending programmes. However, tax reliefs or tax expenditures are as much subsidies as are discounts on valuations of publicly owned dwellings, subsidies for improvement grants or enveloping of owner-occupied dwellings (external and structural improvements carried out without a financial contribution by the owner), or specific subsidies related to low-cost home ownership. To move from a council tenancy to owner occupation, whether as a sitting tenant purchaser or through changes of dwelling, involves a change in level and form of state subsidy. The transformation is immediate and profound. At the beginning of the week Mr and Mrs Tenant are generally assumed to be subsidized heavily through other people's taxes and often assumed to be paying no rates. Neither of these assumptions is accurate. Nevertheless, they serve to support a view that Mr and Mrs Tenant are victims of a drug of dependency. But by the end of the week, through the magic of tenure transformation, they have become Mr and Mrs Homeowner entitled to discounts and tax reliefs that are not referred to as subsidies. They have been cured of dependency and have achieved a new status and respectability without even moving to a new neighbourhood. It is ironic indeed that those who for so long bemoaned the subsidized feather-bedding of council tenants can unashamedly offer a range of more generous subsidies to the same group of households.

As was emphasized in Chapter 2, the notion of a private market in housing, therefore, needs careful scrutiny. We must beware the 'ideological' loading of the term 'privatization'. In housing it begs the question of the extent to which council housing was ever divorced from the market in its production or finance and, of more contemporary significance, how far home ownership is (or ever was) the product solely of the free market. The nearest to a private market in housing is the residue of private renting, which has been progressively deregulated and receives virtually no subsidy. Council housing, on the other hand, is still heavily regulated and receives less and less subsidy. Owner occupation has been affected by deregulation but remains heavily subsidized. The social and individual costs of the extension of home ownership have involved increasing payments from the public purse. In that sense it is not inappropriate to describe home ownership as a 'socialized' form of provision, a form of state-subsidized individualism.

The past growth of home ownership and any future growth depend upon substantial state expenditure. However, it is not evident that that expenditure will be maintained. Restrictions placed on supplementary benefit support for home owners, the removal of tax relief on improvement loans, and targeting of improvement grants through means testing have already emerged as ways of trimming the costs of home ownership. A major reduction in improvement grant aid may ease the burden of expenditure on the owner-occupied market, but it will undoubtedly exacerbate the crisis of disrepair and decay that is emerging in the housing stock as a whole but particularly in that sector. The significant improvement in housing standards over this century has been supported by state regulation, state expenditure in the private sector and the growth of council housing. Many owners simply cannot afford or do not choose to carry out major repair works and in many cases it does not make financial sense to carry them out. A kitchen fitted with the latest consumer durables may be a worthwhile investment, but a new (rather than patched) roof is more likely to represent a loss on resale. Parts of the owner-occupied market have received inadequate investment in maintenance and repair. This may involve major problems for the future which will require substantial intervention and investment. Home ownership in its present form benefits from heavy consumption subsidies to the neglect of production and improvement and repair. As Ball (1986) has observed:

> For 50 years after the start of large scale state intervention at the end of the First World War an increase in state expenditure

164 *Home ownership*

> on housing could be regarded as directly leading to an overall expansion or improvement in the total housing stock. The shift in emphasis to owner occupation in its current form has broken that link. (p.64)

These heavy consumption subsidies are fuelling the transformation of home ownership. There is a paradox that, as owner occupation has expanded, it has become progressively what it is not supposed to be. It has become dependent in its present form on large-scale public support. With the progressive withdrawal of subsidy from council housing, attention will shift (and is shifting) to the extent to which subsidies for home ownership are justified or adequately targeted. Questions about accountability, equity and rationality will be directed at the financing of home ownership. While housing production and direct public provision has been starved of resources through fiscal imperatives, it is evident that these fiscal 'imperatives' have not encompassed home ownership.

Home ownership is also becoming what it is not supposed to be in the sense that social conflict and inequality are finding new expression within the tenure. The problems faced by elderly low-income home owners, or home owners coping with housing costs in periods of unemployment or marital disruption, and problems associated with physical decay, previously tended to be presented as problems confined to public or private renting. The irony is that the more successful policies are in transferring council housing into owner occupation, the more significant are the consequences for home ownership. Problems in council housing are not problems of council housing. Housing provision is overlaid on a highly stratified, unequal and class-divided society. Those stratifications, inequalities and class divisions both reflect and are acted upon by housing market processes regardless of the particular tenure form.

Although problems in owner occupation are visible and others are predictable, there is also remarkable resilience in the system. Some commentators have suggested that the instability in the owner-occupied sectors leaves it prone to collapse. Yet situations of dramatic local economic decline appear to have resulted in only short-term falls in house prices and there is no equivalent of residential abandonment or (pre 1989) the sustained or significant falls in nominal house prices apparent in some other countries. This resilience does not derive solely from attributes of home ownership. The way the sector is financed and organized and the long-term appreciation in property values enable many owners to cope with short-term fluctuations in the market and even crises in their own circumstances. However, the resilience also relates to the

A tenure in transition 165

way the taxation and income maintenance systems work and to the framework of social institutions, which enable households to cope with crises in income, health and family circumstances. The tenure is sustained by family and social care systems that enable households to adapt and adjust to changed circumstances rather than abandon existing arrangements. In this sense the form of home ownership and the way it functions are integrated into a broad social system. While it is characterized by change and instability, it is also characterized by a resilience based in part on its own attributes and on the social framework within which it operates. One element of the latter is the operation of other tenures and the role of local authorities in rehousing and sustaining owner occupiers. Perspectives on home ownership require more than counterposing it with other tenures; they involve recognizing its relationship with other institutions, including other forms of tenure. Home ownership in Britain has mainly grown in an environment of full employment, generally rising incomes, stable family arrangements and comprehensive welfare provision. Declining welfare provision, high and long-term unemployment and a greater incidence of marital breakdown and household fission place a greater strain on the tenure.

Part of the support of home ownership is apparent in its cost to public expenditure. If tax reliefs on capital gains and mortgage interest, discounts on council house sales, improvement grants and the various other subsidies referred to earlier are added together, home ownership not only makes disproportionate demands when compared with council housing, but emerges as one of the major programmes of public expenditure. It exceeds public expenditure on overseas aid; agriculture, fisheries, food and forestry; trade, industry, energy and employment; transport and other environmental services. More relevant perhaps, it exceeds by a considerable margin public expenditure on law, order and protective services.

It is unclear whether this support for the present system of home ownership is either necessary or justified in terms of sustaining the health of society in other terms. It was mentioned in Chapter 6 that the potential gains to be made from owner occupation may be drawing entrepreneurial energies away from more productive activities (Farmer and Barrel, 1981). It may be that the entrepreneurs with Jaguars sitting outside their council houses – figures so beloved by critics of public sector housing – were in fact good news for capitalism. They may have become civil servants with a steady, reasonably paid job, content to channel their wheeling and dealing into the occasional property transaction.

There are doubts about the wisdom of absorbing such a large element of public expenditure in housing consumption to the

166 *Home ownership*

neglect of industry and commerce. While a view of direct competition for funds does not stand up to close analysis, there are real conflicts of interest involved in channelling resources to home ownership rather than elsewhere. If the country cannot afford to maintain and extend home ownership in its present form, what are the political, social and economic consequences of withdrawing such support? As the housing problems of some owner occupiers become more marked and as problems arising elsewhere are increasingly experienced by households who are owner occupiers, so the demand for alternatives to the present form of owner occupation are likely to emerge. The debate is less likely to focus on whether specific tenure forms are 'good' or 'bad' and for whom, than to embrace arrangements that transcend existing tenures, that focus on the material needs and demands of tenants and owners, that are not predicated on false notions of public and private, and in which common interests in respect of mobility, choice, security, costs, housing rights and housing production are stressed.

A bulwark against Bolshevism?

Whether or not home ownership has contributed to political stability is an impossible counter-factual question. It would be equally valid to argue (and it has been consistently argued) that the growth of council housing has made an equally significant contribution to the maintenance of the status quo. Both tenures developed in response to the failure of the free market in the form of private renting to deliver adequate quality housing at reasonable cost.

The nature of the housing debate has been transformed by the growth of home ownership. For most of this century private landlordism has been the dominant tenure. It was the political and social consequences of absentee ownership that was the main preoccupation of Engels in *The housing question* (1975). In the 1950s it was the abolition of private landlordism that was perceived by the Left as the primary task in achieving better housing conditions and opportunities for the working classes. Speaking in the House of Commons in 1951, Bevan stressed that 'I have never felt that there was anything wrong or unsocialistic in a person owning a house. I never thought it wrong to own your own house. I thought it wrong to own somebody else's' (quoted in Murie, 1975). It is now recognized that the eclipse of private landlordism doesn't signify the end of the housing problem and that problems exist in other tenures – including home ownership. Will individualized home ownership be a guarantee of political conservatism if it fails to

A *tenure in transition* 167

deliver what it promises? It has not proved such a guarantee in other countries. In Australia for example, the housing-related concerns of those on the margins of home ownership were a significant factor in the election of a socialist government in 1987. This and the evidence from local elections suggest that connections between tenure and political party allegiance are contingent rather than inevitable. British discussions of the impact of home ownership on working-class solidarity or industrial militancy are bound to point, for a long time to come, to the long drawn out dispute in the mining industry – a dispute involving home owners. Some sections of the working class, it seems, have not been so influenced by home ownership as some theories would lead us to believe.

The discussion of the electoral impacts of home ownership has various dimensions. For example, the support for the Right to Buy among council tenants does not establish that this has been a key factor in voting. At the heart of the debate is a claim that increased levels of home ownership among the working classes have contributed to the decline of the Labour Party. Put crudely, the 'privatized' working class are more likely to vote Conservative. The literature on this topic displays a considerable dispute between those who argue for the continuing importance of class as the basis of British party politics – occupational class and voters' image of their class being major determinants of voting behaviour – and those who argue for a substantial weakening of the ties between classes and parties. In the latter school there is a further split between those who see voting based on class being replaced by volatility or pragmatic voting behaviour and those who see a new basis for electoral divisions. It is in relation to the latter that housing tenure has been identified as an important dimension of voting. Analyses of a 1983 electoral survey show that, within occupational classes, the greater the dependence on forms of collective consumption provided by the state the greater the likelihood of voting Labour. Thus, manual workers in the council-owned homes, without a private car, and reliant on state health, education and social services gave Labour a lead over Conservative of 36 points, but among controllers of labour with three or more consumption items provided by the market, the Conservative lead was 64 points, and among comparable non-manual workers it was 41 points (Dunleavy and Husbands, 1985).

Johnston's analysis of 1983 voting shows that, while the usual relationship between occupational class and voting held (the petty bourgeoisie and salariat strongly pro-Conservative and anti-Labour, the working class the strongest Labour supporters) so did that relating to housing tenure. Home owners preferred Conservative to Labour by a ratio of about 3:1, whereas council tenants preferred

168 *Home ownership*

Labour by about 2.5:1. Home owners were 50 per cent more likely to vote Alliance than were council tenants, who were more likely to abstain. Members of the third tenure category (mainly renters from private landlords) were much closer to the home owners than to the council tenants in their relative preferences for Conservative and Labour. Very substantial within-class variations existed according to housing tenure. Within the salariat and the routine non-manual classes, for example, whereas the Conservative:Labour ratio among owner-occupiers was almost 4:1, Labour was preferred by a 2:1 majority among council tenants. Even in the petite bourgeoisie, support for Labour was almost as strong among the small number of council tenants as it was in the salariat, though Conservative retained a plurality of votes. For foremen and technicians, the ratios were similar to those for the routine non-manual workers. In the working class, Labour had a 3:1 lead over Conservative among council tenants, but a slightly smaller percentage of the vote than did Conservative among home owners (Johnston, 1987).

Johnston adds to this picture by including regional variations. He argues that the evidence for significant spatial variations in voting behaviour within groups of voters defined by both occupational class and housing tenure is strongest for manual workers other than foremen and technicians. Among the owner occupiers in that class, the propensity to vote Labour was significantly greater in the older industrial areas and regions than in the 'booming' areas of small town and agricultural south eastern England (Johnston, 1987, p.118). Among working-class council tenants, the spatial variations are even more substantial. Johnston explains this in terms of different milieux and socialization. His conclusions from this kind of evidence are salutory for the whole debate:

> Most social theory, and certainly most social theory that informs voting studies, is compositional in form: it allocates people to categories (such as occupational class) and assumes that they will act as members of those categories. Such theory pays no regard to the role of context, to the milieux in which behaviour patterns are learned and enacted. Yet membership of a category is something whose meaning must be learned, almost certainly in the local environment, and variations in the nature of milieux can thereby influence how people learn about their compositional situations and how to act according-ly. Thus compositional theories must be complemented by con-textual theories, people learn about what they are, and what that means, in environments which are locally as well as nation-ally structured . . . .

How people voted in 1983 in Great Britain reflected not only their occupational class and housing tenure, but also where they lived. Local context was apparently an important influence on how people interpreted being working class, in both major housing tenures. (Johnson, 1987, pp. 120–1)

The evidence on voting behaviour in Britain is, however, far from conclusive and the changing relationship between tenure and class remains ambiguous. In this debate Heath, Jowell and Curtice (1985) in particular have taken issue with the view that there has been a major political realignment and that there is a new working class who are more inclined to vote Conservative. Moreover, as they point out, *associations* are not necessarily *causal* connections. They suggest that:

Housing does not form the basis for a new cleavage in British politics but rather acts as a separate source for the maintenance of class cleavage. (Heath, Jowell and Curtice, 1985, p. 54)

. . . . changes in the distribution of housing tell us little that the changes in class structure had not told us already.

They continue:

While we agree with Dunleavy (1979) that 'consumption patterns . . . . in housing . . . . raise important questions for political analysis' we disagree that housing has 'political effects cross cutting those of occupational class'. Housing does not form the basis for a new cleavage in British politics, but rather acts as a separate source for the maintenance of the class cleavage.

In a more recent contribution, Marshall *el at* (1988) state:

. . . . insofar as sectoral cleavages in housing and employment are associated with voting intention, these are merely surrogates for social class. Or, at best, class voting is mediated by sectoral differences. (p. 251)

In this debate, it is important to recognize that, while the housing tenure structure is changing, so too is the class structure. Occupational class appears to remain paramount in the shaping of political attitudes because, whilst the level of home ownership has increased, the size of the working class has declined. The proportion of the working class who are council tenants, in these terms, has remained relatively constant over the last 20 or so

170 *Home ownership*

years. And on the same definitions the level of working-class home ownership has shown only a marginal increase. Although the evidence of an independent effect on housing tenure status on political attitudes is far from convincing, politicians remain unwilling to risk fundamental changes to the taxation treatment of owner occupation – especially in relation to mortgage interest tax relief or taxation of imputed rent.

Home ownership and the home

Assumptions that home ownership generates particular political attitudes tend to be linked with more general stereotypes that link different tenures with different attitudes to the home. Home owners are portrayed as home centred, house proud and private. Other tenures are portrayed as providing limited security and limited personal control over environment and as alienating. While these stereotypes appear in simple political slogans, they also relate to academic contributions. Saunders (1984) refers to the significance of private housing as an expression of personal identity and a source of ontological security. His emphasis on private housing is on home ownership and not on the home as private space. It is home ownership rather than the home that is seen as an expression of 'the need for ontological security, for a "home of one's own".' Elsewhere in this book it is argued that such simple, categorical sentiments are misleading. The nature of the tenure and attitudes to it are more complicated. Equally the attitudes of individuals and households to their home are formed by a wider range of experience than their legal tenure status. However, stereotypical views of tenures are so commonly stated in Britain that it is not a diversion to address these briefly.

Various evidence demonstrates both that council tenants' use of and satisfaction with their housing is not diminished by tenure and that owner occupation does not provide the universal satisfaction and security that stereotypes imply. One of the clearest challenges to views that attitudes to house and home are tenure led relates to council house purchase. For example, interviews with council house purchasers in Birmingham (Murie, 1975) showed that households who opted for owner occupation through sitting tenant purchase had rarely sought to buy elsewhere. Where they had done so, they had decided that the qualities of their present rented dwelling were preferable to the qualities of other dwellings where they would be owner occupiers. There is no support in this kind of evidence for a view that tenure or the desire to own is of primary importance in housing decisions or that home ownership creates attitudes to the home. Rather, attitudes to the home, generated independently of tenure or through the experience of renting, inhibited demand to own. Council house purchasers also were more likely to identify rent levels and rent rises as the most important gain associated with buying rather than considerations of investment, security or freedoms and independence associated with ownership. In explaining why council tenants did not move in order to become home owners, it is not adequate to argue that this was a result of the negative experience of state housing, of constrained choices or of fatalism and inertia (Saunders and Harris, 1987). Choices not to move and expressions of attachment and belonging and possession and of home are not restricted to home owners. To explain these choices in a different way than the choices of owners indicates an attempt to argue a case rather than to analyse the facts.

A different perspective on tenure and home-centredness is presented in Anthea Holme's (1985) study of young families in London. This involved interviews with home owners and council tenants. The latter were on estates with most of the features of badly designed and maintained mass housing. However, inside the homes, facilities, decoration and upkeep did not indicate alienation from the home. Sometimes there were unmistakable signs of poverty and a generally depressed standard of living in the condition of the home and its furnishings. In spite of confusions about obligations and responsibilities for repairs, some tenants had redecorated to very high standards and modified fireplaces and kitchens to get it to their 'way of liking'. Holme argued that differences in tenure really bite in the exteriors and immediate surroundings and that tenure also relates to how much you can afford and how free you are to do what you want. However, with some exceptions, the interiors of the homes of home owners and council tenants in 1981 were, compared with the 1950s, more alike and more comfortable.

Matching Laura Ashley curtains and wallpaper, brown corduroy or Dralon-covered sofas, glass-topped occasional tables, thick close carpeting, wall-units – these are what you would now expect to find and what we did find in Bethnal Green council flats as well as Woodford owned houses. Bethnal Green in the 1980s was catching up Woodford more quickly than in the 1950s. Witness the cool immaculate, uncluttered home of the Hills, as described by the interviewer, with its Habitat-style furniture, old-fashioned plates on the wall, a few books around. Or the Masons' reproduction tables with leather tops crafted by Mr. Mason himself, the Tooleys' collection of porcelain figures and the Brogans' well-equipped kitchen. All these were in Bethnal

172 *Home ownership*

Green and all were interiors of council flats. Not so different from the Enrights' careful colour co-ordination in Woodford, the top-quality kitchen of the Evanses, the Reeves's Berber carpet or the Shadwells' pine tables, Sanderson linen curtains and matching three-piece suite. (Holme, 1985, p.111)

Franklin's (1989) discussion of the purchase, decoration and display of a house emphasizes culture and cultural practices. Rather than home ownership creating certain behaviour, cultural practice in relation to housing is argued to have assimilated developments in tenure. Thus the decoration and display reflect culturally appropriate goals within a chosen social reference group. This reference group is likely to reflect the extent to which the household has lived locally throughout its history or has had a migratory pattern of movement. For both groups, however, owner occupation is an appropriate vehicle of achieved status display and recognition. In previous phases, with different tenure structures, a great deal of energy was put into obtaining and displaying household status symbols appropriate to particular stages of the life cycle. In a new tenure system transformed through the investment and disinvestment decisions of builders and landlords, the housing practices of home owners reflect different lifestyles and reference groups. It is the cultural context that is reflected in home ownership rather than culture that is transformed by home ownership.

A clear illustration of the inadequacy of equating ownership with satisfaction and security relates to applications by home owners to become council tenants. Bramley and Paice's (1987) study of waiting lists in the non-metropolitan districts of England in 1987 showed 21 per cent of applicants to local authority housing to be home owners. A rising demand for renting among home owners is apparent and regional variations were significant (ranging from 15 per cent to 34 per cent). A national survey of council house waiting list applicants carried out in 1986 (Prescott-Clarke, Allen and Morrissey, 1988) focused on applicants who were regarded as active cases. Of those interviewed, 31 per cent were home owners. Three-quarters of these had paid off their mortgage, 77 per cent were aged 55 or over, and around two-thirds had low incomes (under £100 per week). As would be expected, very few owners were sharing amenities or had any pressure on space. Their weekly housing costs were very low. Of these home owners, 15 per cent were not at all satisfied with their accommodation and a further 21 per cent not very satisfied, 30 per cent were very satisfied and 34 per cent fairly satisfied. These home owners were predominantly elderly and their reasons for wanting to move from their present home were similar to those of elderly households

A tenure in transition

generally – their present home was too big to manage and they wanted accommodation on one level.

In this same study, 18 per cent of new tenants interviewed had been home owners immediately prior to obtaining a council dwelling. These new tenants had a less elderly profile than home owners on waiting lists, but 56 per cent were aged 55 or over. There were two main reasons why those aged under 55 had wanted to move – marital breakup (34 per cent) and mortgage repossession (23 per cent).

This picture is not surprising. It merely asserts that there is no magic ontological ingredient that transcends and transforms needs experienced at different stages in the life cycle. While home ownership (and other tenures) can deliver satisfactions and be a successful way of organizing and controlling housing, it does not necessarily or inevitably do so; its appropriateness reflects other circumstances and can change.

The position of elderly home owner applicants for council housing can be illustrated from such applicants' comments from the authors' own research in Accrington. Most applicants emphasize health circumstances, but their need for rehousing also relates to the design and condition of the dwelling they own.

'I am disabled, having a bad leg which is next to useless, which leaves me needing crutches. My home is in a poor condition with an outside toilet . . . .'

'I am finding it extremely hard to manage all my repair bills and insurances. I also have great difficulty walking from the main road to the above address, being arthritic . . . .'

'The house I am living in has seven rooms and just two gas fires . . . . This house wants a very large grant which I know I cannot cope with. I have not been able to have a bath owing to an accident in . . . . I feel so desperate in this house . . . .'

'My home is much too large for me and also it is very cold . . . . Apart from my ailment for which I'm on permanent treatment I'm living in fear. I'm alarmed in case of fire due to electric system not being rewired . . . . I dare not put my immersion heater on so I go to my friends for a bath, I sleep downstairs . . . . I can't get my room any higher than 55 with fire full on when it is cold and I find this makes my chest worse. To crown it all part of my bedroom ceiling has fallen in; I sleep downstairs.'

'My house is due for demolition in the near future. The house is large, cold and damp and too costly to heat. My kitchen slates

174 *Home ownership*

are used to repair other people's property. This has caused rain to seep through. The back of my garage is constantly being used as a dumping place for other people's black bags. A few months ago my house was burgled . . . . what next I wonder.'

Such accounts are accurate reflections of the experience of some home owners. They should not be used to argue that 'home ownership makes people desperate and unhappy.' They are not, however, compatible with some of the overstated images of home ownership, which have lost sight of the background in which home ownership works and of variations within the tenure.

The stereotypes that link tenures with alienation and satisfaction with the home do not stand up. Perhaps the ultimate challenge to such stereotypes is when the *Observer* (1988) colour magazine's pretentious 'room of my own' feature, rather than referring to rooms in expensive, conventionally luxurious homes and locations, featured a room in a council tower block. The window cleaner featured had decorated the room with a 'faintly continental air' with Dutch wooden floors, Persian rug, cheese plant, Victorian furniture, African figures, decoy duck and paintings. The image is more like that associated with home ownership in Brighton than council housing in Poplar.

'When I moved in it was hard to let, but now people are clamouring for the top floors, though I wouldn't recommend tower blocks as places to bring up children. On my rounds, I notice people who have done a lot more to their council flats than I have and give them a lot of love and care. When I moved in here, I remember lying in the bath and thinking I never wanted to live anywhere else. A place like this is more than I'd ever dreamt of.'

This discussion of legal rights, material interests and ontological security has become an important one. They represent, along with the discussion of accumulation, an argument about exclusive attributes for home ownership. Essentially the argument is that, even though home owners have become owners for all sorts of reasons and through all sorts of processes, and even though what they own is enormously variable in certain ways, home ownership has certain things that distinguish it from other tenures. These unifying features relate to legal rights and a unique sense of independence and control or ontological security. At times the argument has been closely linked with one that associates home ownership with home–centredness or privatized lifestyles. The arguments presented above and elsewhere relating to this do not

A tenure in transition 175

dispose of ontological security. Peter Saunders' conviction about this is strongly stated:

> The popular and widespread desire to achieve owner-occupation can in my view mainly be explained in terms of a search for a realm of individual autonomy and freedom outside the sphere of production. (Saunders, 1985, p.167)

> The advantages of owner occupation are grounded in the rights of private property and cannot therefore be extended equally to those who are obliged to remain proprietors . . . . council tenants will never enjoy the rights which owner occupiers take for granted until such time as they are handed the title to their properties. That in a nutshell, is why so many would prefer to own. (Saunders, 1989b)

Saunders' own attempt to 'test' the thesis that ownership is a necessary condition for feelings of ontological security and establishing a sense of self and identity rests on an analysis of owners' and tenants' views of the advantages of their tenures. The conclusions that owners identify autonomy (the right to do what you will with the dwelling) and financial security, while tenants identify lack of autonomy and lack of long-term financial security as disadvantages, are said to 'point to crucial differences between the tenures'. This far, the analysis says nothing that earlier studies of tenure attitudes have not said (Murie, 1975). Indeed, it says a lot less because it does not refer to context, to differences within tenure categories (say older owners) or to the disadvantages of owning or advantages of renting. But Saunders acknowledges that these data do not establish tenants' and owners' sense of self or feeling of powerlessness. Saunders (1988) states:

> The concept of 'ontological security' is difficult to define, even more difficult to operationalise. Giddens defines it as 'confidence or trust that the natural and social worlds are as they appear to be, including the basic existential parameters of self and social identity' (1984, p.375). Presumably any rigorous attempt to operationalise this concept would need to utilise sophisticated indicators regarding people's levels of worry, concern and paranoia as well as measures of self-conception and positive social identity. None of this was done in the research reported here which means that we have to resort to indirect indicators.

The indirect indicators include differences related to consumer durables. These seem likely to reflect income and affluence rather

176 Home ownership

than tenure status. It is former council tenants who even more than other owners see home as a place to relax in – but is the implication that these same tenants when they choose to remain as tenants rather than move to buy would not experience the same feelings? Again, this seems likely to reflect other factors rather than tenure. Yet, Saunders' view of what all this means is:

> One possible interpretation is that people may find it difficult to establish a sense of belonging in a house when they do not own it. This does not mean that they have no sense of belonging at all, but rather that they seek this sense of security in other ways.

Saunders' struggles with the council house purchasers:

> Whether it is the people with a different orientation to home who apply to buy their council houses, or whether it is the act of purchase which changes their orientation to home, is extremely difficult to judge – both factors are almost certainly operating together.

This does not prevent a conclusion:

> That owners are more likely than tenants to express a sense of self and belonging through their homes, and that this difference has to do with the different ownership relations rather than any feature of the housing itself.

When asked 'Do you feel particularly attached to this house? Would you be unhappy to leave it?' 64 per cent of home owners and 40 per cent of tenants said that they did; 28 per cent of home owners and 46 per cent of tenants denied any such feelings. This is regarded as highly significant by Saunders. A series of other data with similar measures of difference between owners and tenants relate to pride in the home, decoration and improvement, and form the basis for the conclusion:

> Home ownership, it seems, does contribute to a sense of onto-logical security. Home owners more readily associated positive images of life with the house they live in; they speak readily of pride of ownership; they associate home more strongly with values such as personal autonomy; they are more likely to see the home as a place where they can relax and 'be themselves'; they are much more strongly attached to the houses they live in; they express choice in selection of where they live; and they derive satisfaction from working on their own personal property. All

A tenure in transition 177

of these factors are indicative of the existence of those 'basic existential parameters of self and social identity' which Giddens identifies as the evidence of ontological security.

Saunders then abandons even his indirect measures and plunges into artistic licence:

> Anyone who still doubts this need only observe those council estates up and down the country where recent purchasers have celebrated their release into ownership by personalising both the interiors and exteriors of their houses. The meaning and significance of the new front doors and porches, the garden fences, the replacement picture windows, the stone-clad walls and the crazy-paved paths and driveways is unambiguous, for these homes stand out from the dull uniformity of the corporation-owned houses around them and proudly proclaim to the world: *'This is mine! This is private property! This is where I belong!'*

But what does all this add up to? People in different tenures do not fall into exclusive categories in their responses to Saunders' indirect measures. It is not the case that certain attitudes and responses are exclusive to a tenure. How, then, can it be seen to be about ownership? What Saunders establishes are quantitative rather than qualitative differences. Nor does Saunders adequately discuss the extent to which the quantitative differences could be explained by non-tenure differences such as income, age, household composition, dwelling characteristics, location, etc. And he wears his heart on his sleeve by interpreting council tenants' responses as reflecting powerlessness over matters such as repairs, but not discussing how far owners' responses are *post facto* rationalizations, or affected by expectations and the interview process.

Saunders' data show some tenants expressing more ontological security than some owners. In his own terms, home ownership *contributes* to a sense of ontological security and home owners are *more likely* to . . . . These cautious statements are very different from the unqualified representation of the released council tenant or the form of his conclusion about ontological security. The image of the released council tenant is colourful and amusing, but colourful images of trapped and distressed home owners and of contented council tenants could equally be presented. Anyone who still doubts this should look at the examples in this book and the sources cited in it.

There is no need to dismiss the evidence presented by Saunders, even if his interpretation of what it shows is rejected. His evidence is fully compatible with other data and a less preoccupied explanation.

178 *Home ownership*

This would shift from trying to demonstrate that tenure produces certain attitudes and would regard it as an achieved status reflecting housing histories, strategies, choices, opportunities and constraints. It is the output of processes. Because of that, there are certain regularities, which reflect, for example, that in a particular context households in certain common situations, faced with similar choices and constraints, are more or less likely to make certain choices. It is not necessary to portray some of these choices as based on inertia or as cultural or fatalistic. Indeed, there is a great danger that by presenting home ownership as a superior, exclusive tenure it is implied that anyone not in it has not made rational choices. All housing choices operate within constraints. People in homes that they do not own make choices within these constraints – to move on, not to move on, and so on. Their constraints are often greater than those facing home owners – reflecting different bargaining power – but not always so. And people in homes that they do not own can and do develop attachments to their home, invest in them financially and emotionally, behave in the same basic ways about privacy and security. It is not necessary to own the home to have feelings of possession, personal identity and belonging to the home, any more than it is only tenants who are alienated from their home. The way that people make housing decisions does not suggest that they regard home ownership as the precondition for satisfactory housing.

Tenure is only one consideration and is not usually of overriding importance. Decisions make sense in terms of previous experience and frames of reference, family circumstances and needs. They involve attempts to satisfy a number of wants about the size and facilities of the home, location, ongoing costs, terms of indebtedness, longer-term value, and so on. This means that they may result in decisions not to move or to move to rented accommodation or to home ownership. The likelihood of that decision resulting in housing satisfaction or ontological security will reflect a range of factors that are not products of tenure – including employment, household income and family changes.

A final comment is appropriate to conclude the discussion of Saunders' contribution. The first is the lack of any historical perspective. He associates home ownership with the current features of the tenure. He neglects, for example, the problems associated with home ownership in other periods. One example will have to suffice. Runciman (1966) states, referring to the period before 1959:

> During the Depression home owning was sometimes not an asset at all, but a liability, since it could prevent people from emigrating from some of the areas hardest hit. (p.76)

Saunders' view that 'the advantages of owner occupation are grounded in the rights of private property' should be challenged. The advantages are grounded in the circumstances that obtain at a particular time and in a particular place. Hence they vary enormously over time as well as according to whether the owners have a mortgage or not (and how big the mortgage is), sustain their ownership by sharing or letting part of it, are leaseholders, are owners of caravans or houseboats, own a house that meets their needs in terms of size and design, heating and maintenance costs, whether its absolute value is substantial and is appreciating, and whether they fit the stereotypes of the spiralist in the south of England.

Transitions

Earlier chapters of this book have emphasized that the nature, role, meanings and characteristics of home ownership have changed over time. Attitudes to the tenure are not constant and reflect the changing context in which the tenure exists and has developed. Discussion of home ownership in the 1980s is concerned with a range of problems and dimensions that were not apparent at an earlier stage. In the 1990s the characteristics of home ownership will differ in other ways. In spite of these features, discussion of home ownership tends to refer to the circumstances applying at one point and to treat the tenure as having inherent or permanent or static attributes. A more appropriate framework for discussion of home ownership is one that emphasizes the restructuring of housing tenure. The institutional, legal and financial arrangements surrounding housing and the home have been transformed in this century. The supply, costs, ownership and control of residential property have been dramatically changed. Since the last half of the nineteenth century, this fundamental change has been particularly evident in the way in which housing has been consumed. In the nineteenth century, the most appropriate mechanism for financing housing production and consumption was private landlordism. For various reasons this situation has changed. Individual private ownership (home ownership) has emerged as the most appropriate mechanism in the twentieth century. But the period of transition and transfer, of the decline of rentier landlordism and the growth of home ownership and the institutions surrounding it, involved particular strains and shortages, which (through political action) have been offset by state intervention. Various forms of state intervention have eased and assisted transition. They have, in some cases, been designed to manage and regulate private renting and its decline and to encourage the development of alternative forms of private provision. In addition, direct state intervention through the production of state housing and the development of state landlordism and management of the housing stock has made a major contribution to housing supply during the period of reorganization of the private sector.

The development of council housing has at the same time redistributed housing resources in the interests of the working class and has served the interests of capital and 'social order' by minimizing the effects of the restructuring of the private market. By the 1980s it was arguable that this period of transition was over and the transitional role of council housing was being abandoned. The permanent role of council housing was being redefined as a very limited one. What has occurred in council housing is not simply another phase in development but is a new and changed situation and there is no reason to expect some natural swing in the pendulum to return to a more 'normal' role. The coalition of interests that sustained the growth of council housing arguably no longer exists. And one of the crucial aspects of both the decline of council housing in the 1980s and the continuing growth of home ownership was the transfer of properties from the former to the latter tenure. If council house sales represent a key aspect of the phase of decline of council housing, at the same time they represent a key element in the sustained growth phase of owner occupation. However, this growth phase cannot be sustained for ever. Speculation about how far owner occupation can grow depends crucially on how far government is prepared to finance and subsidize the sector. However, most commentators have been sceptical about expansion beyond a 75 per cent figure. This implies that, in the not too distant future, one key consistent feature of the tenure – its numerical and proportionate growth - will be transformed. While this will be an important development, the transformation of home ownership will not commence with it. The dramatic changes in the tenure structure of British housing through the present century, since 1945 and over the last 10 years have involved dramatic changes in each of the tenures. Owner occupation at the end of the period is profoundly different than at earlier stages.

This change has involved a switch from a minority to a mass tenure and a shift from a newly built tenure or a tenure growing through new building to a second-hand tenure. Tenure transfers have been an important element in the growth of the tenure throughout but, as was noted in Chapter 3, have been particularly important in the 1980s. As properties have aged, questions of maintenance and repair have increased in importance.

The declining importance of new dwellings has been illustrated in other ways. In 1976, 18.6 per cent of all dwellings mortgaged in the United Kingdom were new dwellings. By 1986 this figure had declined to 10 per cent. Regional variation was also significant. In Greater London the comparable figures were 3.2 per cent and 5.3 per cent. New dwellings also represented a small proportion in Northern regions. In contrast, in Northern Ireland the proportion of new dwellings remained buoyant and showed a slight increase to 27.7 per cent in 1986.

Table 7.1 summarizes key features of the changing nature of home ownership. As was emphasized in Chapter 3, home ownership in Britain is still a relatively new tenure. Its nineteenth century origins are associated with newly formed working–class organizations or with the wealthy employer class. Small-scale, purpose-built (sometimes self-build) housing was not state subsidized and was financed through mutual organizations (the terminating building societies are the best example) or in the same manner as other investment. The sector was restricted to new building largely by small builders in urban areas and no second-hand or mass market existed. A socially distinct and selective system had little impact on overall patterns of segregation and life chances because its development was so limited. The form and nature of home ownership as it developed into a more mature tenure was strongly influenced by this early phase, but has changed considerably.

Home ownership developed into a mass tenure between the wars. In this middle phase it was still largely formed in terms of new development but as detached and semi-detached homes with gardens in leafy suburban areas built by a developing speculative building industry. These 'middle–class' suburbs derived their characteristics partly from who was able to become a home owner. With limited state subsidy, access was restricted according to income and credit status. In a period of high unemployment, it was white–collar and skilled workers' families and those in stable employment who were most likely to become home owners. Building for this market was no longer organized on a small scale through mutual organizations but predominantly involved speculative building ahead of purchase and for profit. Credit institutions had, in the same mould, developed into permanent building societies, sometimes with very close links with builders (Craig, 1986). In some cases, the terms and rights associated with the emerging form of home ownership bore a very close similarity with renting. Builders and investment organizations were developing home ownership on a renting model. The unsatisfactory nature of this model resulted in mortgage strikes and other action and, in turn, in changes in legislation to significantly change the rights

Table 7.1 *Home ownership: stages of transition*

Dimension	Early stage	Middle stage	Late stage
Users/clientele	Established families	White affluent families with incomes and jobs enabling them to live in suburban locations	Mixed ages, incomes and family structures
Social class	Select polarized: upper and working class	Increasingly middle class	Increasingly including skilled and semi-skilled workers (proletarianization) Class differentiated
Stock	Small-scale, new build and self-build	Mass suburban new build and transfers from private renting	Declining importance of new build Mixed age, quality and location Substantial transfers from public and private renting
Organization	Terminating organizations Small investors and mutuality	Speculative builders and permanent building societies	Rationalized structure of building societies and builders Cartels and large centralized organizations Closer corporate links with government Increased competition and integration with financial markets
Financial basis	Credit for building	Credit for home purchase Growth of building societies linking small savers with purchasers	Credit for other consumption as well as home purchase Rationalization and competition resulting in more complex financial arrangements

Table 7.1 *Continued*

Dimension	Early stage	Middle stage	Late stage
Economic function	Minor significance	Major role in meeting housing needs and in economic growth	Major user of savings and base for expansion of credit Less directly linked to new investment
Production	Small firms and self-build to contract	Wide range of speculative builders	Rationalized structure of larger speculative builders less dependent on housebuilding and catering for specialized markets
Market structure	Very localized new build	Stock transfers and regional/local new build	Predominantly second-hand market National but highly segmented
Relationship to renting	Junior partner in parallel development	Replacing private renting only	Replacing renting generally
Risk	Borne by investors in building process	Borne by depositors/savers	Borne by users/owners
Role of state	Passive/minimal	Establishing and guaranteeing legal rights of owners and status of credit institutions	Regulation, sponsorship and subsidy Encouragement through active intervention and privatization of public housing
Value orientation	Use value	Use value	Accumulation and speculation more prominent Greater emphasis on exchange value

of home owners and the legal relationship between them and their building societies or mortgager. At this stage, home ownership was still a new tenure mainly growing through new building and transfers from private renting. There was a limited second-hand market and little resale and accumulation.

In terms of this pattern the postwar period saw the transition from a middle to a late stage. New building became less important than second-hand transactions. Estate agencies handling the increasingly complex chains of transactions grew as the number of second-hand transactions grew. Growth of the tenure continued to involve transfers from private renting – but, increasingly, from older, working-class and inner city neighbourhoods. Latterly, growth has been dominated by substantial transfers from public sector renting. These tenure transfers form one dimension of gentrification or changing social composition of areas of council housing and private renting. At the same time, some areas of home ownership are increasingly working class or proletarianized! In the late stage, home ownership has also become less exclusively housing for middle-class and affluent families. Household characteristics of home owners have become more varied – partly as a product of the ageing of the first cohort of home owners and partly because of changing recruitment, with changes in access to subsidy and finance.

Differentiation in the sector has become more obvious in other ways. The relative uniformity in price, age and quality no longer exists. While the ideology and imagery of the property-owning democracy and popular capitalism are more strongly associated with home ownership, the reality of instability - of fluctuations in house prices and interest rates and in debt encumbrance - is more apparent. Differentiation in home ownership has increasingly involved problems of mobility (and labour mobility), polarized subsidy, mortgage arrears, and repair and maintenance problems. Leakage and realization of wealth have become more important. In addition to gentrification, home ownership is associated with 'proletarianization' as some areas of owner occupation cater predominantly or exclusively for marginalized groups. As non-family households, black households, female-headed households, and non-wage-earning households become more numerous among home owners, it is apparent that such households are concentrated in neighbourhoods and price bands. Differentiation in the sector is associated with differential rates and routes of residential mobility.

The late stage of development of home ownership has also seen a major rationalization and centralization of housing finance arrangements. Amalgamation and branching as features of building

A tenure in transition

society finance have, with the Building Societies Act of 1986, developed into acquisition and development into insurance and estate agency and the provision of a wider range of financial services. The reorganization and changing role of housing organizations in this late phase have not been restricted to the private sector. State sponsorship and subsidy of home ownership have become important. Fiscal subsidies have been crucial to the development of the sector, but so have grants for improvements, special subsidies and grants for low-cost home ownership and council house sales schemes and the general treatment of home owners' housing costs by the supplementary benefits system. There can be no doubt that the resilience of the sector and the capacity of building societies to postpone and adjust payments in periods of unemployment or other crisis have been built upon the knowledge that supplementary benefit entitlements take into account mortgage interest repayments.

As well as altering the financial environment for the growth of home ownership, the state, and especially local authorities, have regulated private provision and had an impact on standards of accommodation in home ownership; contributed significantly to the production of dwellings for home ownership (especially through privatization schemes); provided management and agency services in respect of financing, carrying out transactions and developing repair and related packages; and provided a 'last resort' service in respect of certain types of defective dwellings, actions in relation to other unsatisfactory dwellings, and acquisition and clearance.

In the late phase of home ownership, the mass housing of its middle phase is now getting old and its environment has changed with urban growth. The interwar suburbs, which were attached to rural and agricultural areas, have been engulfed by later urban development. Perhaps even more important, the owner-occupied sector has grown through transfer of properties from the rented sectors as well as through new building. The locations, ages, dwelling types and conditions of transferred properties are very mixed. Some 5 million of the 14 million dwellings in the owner-occupied sector were at some stage rented dwellings. Over 1 million of these are former council houses – with locations, ages, designs and maintenance histories associated with who they were built by and for. And the dwellings transferred from private renting have characteristics reflecting who they were built by and for, and when they were built. The nineteenth century tunnel-back terraced house in an inner city area and with a history of neglect of maintenance and repair by an absentee landlord is just as much part of the owner-occupied sector as the suburban 'semi' built for the affluent middle classes between the wars. An increasingly ageing and differentiated stock is as important an aspect of the transformation of home ownership as is its growth.

The characteristics of who uses the tenure have also changed. The cohort of home owners in the middle phase when home ownership developed as a mass tenure appears to have been relatively young, white, white-collar worker families. But these younger households have grown old and some older owners have low incomes. At the same time, access to owner occupation has widened and moved down the income and occupational ladder. Younger and single-person and childless couple households, the unemployed and others on low permanent incomes are strongly represented among owner occupiers. The number of home owners on supplementary benefit grew from 362,000 to 793,000 between 1967 and 1986. Redundancy and changes in economic circumstances have affected households in all tenures. Demographic changes, including the increase in the aged population, single-parent families, and female-headed households and the importance of divorce and separation have contributed to a changed profile and a changed (less stable?) experience of home ownership. Racial discrimination and changes in the mechanisms determining access to home ownership and to loans for house purchase have added a further dimension. The changing availability of private renting has led to an increase in the use of home ownership by newly formed households and as 'starter' housing. At the same time, those households with least choice in the housing market, those unable to obtain council housing or unable to afford it, have increasingly looked to the bottom end of the house purchase market. Some households have become home owners because of lack of choice and as a last resort – quite out of character with images of the tenure.

Major changes are also evident in the way home ownership has been financed and subsidized. Prior to the 1960s, tax expenditures on home ownership were negligible and benefited only the relatively small proportion of the population paying tax. Payment of Schedule A tax largely cancelled out the advantage. Council tenants benefited from Exchequer and rate fund subsidies, although various devices including rent policy and rent rebates were used to restrict their growth. By 1985, however, the steady growth of tax relief had taken it to a level that both in total and per capita was greater than subsidy to council tenants. Many council tenants no longer benefit from any form of non-means-tested subsidy. But for owner occupiers both tax relief gains and gains from appreciating property values are extremely uneven. Improvement grants and discounts on council houses sales have added to the financial opportunities available to home owners and to the uneven pattern of benefit.

A tenure in transition   187

Finally, the control and management of home ownership have changed. Local authorities have largely ceased new lending for house purchase except in connection with the sale of council houses. New organizations have become involved in financing house purchase, and building societies, which have retained the bulk of the 'market share', have expanded, branched, amalgamated and reorganized to present a very different face. They have changed their methods of operation and, even in recent years, their policies in relation to lending and borrowing. Other parts of the owner occupation industry have also developed – builders have amalgamated and developed more specific products for particular markets (from starter homes to sheltered units). Local authorities' role in the home ownership industry has shifted from lending to sales of their own stocks and the development of special schemes. In some areas, local authority activity has contributed more to the growth of owner occupation than has private speculative activity.

The administration of improvement grants and development of local authority agency and other services for owner occupiers mean that local authorities are involved in the resourcing and management of home ownership. Voluntary sector agency schemes such as Care and Repair and the Neighbourhood Revitalisation Service are also involved in this way – often considerably dependent on local authority support through grants. New financial arrangements to release the equity tied up in home ownership (for repair and maintenance or general consumption expenditure) represent ways of releasing house savings and dissaving in old age. They are important (although as yet minor) developments.

In all of these changes local variation is considerable. In some localities, renting or even council renting is the dominant tenure; in others there is very little rented housing and the market is a private one managed and organized by agencies involved in home ownership. National average figures give little feel for the variation between localities and the striking differences that result. In each of these and in other ways the statistics of tenure change fail to indicate the full story of changes in tenure. And the failure to grasp some of this story is a problem in current policy debate in which it is too often implied that the main tenures are still what they used to be, or are relatively homogeneous.

In the current debate over what is happening in housing these themes appear in a number of ways. Sales of council houses have sharpened rather than reduced local variation in tenure structure. The highest levels of sales have occurred in England rather than Scotland, in the south rather than the north and in shire districts rather than metropolitan areas. By 1989 over 1 million council dwellings had been sold in England – representing over 15 per cent of the council stock. The trend results in increased spatial and social polarization, with many areas of high home ownership experiencing a more rapid decline in renting than elsewhere. Variation of property types has become more striking between tenures. Council house sales have been disproportionately of houses. Council tenants consequently are increasingly likely to live in flats or maisonettes. And the evidence suggests that these properties are increasingly likely to be defective. In owner occupation, the evidence on house condition and disrepair suggests a growing inequality within the tenure.

As the owner-occupied market develops, so the importance of newly built stock declines. Second-hand properties are increasingly important and more transactions involve such sales and chains of sales. As the market becomes more dependent on the successful completion of complex chains of sales, so it becomes less stable and involves more costs for buyers and sellers. This becomes a *general* problem of organizing and paying for mobility and exchange in owner occupation, not just a problem for the marginal few.

The withdrawal of general assistance subsidy from council housing and the switch to means-tested housing benefit are furthering the process of residualization. As rents rise and housing benefit tapers steepen, the least affluent become trapped in council housing and the more affluent are under greater pressure to move out. The continuation and growth of tax relief increase the pressure. Rising rents, declining quality, means testing, residualization and falling supply in the council sector all contribute to the demand for home ownership. That demand is not natural or fixed. It grows and is fostered by changes in each of the tenures and by comparisons between them. Many of the changes and failings in council housing have led to a loss of support for it. But the demand for owner occupation has always been built up by different considerations. For some, owner occupation has been a way of reducing current housing costs. This has been the case in the past but it is an increasingly important consideration at present. Buying your council house in some areas means an immediate cut in housing expenditure.

New policies

The priority given to the promotion of home ownership since 1979 has been evident in two ways. First, the existing mechanisms that encouraged home ownership were maintained and enhanced. In this context it is the growing cost of tax relief associated with mortgage interest that is most striking. In a period when housing

A tenure in transition

public expenditure has been cut, this element has grown (from £1,639 million in 1979/80 to £7,000 million in 1990). This has occured in spite of reduced tax rates and because of increasing house prices, interest rates and levels of home ownership. The increase in the qualifying ceiling from £25,000 to £30,000 in 1983 involved a direct increase of some £60 million. Secondly, by giving local authority and new town tenants the right to buy their homes at substantial discounts, the government introduced a major new element that radically broke with the past and did so in a way that had major implications for the role of local authorities.

While local authorities had previously had powers (and had used these powers) to sell council dwellings, the Right to Buy clauses of the Housing Act 1980 almost completely removed local discretion on this issue. The majority of local authority tenants became entitled to buy and also obtained a right to a mortgage. The terms and procedures for sale were laid down in unprecedented detail and the Secretary of State was given very strong powers to intervene in local administration of the scheme. Consistent with its policy commitments, the government, both in drafting legislation and associated regulations, and in its actions in connection with this policy, has sought to limit local policy obstruction, to minimize and reduce the numbers of properties and persons excluded from the policy and to adopt an approach that would maximize the opportunities to buy. Other contemporary policies, and notably policies towards rents and subsidies, have reinforced this policy by increasing the relative advantages associated with purchase.

The new policies pursued and introduced in the 1980s have and will continue to have an important impact on the future development of home ownership. Deregulation of the private rented sector and rising rents in all parts of the rented market will increase the relative attractions of home ownership. Privatization of council housing estates as well as the Right to Buy are likely to contribute to the growth of home ownership. While some estates will have a greater mix of tenures than was the case in the past, increased social polarization between tenures will in some cases involve greater geographical segregation and form part of a more general trend for income and poverty to be more strongly associated with housing quality and value, both within and between tenures.

One striking feature of the dramatic house price inflation between 1986 and 1989 is how the emphasis in media debate has been on the gains made by owners rather than on the problems faced by first-time buyers. While some comment on shortages of houses to purchase and pressures for land release for new building in the South East emerged latterly, and comment was made on problems of labour

190 *Home ownership*

mobility and on gazumping and the process of exchange, there was little or no discussion of the need for intervention to slow down or deal with the effects of house price inflation. It seems unlikely that government will in the future step in, as it did in the 1970s, to protect the building industry from the collapse of demand or in order to hold mortgage interest rates down. The relationship between government and building societies has developed from the 1970s and moved to one of closer negotiation and collaborative mutual dependence.

New policies have operated against a continuing environment of financial and ideological support for home ownership. However, neither of these features is as significant in explaining the way in which home ownership has changed and developed as are the ways in which corporate and financial changes have impinged on owner occupation. The way in which the building industry, the financing of home ownership and the management of exchange transactions have changed is crucial to the reshaping of home ownership. But these changes have not occurred because of changes within the housing or owner-occupied market. They are responses to broader economic pressures and changes. Increased competition and integration with other financial institutions have affected the operation of building societies and other house purchase finance agencies and had repercussions on home ownership. Reorganization and amalgamations among construction companies have occurred for reasons not directly associated with house building output, but have consequences for that output. Both of these examples are pursued in the next chapter.

8 Home ownership: deconstruction and reconstruction

Previous chapters of this book have emphasized change as a feature of home ownership. The position that was reached at the end of the 1980s was not a stable, equilibrium position that will remain for home ownership in the future. The restructuring of housing tenure in Britain and the changes affecting building societies and the financing of home ownership will continue through the 1990s and beyond. This chapter pulls together some of the key arguments presented earlier and goes on to address how home ownership is likely to change in the future. This discussion of future situations is grounded in features of the current situation and in tensions and trends that are already apparent. Reference to issues relating to the organization and financing of owner occupation and to demographic and social trends affecting the sector identify a number of emerging themes about the future of the tenure.

Key perspectives on home ownership

Earlier in this book it was suggested that the appropriate point of analytical departure for understanding home ownership was the process of commodification. Whilst housing has certain peculiarities in terms of its longevity and cost and plays a pivotal part in individual experience and social structuration, it is, nevertheless, appropriate to set developments in housing alongside more general processes associated with the extension of credit-based, individualized consumption. Certain key themes and arguments have emerged, which can be summarized as follows:

● Whilst we cannot read off the relations of consumption from traditional class categories determined at the point of production, neither can we understand the processes leading to consumption divisions without that analysis being related to inequalities generated through the production process.

192   *Home ownership*

- Analyses that emphasize housing tenures as a key source of divisions in society imply that tenures are uniform and underestimate the spatial and temporal differentiation within all tenures and the determinants of change in housing consumption.
- Segmentation and stratification within the owner–occupied market are no less significant than divisions between the tenures. The potential for accumulation and money gain is highly varied and relates to class divisions, determined by differential bargaining power.

Arguments such as these inform a view that all-embracing labels such as 'council housing' or 'owner occupation' conceal substantial variations in households, dwellings, quality and conditions within each of the major tenures. Moreover, the growth of home ownership has taken place under very different conditions, drawing in different groups at different times in a constantly changing social and economic environment and as a result of the decisions of key institutions and supply-side agencies as well as individual consumers.

The instability of the owner–occupied market deriving from the existing structure of housing production (Ball, 1983) has created a situation in which the tenure does not deliver in terms of either numbers of dwellings or price. The structure of housing production has been unable to deliver new building to sustain the rapid and continuing expansion of home ownership that political support has demanded. The ideological support has run ahead of the organization of production. As the scope for transfers from private renting has declined, the privatization of public housing has become the only way of maintaining the rate of growth of owner occupation. At the same time, privatization fits with other fiscal and ideological concerns. But if privatization has partly proved necessary because of failures in production, it deepens the instability of the owner–occupied market. Privatization increases the extent to which the demand for new production is dependent on existing owners, mobility and resale. Privatization, however, also highlights other aspects of home ownership. The mechanisms used for privatization include encouragement to buy in order to reduce current housing costs and they are likely to increase the extent to which the promise of home ownership is diminished by experience later of problems of cost, mobility, choice, resale and repair. The failings of the present structure of home ownership are rooted in production, but are mediated through and can be exacerbated by processes in consumption and exchange.

Table 8.1 summarizes some of the main propositions put forward in the literature concerning home ownership in Britain and summarizes the discussion in this book about the accuracy of these propositions for a sector affected by increasing market penetration and segmentation. Essentially the message is that propositions that treat home ownership as a significant analytic category are flawed. Home ownership is a descriptive category – it describes a particular legal and tenure status. But it is an output of a widely varied range of situations and relationships. As Barlow and Duncan (1988) have argued, tenures are assumed to correspond with significant break-points in concrete real world categories like housing quality, social status or financing mechanisms. In fact, while households in a specific tenure share certain formal attributes,

Table 8.1 *Perspectives on home ownership: propositions about home ownership and the implications of market segmentation*

Home ownership involves substantial real capital gains. These capital gains are realizable, if only through inheritance. Home owners regard their housing as an investment and their decisions reflect this.	These attributes do not apply for all sectors of home ownership or all home owners at all stages. Not all home owners gain or gain to the same extent on a continuing basis. Housing movement decisions are generally made with some concern about investment aspects but these are rarely the primary considerations in choice of dwelling or trigger decisions to move. Home ownership does redistribute the pattern of housing costs over lifetime and may provide a mechanism for dissaving (equity release) in old age. The significance of this will, however, vary according to property values and is likely to reflect aspects of job history.
The wealth associated with home ownership means that home owners have a stake in the system. Their political attitudes reflect this and are innately conservative and anti-collectivist. Home ownership has an independent effect on political attitudes and behaviour and this effect is not mediated through class.	Evidence on voting behaviour and other evidence on political attitudes and behaviour suggest that housing tenure is only one of a range of factors affecting political attitudes. It is not the dominant factor and knowledge of tenure alone is not a good basis for predicting political attitudes. Class and locality factors remain important determinants of voting behaviour.

Table 8.1 *Continued*

Home owners are more private and home centred and take more pride in and care of their home.	This view is not supported by evidence relating to behaviour in other tenures and does not stand up to historical or critical examination (Franklin, 1986). The greater affluence of some home owners and some tendency to express ownership through exterior symbols are more significant features than any other behavioural differences peculiar to home owners as a group.
There is an innate desire for home ownership and the growth of the sector has been in response to consumer demand.	Demand and preference for home ownership vary regionally and over time. They reflect various contingent factors (Merrett, 1982). The pattern of growth of the sector has also been determined by policy and supply-side factors, factors that have influenced investment and disinvestment decisions by builders, landlords and the state.
Home ownership provides a sense of autonomy and control over personal and family life and provides ontological security.	This view rests on a contrast between home owners in general and those in other tenures. It does not stand up to tests in terms of 'are there home owners who feel differently?' or 'are there non-owners whose home provides these?' More fundamentally it isolates the home and ownership from other factors that affect attitudes.
Home owners have certain common material interests.	Changes in rates of house price inflation, costs of credit, house prices and systems of taxation have very different implications for different groups of owners (outright, with mortgage) in different regions and sectors of the market, with different work and taxation status, at different stages in the life cycle and in their housing history, and with different expectations and aspirations.
Home ownership represents a democratic system based on dweller control and accountable to individual households.	The growth of home ownership and what is available, when, where and at what cost reflect investment and market processes in which consumer pressure is relatively insignificant. The degree of choice and

Table 8.1 *Continued*

	autonomy experienced by owners will reflect their financial and bargaining power rather than any inherent feature of the tenure as a whole.
Home ownership is associated with rising material standards of housing and facilitates mobility and choice.	Home ownership has grown in a period of rising housing standards and has contributed to this improvement – as have other tenures. Increased market segmentation has involved greater disparities in conditions and costs in different parts of the market. Low standards, lack of mobility and severely restricted choice apply in some segments.
Home ownership represents the unsubsidized free market tenure in housing.	Regulation and subsidy are essential features of home ownership and some sectors of the market and some groups of home owners have only been able to enter the sector or remain in it because of systems of grant and subsidy.
The home ownership sector will experience a major collapse, especially in house prices.	The sector is marked by instability and volatility, with changing rates of investment, rates of price inflation, interest rates, and levels of activity. However, there is a resilience based not just on the institutions directly associated with home ownership but on family and welfare state institutions and household coping strategies. In general, these enable households to survive fluctuations. In some phases (and as the sector includes more lower-income households or those affected by sharp falls in income or sharp increases in mortgage interest rates) the number of home owners coping with difficulty or failing to cope will increase. In general, however, while the wider institutional arrangements that sustain the sector operate, it is likely to continue to grow rather than to collapse. Ability to cope will become more differentiated according to which part of the market households are in and what sources of support they are able to draw upon.

196 *Home ownership*

they are not always subject to the same pressures and processes which determine their situation. The use of tenures as approximate shorthands ceases to be valuable in this situation and imposes a spurious framework for analysis. In British literature, tenure-based analysis gained prominence because key divisions in access and opportunity related to tenure and policy and ideology were tenure specific. Analyses that focused on dwelling location, cost, value, type, age or on household income or other characteristics, but that did not acknowledge the role of tenure in the process of sorting and sifting households between dwellings and localities, ignored the real world processes involved (Murie, Niner and Watson, 1976). Tenure is still an important aspect of housing in this sense, but, where the questions being addressed relate to attitudes or values or to the specific processes determining housing situation, tenure does not provide a sufficient picture. Contemporary analysis of key processes and divisions in housing has to look beyond tenure labels, which presuppose too much similarity. Tenure labels or categories within tenures are only of value where they do reflect some real similarities in circumstances and therefore provide a relevant way of identifying key divisions. In this book it has been argued that the ways in which home ownership has developed in Britain have rendered it a less homogeneous unified sector. As differentiation and segmentation become characteristic, so it is important to use analytic categories that reflect that situation. Categories should be tenure sensitive but not tenure wide. Tenures represent points of departure rather than undifferentiated categories to be uncritically applied. Mainstream housing research has become increasingly sensitive to the limitations of using tenure as the key to analysis and has alternatively emphasized intra-tenure differentiation in relation to race, class, gender and locality or emphasized the structures of provision that lead to tenure change and development. At the same time, mainstream urban sociology and political science have become increasingly preoccupied with divisions within consumption and particularly the sectoral cleavage between owners and renters (e.g. Dunleavy, 1986a; Saunders 1986b).

The propositions referred to in Table 8.1 are generally based on assumptions that social behaviour is related to tenure – that tenure categories do refer to households that relate to each other causally or structurally, and that their tenure status represents a powerful independent influence on behaviour. They reflect views that the division between those who own privately and those who rent (especially in the public sector) is a central pivot in a broader division between new privatized forms of provision and residual collective forms. Within general debates regarding the sociology of contemporary processes of consumption, such sectoral divisions

Deconstruction and reconstruction

between privatized majorities and state-dependent minorities are posed as potentially of equal if not greater importance than class divisions. This has become a complex and multi-dimensional debate, which has, to some extent, reintroduced notions of homogeneity within home ownership in the sense that those who own may share broad material interests regarding the asset appreciation and accumulation potential of their dwellings or less hard and tangible feelings of security and well being that ownership may generate (for a discussion of some of these aspects see, for example, Saunders and Harris, 1988; Forrest and Murie, 1988b). And there is a broader political dimension to this debate in the sense that the material and attitudinal dimensions of residential property ownership are seen as both impacting upon and reflecting a pervasive, privatized world view.

The commentary that is offered on these views derives from an emphasis on divisions within the tenure and is incompatible with the propositions. However, it is important to stress that it does not support the opposite case about the tenure category. It does not deny that capital gains are made through home ownership, that wealth is redistributed, that there are influences on political behaviour, and so on. Such a stance would equally be to assert some consistent and categorical features that apply to the tenure. The response to the propositions offered involves a series of questions:

● Can the proposition be sustained as peculiar or exclusive to home ownership or does it apply in other tenures?
● Can the proposition be sustained as universal within home ownership?
● Can the proposition be sustained as attributable to home ownership rather than being determined elsewhere but correlated with tenure?
● Can the proposition be sustained as only capable of being associated with home ownership or the particular form that home ownership currently takes?

The commentary provided particularly emphasizes the first two of these questions. A different response to these propositions would simply argue that any account of attitudes to the home or of housing mobility decisions or of the effects of ownership on attitudes and interests will be affected by a much wider range of social experience than is implied by a one-dimensional view of the home owner. Home owners' attitudes – even their attitudes to home ownership – are products of a wider range of experience. And this is not just housing experience and history, but involves locating households in a broader social context. The attempt to attribute behaviour to one dimension of housing experience is misguided and the case for attributing dominant importance to tenure must be weak when the category itself has such diverse components and meanings.

The pattern of change for home ownership outlined in this book has been one of fragmentation. Fragmentation as used here means not disorganization but rather a new arrangement related to the process of commodification. From being a relatively uniform tenure, home ownership has become differentiated. It is increasingly important to indicate which part of home ownership is being referred to rather than to refer to home owners or home ownership as a consolidated homogeneous group with common features and interests. A commodified market system of home ownership is characterized by market segmentation and differentiation, with privileged, elite, high-status sectors at one extreme and state-dependent sectors at the other. As the tenure has become a mass tenure, its social meanings and significance have changed and the status at one time attributed to ownership attaches itself only to certain sectors and locations. As home owners move through the family life cycle and lifetime earnings cycle, so the association between ownership and affluence breaks down at an individual household level. Different features of home ownership – in this case those connected with repairs and maintenance and mobility and social care – become prominent and problematic. The effectiveness of the tenure and the way it works reflect the changing needs and demands of those in the tenure.

Whilee fragmentation, market segmentation and differentiation are perspectives that highlight discontinuities and deconstruct home ownership, the pattern that exists is not without structure. The emerging nature of home ownership, however, involves different forms and types of relationship. A reconstructed view of the nature of home ownership would seek to specify these different forms and types of home ownership. One perspective on this is to see home ownership in terms of a continuum that at the one end is indistinct from renting. The owner has a continuing mortgage commitment and limited choice and autonomy in sectors of the market that do not keep pace with the general rate of accumulation of housing. Low-paid or insecure employment leave the owner with important periods of dependency on state benefits and paternalistic management. Problems in maintaining home ownership status and in maintaining the fabric of the dwelling in old age result in a continuing dependency on benefits and external support. At the other end of the continuum, home ownership involves independence, autonomy and high rates of accumulation, which provide opportunities in other spheres and the attributes of positional

Deconstruction and reconstruction

goods. For this latter group, home ownership provides enhanced choices, not just in housing, and these advantages continue into old age. Households at different points on this continuum are all affected by constantly changing patterns of investment and disinvestment in home ownership and by the instability that marks patterns of investment and rates of house price inflation. However, the impact of these variations is not uniform. Rather it reflects the resources and circumstances of the households involved. Employment and job situation are critical factors in this. Those employed in certain sectors of the economy will more easily cope with variations in the market either because of high levels of earnings, or because of specific employer assistance, or because their status has enabled them to negotiate different financial packages for house purchase. Those whom financial institutions particularly wish to attract – the best-risk groups – are able to bargain for better house purchase packages. These may include employer assistance and may anyway include fixed-interest or marginally lower interest payments on large loans, insurance packages, and a variety of preferential treatment. Differential bargaining power deriving from occupational, income and wealth status will enable some owners to operate within a different regime than others. And this pattern is likely to be cumulative through the life cycle, if only because of the rate of accumulation of housing wealth and the size of asset holding. Increasing market segmentation provides the preconditions for the development of new differential arrangements at the top end of the market. On the same logic, provision for those with less bargaining power will also develop to reflect their market position. The way that home ownership is reconstructed will reflect competition among key private sector agencies and the economic and financial environment within which that competition takes place.

The nature, form and rate of growth of home ownership have not simply reflected demand. What happens is owner occupation is a product not of the decisions of individual home owners but of the way the market has developed and of the decisions of key agencies in the market. The most striking examples of this relate to decisions that have led landlords to sell their stock to owner occupiers. The growth of home ownership through transfers from private and public landlords has left tenants with opportunities to buy on preferential terms. The growth of owner occupation in these situations has been contingent on landlords' decisions. Similarly, the decisions of builders and developers to build for sale rather than rent have been crucial in the pattern of opportunities faced by those seeking housing. Those wanting modern, newly built housing, or housing in particular localities, have increasingly found that becoming a home owner is the only way of achieving

200 *Home ownership*

this. The decisions of supply-side agencies are determined by a range of financial calculations, but it is judgements made by these organizations at particular times that have determined the growth of home ownership and have affected the decisions open to the large number of individual households seeking housing.

The changing organisation of home ownership

From this perspective, the future of home ownership will be fundamentally affected by changes in the organization and financing of housing production and investment. While economic and demographic changes will affect housing demand, it is futile to construct elaborate models of future demand and imply that the determinants of the past or future of home ownership are related to these processes and ignore institutional and policy changes. While attention should be paid to such models (e.g. Dicks, 1988), they should not be regarded as sufficient. The pattern of amalgamation and operation of the building industry consequently has an important role. Reference was made to this in Chapter 1. Recent trends have involved increasing concentration in the industry and only a limited expansion of the total output of speculative building – by no means offsetting the decline in building carried out by or (more importantly) for local authorities. The building industry has tended to seek specialist markets, including more expensive dwellings and dwellings for elderly people. It has also increased its role in rehabilitation projects. These features seem likely to continue to characterize the activities of builders. The largest profits are to be made from building for home ownership, up-market and in the south of England, and the way that home ownership develops will reflect these elements. Land banking will continue to be key to the profit-making process and company take-overs will continue to be influenced by land acquisition. Perhaps more importantly, levels of speculative housebuilding will fluctuate and, without a cushion of relatively sustained council house building, the impact of this volatility will be more severe than in the past.

The clearest example of institutional changes that are likely to affect the future of home ownership relates to developments in the building society and financing areas. As has been described earlier in this book, building societies have developed from very different origins into large mutual, permanent organisations. They have changed from being glorified landlords and developed a different relationship with mortgagors. They have gone through a dramatic rationalisation with the number of societies declining from 835 in 1950 to 137 in 1987. Variations in size and coverage remain. The number of branches has grown from 756 in 1955 to 6,962 in 1987. Their activities have increasingly been linked to government and policies promoted by government. The collapse of the cartel over interest rates has resulted in increased competition since 1984 and the Building Societies Act 1986 has increased the range of ways in which societies can compete both with each other and with other financial institutions. One of the important effects of these changes, of the increased willingness of banks and insurance companies to lend to house purchasers and of the advent of mortgage companies and new competitors for lending has been the ending of the rationing of mortgages through a mortgage queue.

Access to credit to enable house purchase still involves tests of credit worthiness, but for those who pass such tests, there are no long queues and additional tests of 'membership' (having been a depositor) rarely apply. The system is one under which mortgages are obtained on demand and loans will relate to the full value of the property. Because of the breakdown of the cartel and the existence of other willing lenders those institutions wishing to stay in business must attract borrowers and meet their demands more fully than was the case, up to the limits of good judgements. The dynamics of change involve competition for lenders to the societies rather than borrowers from them. To operate in this environment building societies (and other financial organisations) borrow to meet the demand rather than lending to the limit of current borrowing. This involves taking steps necessary to attract sufficient borrowing and has meant offering higher rates of interest drawing on institutional lenders and on non-retail borrowing. The cost of credit associated with house purchase and the accessibility of credit for house purchase have both risen. Both developments have mixed advantages. They widen access to credit and home ownership and reduce paternalistic rationing practices for which building societies were criticized in the 1970s; but by doing this they may increase the likelihood of borrowers being overcommitted. The volatility of mortgage rates is also increased – in the past societies' decisions to reduce lending rather than raise rates to attract depositors dampened the effects of market changes on borrowers. In an environment of meeting demand the industry is more integrated into the financial system generally.

As the mortgage market has become increasingly competitive, so the mortgage rate has much more closely mirrored market interest rates and has tended to operate at a level between 1 per cent and 2 per cent above money market rates. At this level, given that the loss experienced on mortgages is negligible and that servicing costs are tiny, investment in building societies is attractive to institutional lenders. Building societies have increasingly met the demand for mortgages by drawing in these institutional funds and have become less dependent on their traditional retail savings market of small savers making short-term unsecured loans. The cost of this adjustment is that home ownership is more open to the effects of changes in the general financial market. It can be cheaper to borrow on the wholesale money market, and banks that do borrow on that market can gain a competitive edge as a result. For building societies to maintain the flow of funds and to compete with other institutions, borrowing wholesale has become increasingly important. In order to continue to meet the demand for mortgages, building societies have argued that limits on their dependence on non-retail lending should be relaxed and government has responded to this to some degree. However, it has also been argued that societies will have to change their status to become private companies in order to escape these regulations. The market is moving so rapidly that either regulations will have to change further or the industry will have to change its form in order to compete. Furthermore, it has been argued that specialist mortgage companies will become more important and that a secondary mortgage market will emerge. Finally, it has been argued that it is the increased competitiveness of the market that has led building societies, banks and other financial institutions involved in mortgage lending to offer a wider range of services and acquire estate agency brokerage outlets – a step that increases their ability to ensure that their services as lenders continue to be used even when there is little or no competitive edge in what they can offer. Lower interest rates can be and are charged on larger house purchase loans, reflecting the costs of administering such loans and the advantages in a competitive market of making such loans.

It is not only building societies that have moved into the house and estate agency business. Insurance companies and banks have also moved rapidly and significantly into this activity in recent years. The acquisition of estate agencies by large financial institutions is visible in the names appearing on shop fronts and advertising material. A recent league table of house agents produced by *Chartered Surveyor Weekly* (18–25 August 1988) showed 16 agents with 100 or more offices world-wide. Nine agents had more than 250 offices and five had more than 500. The top two agents were both owned by insurance companies. The three largest building societies owned agencies included in the top nine. With the exception of one agent owned by a bank, the other agencies in the top nine were all owned outright by or had substantial shareholdings by insurance companies. While substantial and even growing independent house agents remain in this list, the process of acquisition and centralization of estate agency services is a major

Deconstruction and reconstruction

feature of the contemporary reorganization of the management of home ownership, and of its increasing commodification.

This perspective on the way that building societies and the provision of lending for house purchase have developed emphasizes integration and competition in the financial market. Future scenarios involve more competition, heightened by the development of a secondary mortgage market through which mortgage portfolios are sold, and increasing rationalization and specialization in the market. The nature of the impact of financial deregulation in the European community in 1992 is unclear but will be significant. Estate agency, relocation and chain-breaking services are likely to continue to develop, and the domination of the market by a small number of organizations able to take advantage of economies of scale and to provide an integrated range of services will become more profound. One view is that mutual organizations will give way to private companies. The decision in 1989 by the members of the Abbey National Building Society (the second largest in Britain) to follow this route may not have a large number of imitators. However, in the longer term a changed saving market – and perhaps a recovery of the stock market – could affect this. Whether or not this is the case, it is likely that the organization and financing of house purchase will become more concentrated. There will be less choice of agency, although concentration need not result in the development of new cartels. It could be, for example, that the costs of estate agency services will fall, as the real purpose of such agencies will be to make loans. Competition to make loans may involve subsidizing other transaction costs, compared with a situation where different agencies are seeking to make profits from different services in the process. Furthermore, pressures to reduce the costs and complications of purchase and sale are likely to be reflected in policies pursued by government and financial agencies. The general picture is one of increasing vertical integration of financial and other services in the home ownership sector – of large financial conglomerates seeking greater control through mergers between estate agency chains, building societies, insurance companies and legal services.

The implications of these changes for individual home owners are not necessarily all adverse or dramatic. However, one consequence is likely to be greater volatility and an increasingly commercial approach to mortgage debt. Repossession is not a sensible step, especially in periods when properties are slow to sell. Furthermore, the industry will not want to see the bad publicity associated with repossessions and will no doubt develop practices to avoid this. Part of this process will involve more attention to aspects of the management of home ownership and the development of

204 *Home ownership*

flexible arrangements to enable mortgage terms and conditions to be adjusted. In this context it is relevant to note that the changed legislative basis for building societies enables them to become involved in the provision of rented housing and in a wider range of partnerships, which include periods of direct ownership or shared ownership of property. Services to assist sale (including chain-breaking and relocation services) are feasible in this situation. It may be argued that, while building societies will not develop significantly as private landlords, they will develop a greater variety of specialist services to maintain their investments and assist borrowers. This sensitive, commercial response is unlikely to be adopted by all lenders for home ownership. It will not only be fringe agencies that will regard mortgages simply as an income stream and will treat problems arising from the volatility of the market in the same way as for any other loan.

One possibility in this environment is that certain categories of borrower will be more at risk. They will be more vulnerable to market changes and their lender will have a less-than-flexible approach to problems. Problems associated with indebtedness, especially connected with fringe agencies and (possibly) secondary mortgage markets, are more likely for certain categories of borrower. The operation of codes of practice (e.g. relating to secondary mortgage markets) and the effectiveness of the building societies' ombudsman will be of key importance. None the less, it is reasonable to argue that the experience of home owners will vary. For some owners, the volatility of markets and the policies of lenders will result in forced sale and movement; for others, in periodic crises and close 'supervision' or 'management' by a lender; for others, in changing contracts with lenders involving changing status, services and responsibilities; for others, it will represent an easily managed continuing arrangement. The relative importance of these categories is difficult to predict. In the past, the vast majority have fallen into the last category. In the future, and depending on the performance of the economy and the housing market, this may not be the case.

The degree of risk associated with home ownership can be modified by two other factors. First, if government financial support of home ownership is reduced (say, by the reduction of tax reliefs), some consumers would be more exposed to changes in interest rates. This has in practice already begun to happen. The impact of rising interest rates in the late 1980s has been less cushioned by tax relief than in the past because more home owners have mortgages above the ceiling for tax relief. Secondly, arrangements to smooth fluctuations and spread risks are possible. Various insurance schemes already exist for this purpose, and employer schemes for job-related moves also ease mobility for some home owners. While such schemes can be developed, it may be argued that they will be selective and restricted to more affluent, employed groups. Other households are less likely to be eligible for such schemes or to be able to afford them. Differences within home ownership are likely to relate to income, economic status, occupation and job history. For those with least ability to obtain preferential credit terms, choice will be of low-priced and low-quality dwellings and the modification to consumption arrangements are more likely to involve various hybrid schemes under which home ownership becomes more like renting. The obvious examples of such arrangements are shared ownership, rental purchase (under which purchase is through a hire purchase arrangement with repossession in the event of arrears), lifetime mortgage arrangements, or (for elderly people) annuity schemes.

A key area relating to the risks associated with home ownership is the treatment of repairs and maintenance. As dwellings in the sector age and as differentiation is more marked, so the quality of dwellings in the sector will vary. These differences will mainly be reflected in price. The tendency for lower-income owners to own dwellings in less good repair is already apparent. The treatment of repairs expenditure by the supplementary benefits system does not relieve the situation. In the budget of 1988, the tax reliefs associated with improvement loans were removed. While this no doubt reflected a correct view that such relief was not well targeted, its withdrawal seems likely to have had a real impact on some owners. Changes to the improvement grant system will also have an impact. The means testing for these grants takes no account of other housing costs (especially mortgage repayments) and many purchasers with a mortgage that leaves them with little cash for repairs and improvement will be unable to obtain a grant. The elderly with low incomes are less likely to be affected by this. The future of home ownership seems likely to include an increasing number of owners experiencing continuing or worsening disrepair problems. For these households, ownership will not be equated with high-quality housing. It is also less likely to be associated with favourable financial arrangements and will reflect the regressive nature of tax relief. One response to these developments has been the evolution of agency services providing aid and advice services and perhaps some subsidy of costs relating to repairs. A fuller development of these services (possibly targeted on elderly or low-income owners) represents a revision of the traditional package available to owners. Without such a development, the differential experience of home ownership and of the financial and housing quality risks of home ownership could be substantial.

206   *Home ownership*

The discussion of differential experience and risk associated with home ownership raises a key issue for the future – the continuing fiscal and policy support from central government. Earlier chapters of this book have emphasized the nature of home ownership as a welfare state, subsidized tenure. While subsidies to council housing have been reduced and the private rented sector has been deregulated, the economics of housing remain affected by increasing fiscal support for home ownership. A growing subsidy bill is not well targeted; indeed, it continues to benefit those on higher rates of tax and with larger (more recent) mortgages most. The inequality of these arrangements has been generally recognized. The bill involved will continue to rise even if the ceiling on tax relief is not raised. The percentage of mortgages of £30,000 or over and therefore qualifying for maximum £30,000 tax relief was 44 per cent in the first quarter of 1988. This reflected a steady quarterly increase from 15 per cent in the last quarter of 1984. A rough calculation suggests that only some 10 per cent of home owners had mortgages qualifying for maximum tax relief. The implication of this is that, even if the tax relief ceiling remains at £30,000, the costs of tax relief will rise as owners trade up or as new purchasers take on larger loans than are being repaid by other households. The potential costs of mortgage interest tax relief with the existing ceiling in operation depend on rates of interest and tax rates as well as levels of mortgage debt. Eight million mortgages of £30,000 or over with a tax rate of 25p in the pound (and ignoring higher tax rates) and an interest rate of 12 per cent would generate some £7,200 million tax relief. The tax relief bill will clearly increase considerably before it withers away, unless it is reformed.

The privileged taxation treatment of home ownership affects the potential revival of private renting. Those who could afford higher rents will buy rather than pay such rents. The pressure to reduce financial support for home ownership is significant and is likely to grow. Reductions in supplementary benefit support, in tax reliefs for improvement loans and in improvement grants could be precursors to other reductions. Redirecting support to home ownership may also become more obviously needed as house price inflation affects first-time buyers, as builders' preferences for building larger dwellings increase problems and as disrepair in the old owner-occupied stock becomes more evident. One obvious response is to target assistance or to develop selective schemes. There is a history to such schemes, with the savings, bonus and loan scheme targeted at first-time buyers and with subsidies associated with homesteading and improvement for sale. Past experience suggests that, if subsidy reduction does become important, rather than a rational, general reorientation of subsidy emerging, general subsidy will be focused on key sectors of the population and withdrawn from those in more marginal situations. While the latter group might be dependent on the system of income support or on an adapted housing benefit system, the former would benefit through continued tax relief or employment-linked support (built on tax arrangements). Whatever other arguments are raised about the removal of tax relief, such a step might have less impact on more affluent owners than on some first-time borrowers and lower-income mortgagers. The social division of financial support for owner occupation may become more regressive and build on arrangements already becoming more apparent in the 1980s.

Other considerations are likely to influence the development of public policy in relation to home ownership. Increasing evidence of labour mobility problems associated with regional differences in house prices and in rates of asset appreciation may lead to a review. They are more likely to result in the encouragement of employer assistance as indicated above. Increasing comment on the links between home ownership, inflation and credit-based consumer spending linked to house purchase seems unlikely to lead to revision of housing finance in preference to the adjustment of monetary policy more generally. Finally, the harmonization and homogenization of European markets in 1992 seem likely to affect the size of the market rather than the form of home ownership.

The pressures that are likely to affect key financial and organizational determinants of the way that home ownership changes are not the only issues influencing the future of the tenure. Who the tenure houses and what its social role will be relate to who moves into the sector – to changes in the means of access – but also to who already are home owners. New entrants to owner occupation will continue to include households benefiting from special advantages associated with sitting tenant purchase (mainly from the public sector). The role of new building for home ownership and more significantly the purchase of properties already in the home owner sector will be more important. As special sitting tenant routes into home ownership decline, the quality and price of housing bought is more likely to relate to the income and wealth (rather than other attributes) of households. The circumstances that determine the price and quality of house purchased have a lasting influence on housing experience. They are modified by length of residence and the resources spent on repairs and maintenance. As properties age, and where they are owned by households with low and declining incomes, the quality and condition of the sector will change.

Recent evidence on house condition and the fact that an increasing proportion of home owners have lower incomes (especially

208 *Home ownership*

through a period of recession) suggests that, without policies to alter affairs, the sector will be marked by increasing differences in quality and condition. The proportion of elderly home owners will continue to increase and this is likely to further deepen this tendency. The future age profile of home owners is predictable. The population aged 65 or over is projected to increase from 8.7 million to 9.2 million between 1986 and 2001. The increase is sharper for those aged 75 and over (from 3.7 million in 1986 to 4.4 million in 2001). But the proportion of elderly people who will be home owners in 2001 will initially reflect the higher rates of home ownership among younger age cohorts today: 65 per cent of those household heads aged 45–59 in 1985 were home owners compared with 48 per cent of those aged 70 or over. A simple cohort projection indicates that a higher proportion of the larger elderly population will be home owners. Such a calculation assumes that movement out of the sector is likely to be limited. Movements through marital breakdown and mortgage default have grown in recent years and will continue to do so. Opportunities to move to other tenures except in these circumstances are likely to continue to decline. The exceptions to this picture are, however, elderly home owners. There is a substantial expressed demand from this group for council housing, but there is likely to be no increase in capacity to meet it. Other 'destinations' include nursing homes, other institutional care and moves to live with sons or daughters. However, the recent development of specialist private sheltered housing seems likely to continue to play an increasing role in the future, as do equity release schemes for the elderly. The low-income, asset-rich home owner is likely to be faced with a variety of proposals to release equity in the future.

The implications of all this are of a wider range of age groups in owner occupation, a wider variation in incomes, a greater variation in housing quality and condition, and a wider range of specialist segments of the owner-occupied market. The tendency to fragmentation and differentiation will become more marked. It will occur alongside and be exacerbated by increased competition and volatility in the market. The inflation of house prices will be affected by the growth in inherited wealth referred to in Chapter 6. Recent research cautions against assumptions that inheritance will have dramatic effects – and equity release schemes, if they develop significantly, will upset even these calculations. The pattern of inheritance, however, is likely to reinforce rather than cut across other aspects of capacity to pay for housing, to deepen differences within the market and to make movement between sectors more difficult.

Compared with other European countries, the home ownership market in Britain is more fully developed. It is less based on new building, the second-hand market is better developed and access is extended further down the income scale. Against this background, increasing differentiation in home ownership will more rapidly involve low-cost housing and both changing social roles and changing needs. Segments of the home ownership market rather than the market in general will be high status and have the attributes of positional goods. Other sectors of the tenure will provide marginal dwellings for marginal groups. The interests and attitudes of owners in these very different parts of the market may have little in common – certainly common tenure status is unlikely to impart such solidarity. Owners in different parts of the market will have very different housing needs and resources. For the marginalized owner, assistance with repairs and maintenance, with the process of mobility and exchange, and with the costs of use may be more immediate and real and aspects of accumulation and schemes for equity release be less relevant.

As home ownership expands, the processes of marginalization will not be restricted to council housing and will increasingly spill over into that tenure and erode the perceived connections between owner occupation and social status. For some there will be an increasing discrepancy between its ideological promise and its material reality. In this sense the problem of the extension of home ownership is that as it grows so it becomes more stratified and differentiated. As a significantly higher level of home ownership is achieved, the greater will be the association of processes of deprivation and stigmatization with sectors of home ownership. As present, the drive toward a higher rate of home ownership continues to be refuelled by the contrast with council housing, but that contrast will become less stark in some areas.

The reconstruction of home ownership?

It is appropriate to describe recent trends in housing as part of the erosion of the collective welfare state, as part of the subsidization of market processes combined with a strong centralist state. But the seeds of future forms of collective provision and state intervention are contained as much within the contradictory features of home ownership as they are within a declining council housing sector. As the problems of home ownership become more marked and as problems arising elsewhere are increasingly experienced by households that are home owners, so the demand for alternatives to the present form of home ownership is likely to emerge. The

210   *Home ownership*

dependence on the private sector seems likely to involve revival of private renting or a situation of permanent mortgage indebtedness as new loans for property maintenance and repair are required. Those in low-valuation properties will (in financial and housing terms) find the options and advantages available to them very different from those in higher-value properties.

The alternatives to continuing in the current direction are not a reversion to some previous consensus. For example, there have been more radical proposals to demunicipalize housing than are represented in current policies. The Conservative politician Peter Walker has periodically over recent years urged the simple conversion of rent to mortgage and tenant to owner and this has recently been treated as a serious proposition. At the outset, these suggestions did not sound as if they had been thought through and it remains to be seen how they develop, especially in relation to those occupying the least satisfactory and saleable properties.

The shortcomings of private renting in terms of control, quality, accountability and tenants' rights have long been recognized, but responses have largely involved simple conversion to one of the dominant tenures. And the current offering of individual ownership in contrast to the shortcomings of public housing is a demonstration of the sterility of active debate about transforming the dominant tenures. There are alternatives, however. Although most of the innovations in policy for owner occupation have been designed to ease access to the tenure rather than change the tenure generally, there is scope to give further attention to developing forms of tenure that incorporate the best elements of each of the main tenures. Some proposals for developing parallel tenures – providing, say, the rights of individual ownership with access to collectively organized repairs and exchange/sale services – do not involve changing the rights of existing owners but rather offer an alternative home ownership package supported by public subsidy directed to achieve clear social objectives. It may be argued that such arrangements could be developed to enable local authorities to redirect their attention to investment and repair, intervention in access/exchange, provision of aid and advice and using the full range of their resources to deliver housing to households rather than day-to-day management in the model of the private landlord.

The range of possibilities here is considerable. They offer a means of changing both the structure and nature of tenures. But such changes would be nominal without resources to back them and an examination of how taxation and subsidy are best constructed to achieve policy ends.

Finally, discussion of alternatives to continuing in the direction of current policy need not neglect the organization of housebuilding

Deconstruction and reconstruction   211

and production. Reducing the tenure-related anomalies in housing finance will not result in the right number of dwellings being built when they are needed, where they are needed, at a reasonable cost. Nor will it solve problems of maintenance and repair. As with issues of transaction costs and exchange, there is a need to reconsider the way housing production is organized, including the provision of land, infrastructure, planning, the organization of building and determinants of housing cost. The nature of costs of housing in each tenure are formed by what happens in production as well as other aspects of the housing process.

The conclusion to this is a simple one. What the tenure structure and nature of various tenures will be in, say, the year 2001 depends on what happens during the next phase of policy. But public policy will not develop in a vacuum and will not be the only or even the major influence. As Ball has argued, in the development of home ownership the state has not been the great orchestrator, and other financial and economic pressures have been more critical in determining what key supply and financing agencies do. Nevertheless, it is likely that in 2001 there will be more marked problems in both tenures – with council housing a confirmed and irrecoverable welfare sector and with owner occupation generally affected by problems of disrepair, chains of sales and transaction costs, as well as including parts of the market with a concentration of problems. These tenure developments are likely to feature in increasing gaps in the housing situation between the north and the south and between inner and outer city areas. If there is a concern to find a way of avoiding this future, there are a wide range of alternatives. Neither the present direction of policy, nor alternative forms of privatization, nor a reversion to previous policies seem likely to succeed in this respect. Simply throwing more money at housing or addressing anomalies in the financial treatment of tenures will also not be sufficient.

What is possible is a broader-based review that is not restricted to tenure, that embraces the volume, costs and organization of building and repair, that addresses problems of exchange and sale, and that is designed to deliver housing resources and services to households.

Greater differentiation in home ownership need not have a damaging impact on home owners. Key issues will relate to how the needs of those in the least-favoured positions, in different parts of the market and at different stages of the life cycle and of housing histories are responded to. Although the record of the sector is of reasonable responsiveness and flexibility, the ability to respond will be affected if the balance within the sector changes - as it will do - towards those not in employment and with limited resources;

if the competitiveness of the market leads to selective marketing – to specialization that offers different and better services to those with the most secure incomes and representing the lowest risk to lenders; and if the context within which home ownership operates provides fewer supportive mechanisms. The latter point does relate to previous discussion of financial support. But it also relates to the opportunities provided by the rest of the social system. The costs of problems experienced in home ownership are borne by the social security system, family and kinship support (financial and care), and local authority and housing association willingness and ability to rehouse. These are important sources of support, which limit the risk of market collapse and of large-scale residential abandonment. The erosion of these sources of support rather than changes wholly *within* the owner–occupied sector are of key importance.

These various considerations suggest different possible futures for home ownership. The sector will be marked by growing variation and inequality. A housing debate that has been mesmerized by tenure categories is likely to be increasingly concerned with differences within the sector – differences in source and level of subsidy, rates of accumulation and exchange value, differences in quality, condition and use value, differences in choice and mobility, the further development of second home ownership alongside abandonment, tensions between the impact of high rates of house price inflation on existing wealth owners and on first-time buyers without the resources (perhaps from inheritance) to supplement credit based on income, differential access to special services and provision, differential gains and opportunities in different areas and sectors, and the different capacity to withstand or cope with instability in the market. While general differences within home ownership are likely to relate to employment and class differences, these will be modified by housing history and inheritance – including the nature of parental housing history and *where* histories have taken place. The gap between the top end of the owner–occupied market, in which positional good status remains, and the no-choice, low-quality and abandonment end will be wider than differences between tenures. But the implications of these growing differences are less easy to assess.

Essentially it depends on how home owners collectively respond and how the institutions involved in the financing and management of home ownership respond. New forms of ownership, including cooperatives, may emerge and various support services and forms of consumer protection could emerge. Some of these forms and protections are likely to involve a significant role for the state or for state-funded agencies. Others will involve self-regulation by key agencies. The development of agency services, the discussion of property log books and warranty systems, criticisms of estate agency services, conveyancing and gazumping, and proposals for leasehold reform can all be seen as preludes to legal and organizational changes. Unless such changes emerge to protect owners with limited political and economic power and resources, the position of low-income groups in home ownership will be no better than that in the rented sector. The party politics and political discussion around home ownership are likely to develop from competition to identify with the tenure and to respond to the needs of particular groups within the tenure.

Concluding comment

The main themes in this book have been about growth, change and differentiation in home ownership. This chapter has also included some discussion of the ways in which the tenure is changing now and in the future. In this brief concluding section it is appropriate to draw out a limited number of points which particularly relate to the future of home ownership and of housing in Britain.

The period 1987 to 1990 has demonstrated the volatility and instability of the home ownership market. A dramatic house price boom spreading outwards from the South East has been followed by what is presented as a collapse. The language of a buoyant market generating substantial gains for buyers, sellers, exchange professions and builders has given way to problems among these groups. The home ownership success story has been replaced by accounts of mortgage repayment difficulties, problems of selling, pressure to cut prices, closures and redundancies among estate agents. The slump in 1988/89 is associated with the ending of the system under which joint purchasers of a dwelling could both qualify for tax relief (up to £30,000) on mortgage interest payments and under which loans for house improvement qualified for tax relief. It is also associated with the impact of rising interest rates. Such rises are associated with the government's policy to counteract rising inflation. Finally, the volatility of the market can be interpreted as a consequence of the way it is organised and profits are made – in ways argued particularly by Ball and referred to elsewhere in the book.

Some caution should be used in discussing collapse or slump. Undoubtedly 1989 has seen a much lower level of transactions. It has also led builders to postpone and reschedule their activity. One major builder (Kentish Homes) has gone out of business, other builders and building materials companies have laid off staff and others may have obscured the extent of their problems by using various devices including sales of dwellings to holding companies. The impact of low levels of transactions is severe on estate agents and especially on small independent agencies. While the larger national networks can rationalise staff and branches and sustain losses, smaller agencies are forced to close. Other specialist operations such as relocation agencies find their services in greater demand because relocating employees are having problems in selling property.

For building societies and other lenders the reduced level of house purchase transactions has been balanced by increased lending to reschedule loans or remortgage. Some of this business involves people switching away from newer lending agencies which lost their attraction as interest rates rose. Some involves further advances for home improvement. Some of this and some explicitly borrowed for the purpose, is to consolidate other (consumer) debt. For the householder such further advances will be at a lower interest rate and over a longer period and may provide some cash in the pocket. In effect such advances involve leakage or disinvestment from housing. They maintain building societies' lending and solve consumer credit problems but obscure the reduction in housing activity and lending. In this context it also seems likely that building societies' attitudes to debt management may have become more flexible and responsive. While mortgage arrears rose in 1989, lenders were reported to be increasing counselling and the number of repossessions in a buyers' market had fallen. A greater willingness to agree interest-only payments or to reschedule payments prevents a crises for the household but may prolong indebtedness and is relevant to discussion of accumulation and of blurred distinctions between owning and renting.

The changes affecting mortgagors in 1988/89 were substantial. When interest rates rose to some 14.75 per cent in October 1989 it was the fourth rise in less than 12 months and had lifted rates by as much as 5 per cent over the period. A large proportion of building society borrowers with their monthly payments adjusted annually, experienced changes only at these annual reviews. For all borrowers, and especially those using banks and specialist lenders funding their mortgage business from the money markets, monthly payments rose by some 50 per cent or more. In this environment seeking a cheaper source of finance or rescheduling payments is a logical step even though there are costs incurred in transferring a mortgage. All of this involves a different environment for home ownership than is often presented. It highlights that prices come down as well as go up and that payments rise steeply as a result of wider economic pressures. It also highlights the integration of housing finance into the wider financial system.

Deconstruction and reconstruction 215

Three further related points arise from this discussion. First the movement of prices and interest of prices and interest payments affects the rates of return discussed in Chapter 6. Some purchasers buying just before the decline of house prices and affected by subsequent interest rate increases will have experienced negative rates of return (in Saunders and Harris terms). However these are paper losses. Only if owners cannot wait for prices to rise again would these be real losses. Some owners will be in this position. Others will not make such substantial gains as they had hoped but will still sell for more than they bought. Second is the question of whether the slump is short lived. It is cautionary to reflect on the widely publicised views of Bob Beckman, a US investment analyst who in 1981 and 1982 forecast an imminent slump in the housing market. He was wrong and the opposite happened. The likelihood is that the 1989 slump will be followed by a period of buoyancy. Volatility and instability is likely to speed up rather than delay the reorganisation of the market. Rationalisation and increased competition is apparent in the building industry, estate agency and among lenders. Advertisements to poach lending business are more common. Building societies' links with insurance companies and plans to provide conveyancing services are steps in further vertical integration of business and attempts to attract business through reducing costs to home owners.

As has been said before, many of these developments may prove to be in the long term interest of home owners. Some other developments are less so. The collapse of Homes Assured in 1989 threatened losses for home owners who had made payments for services they had not received. It is reasonable to argue that the amount of business involved in home ownership will draw in some activities which are undeniably exploitative. Rental purchase schemes and some activities of estate agents and solicitors in recent years have been regarded in this way. Indeed the low public esteem in which estate agents are held is perceived as a problem to the profession. And this low esteem does not derive only from periodic complaints over gazumping. The problems experienced by the Abbey National Building Society in its embarrassing loss of documents for potential shareholders have not been good publicity and may influence other societies to hesitate from stock market flotation. These examples of a mixed history do not however deny the continuing process of reorganisation of the home ownership industry in general.

One key issue in some discussions is the possibility of universal home ownership and limits to the growth of home ownership. Much of this rests on what forms and levels of state assistance are envisaged to enable entry to home ownership and to sustain home

216 *Home ownership*

ownership. Some further growth will derive from demographic processes. However, high interest rates, affordability and choice for lower income buyers and greater regional differentials in house prices provide a different context for discussion than in the past. In addition further growth will change the tenure. It is not evident that questions of how to bring non-owners into home ownership do equate with how to extend the benefits of home ownership. It might extend problems and disadvantages. It is at least as important to carry a parallel policy concern which is about how to protect home owners and regulate the market to ensure that those entering and those in the sector do have security and do benefit.

It has been argued in this book that the widely assumed benefits of home ownership do not flow inevitably. They are not inherent or necessary attributes of the tenure but are fostered and sustained by a range of institutional, financial, family and state mechanisms. It has been argued that it is important to acknowledge and develop these mechanisms. Examples such as support for improvement and repair costs and agency services could be broadened to emphasize the need for consumer protection. Perhaps more fundamental than this is the argument that home ownership has grown because it has operated alongside council housing and not in spite of it. The future of home ownership is likely to be more assured if council housing continues to provide a route into home ownership and a route out of it for those seeking it as a result of homelessness, age, infirmity or problems of meeting repair and maintenance costs. In this way a policy for home ownership needs to be located in a broader housing policy and a continuing active role for the state, the local authority and housing associations should be regarded as a necessary complement.

This view further relates to the volatility of the home ownership market. Dramatic fluctuations in house prices, interest rates and levels of investment create problems for home owners. While it may be argued that over a lifetime of home ownership such fluctuations will be looked upon as temporary inconveniences, they can cause extreme hardship. Furthermore, the instability of levels of investment makes these problems greater. The tendency for investment to fluctuate exacerbates house price inflation. A more stable building output would prevent the coincidence of rising demand with low rates of production. The role of the state in sustaining building output related to demographic and other aspects of need is justified both in preventing long-term shortages and reducing the conditions that create hyper inflation in housing. Levelling out the peaks and troughs would be an appropriate aim for housing policy and questions of what tenure building was for would not be of key importance.

Deconstruction and reconstruction 217

Both the volatility of the market and the problems associated with high house prices and high interest rates lead to a final concluding point. In a period of mass home ownership with more households with substantial housing debts and perhaps combining housing debt with debts incurred from other consumer expenditure, movements of interest rates have considerable importance. They mean that the manipulation of interest rates has a more direct impact on household budgets. At the same time, governments are more vulnerable to voter reactions to this situation. The voting behaviour of home owners may relate in future to the impact of volatility and instability in the market, to changes in house prices and interest rates. Rather than assuming that home owners will respond in a similar way to these factors it would seem probable that reactions will reflect their different material interests and social circumstances.

At the end of the 1980s and the beginning of the 1990s high interest rates, a stagnant housing market and declining house prices have highlighted the diversity of experience within home ownership. Some households can cope with this situation. For others it can mean serious financial difficulties, enforced sale, repossession of homelessness. The longer this situation obtains and the more extensive the problems become the more clear cut will be the social divisions within home ownerships. Rather than ameliorating these problems the taxation and interest rate policy of government are widely regarded as having contributed to the speculative boom in housing, the inflationary effects of this and the consequent pressure on interest rates. Uncertainties in the housing market have been increased by the introduction of the poll tax. All this calls further into question approaches which assert a common set of values, common interests, similar experiences and shared benefits among home owners. As more of the nation become home owners, so there are more nations within home ownership.

References

Advertising Service Guild (1943), *An enquiry into people's homes* (London: John Murray).

Ashworth, H. (1980), *The building society story* (London: Franey).

Association of Metropolitan Authorities (1986), *Mortgage arrears: owner occupiers at risk (London: AMA)*.

Atkinson, A. B. and Harrison, A. H. (1978), *The distribution of personal wealth in Britain* (Cambridge: Cambridge University Press).

Ball, M. (1982), 'Housing provision and the economic crisis', *Capital and class*, 17, pp.66–77.

Ball, M. (1983), *Housing policy and economic power* (London: Methuen).

Ball, M. (1986), *Home ownership: a suitable case for reform* (London: Shelter Publications).

Ball, M. (1988), *Rebuilding construction* (London: Routledge).

Ball, M., Harloe, M. and Martens, M. (1988), *Housing and social change in Europe and the USA* (London: Routledge).

Bank of England (1985), *Quarterly Bulletin*, March.

Barlow, J. & Duncan, S. (1988) 'The use and abuse of housing tenure', *Housing studies*, 3 (4) pp.219–31.

Barrett, S. and Healey, P. (1985), *Land policy: problems and alternatives* (Aldershot: Gower).

Bellman, H. (1927), *The building society movement* (London: Methuen).

Bellman, H. (1938), 'The building trades', in British Association, *Britain in recovery* (London: Pitman).

Black Horse Relocation (1986), *Point to point*, Autumn.

Board of Inland Revenue (1987), *Inland Revenue Statistics 1985*, (London: HMSO).

Boddy, M. (1980), *The building societies*, (London: Macmillan).

Boddy, M. (1989), 'Financial deregulation and UK housing finance: government–building society relations and the Building Societies Act, 1986' *Housing studies*, 4 (2), pp.92–104.

Boddy, M. and Gray, F. (1979), 'Filtering theory, housing policy and the legitimation of inequality', *Policy and politics*, 7 (1), January, pp.39–54.

Boleat, M. (1976), 'Home ownership will not rise above 60% on present policies', *Building Societies Gazette*, June.

Boleat, M. (1982), 'Home ownership in inner city areas', *Policy analysis for housing and planning*, Proceedings of PTRC Annual Meeting, 1982.

Boleat, M. (1985), *National housing finance systems* (London: Croom Helm).

References   219

Borough of Hyndburn (1982), *Report of Borough Planning Officer.*
Borough of Hyndburn (1985), *Housing investment programme submission 1986/87.*
Bournville Village Trust (1941), *When we build again* (London: George Allen and Unwin).
Bramley, G. and Paice, D. (1987), *Housing needs in non-metropolitan areas,* Report of research carried out for the Association of District Councils, University of Bristol, School for Advanced Urban Studies.
British Market Research Bureau (1977), *Housing consumer survey,* NEDO.
British Market Research Bureau (1986), *Housing and savings* (London: Building Society Association).
British Market Research Bureau (1989), *Housing and savings* (London: Building Society Association).
Brown, C. (1984), *Black and white Britain: the third PSI survey* (London: Gower).
Building Societies Association (1983), *Housing tenure* (London: Building Societies Association).
Building Societies Association (1984), *Leaseholds – time for a change.*
Building Societies Association (1985a), 'Trends in personal sector wealth', *BSA Bulletin,* no.144, October pp.16–19.
Building Societies Association (1985b), *BSA Bulletin,* no.43.
Building Societies Association (1988), *BSA Bulletin,* no.55.
Building Societies Association (1989), *Housing Finance No 1.*
Burman, S. (ed.) (1979), *Fit work for women* (London: Croom Helm).
Burnett, J. (1978), *A social history of housing 1815–1970* (London: David & Charles).
Burnett, J. (1986), *A social history of housing 1815–1985* (London: Methuen).
Butler, D. and Sloman, A. (1975), *British political facts 1900–1975* (London: Macmillan).

Carchedi, G. (1975), 'On the economic identification of the new middle class', *Economy and Society,* 4, pp.1–86.
Central Statistical Office (1988), *Regional trends,* no.23 (London: HMSO).
CES Ltd (1987), *People and places: a classification of urban areas and residential neighbourhoods,* CES Paper 53, 5 Tavistock Place, London.
Champion, A. and Congdon, L. (1988), 'Recent trends in Greater London's Population', *Population Trends 53* (London: HMSO)
Chapman, S. D. and Bartlett, J. N. (1971), 'The contribution of building clubs and freehold land society to working-class housing in Birmingham', in S.D. Chapman (ed.), *The history of working class housing* (London: David & Charles).
City of Bristol Planning Department (1985), *Moving to Bristol.*
Cleary, E. J. (1965), *The building society movement* (London: Elek).
Confederation of British Industry (1988), *Special survey of company housing needs in the South East* (London: CBI).
Conservative Central Office (1979), *The sale of council homes – model scheme, guidance notes.*
Conservative Party (1979), *Conservative manifesto.*
Council of Mortgage Lenders (1989), *Housing finance* 3, July.
Cowling, M. (1987), 'The regional impact of the Channel Tunnel', Paper

220 *Home ownership*

presented at conference on 'Divided Britain', Northern College, 2–4 October.

Craig, P. (1986), 'The house that Jerry built? Building societies, the state and the politics of owner-occupation', *Housing Studies*, 1(1) pp.87–108.

Craig, P. (1987), 'Public authority and private purposes, building societies, the state and the politics of housing', unpublished PhD thesis, University of Bristol.

Craig, C., Rubery, J., Tarling, R. and Wilkinson, F. (1985), 'Economic, social and political factors in the operation of the labour market', in B. Roberts, R. Finnegan and D. Gallie *New approaches to economic life* (Manchester: Manchester University Press).

Crossick, G. (1977), 'The emergence of the lower middle class in Britain: a discussion', in G. Crossick (ed.), *The lower middle class in Britain* (London: Croom Helm).

Daniels, S. (1980), 'Moral order and the industrial environment in the woollen textile districts of West Yorkshire, 1780–1880', unpublished PhD thesis, University of London.

Daunton, M. J. (1977), *Coal metropolis: Cardiff 1870–1914* (Leicester: Leicester University Press).

Daunton, M. (1980), 'Miners' houses: South Wales and the Great Northern Cornfield 1880–1914', *International Review of Social History*, 25, pp.143–75.

Daunton, M. (1987), *A property owning democracy? Housing in Britain* (London: Faber & Faber).

Dennis, R. (1984), *English industrial cities of the nineteenth century: a social geography* (Cambridge: Cambrige University Press).

Department of Employment (1986), *Family expenditure survey* (London: HMSO).

Department of Employment (1986), *Labour force survey 1986* (London: HMSO).

Department of the Environment (1977), *Housing policy: technical volume III* (London: HMSO).

Department of the Environment, Scottish Development Department and Welsh Office (1987), *Housing and construction statistics 1976–1986* (London: HMSO).

Department of the Environment (1988), *Queuing for housing: a study of council housing waiting lists* (London: HMSO).

Dickens, P., Duncan, S., Goodwin, M. and Gray, F. (1985), *Housing states and localities* (London: Methuen).

Dicks, M. J. (1988), *The demographics of housing demand, household formations and the growth of owner occupation*, Bank of England, Discussion Paper No.32.

Doling, J., Karn, V. and Stafford, B. (1986), 'The impact of unemployment on home ownership', *Housing Studies*, 1(1), pp. 49–59.

Doling, J. and Stafford, B. (1989), *Home ownership – the diversity of experience* (Aldershot: Gower).

Dunleavy, P. (1979), 'The urban basis of political alignment: social class, British domestic property ownership and state intervention in consumption processes, *Journal of Political Science*, 9, pp.409–443.

References 221

Dunleavy, P. (1986a), 'The growth of sectoral cleavages and the stabilization of state expenditure', *Environment and Planning D: Society and Space*, 4, pp.129–44.

Dunleavy, P. (1986b), 'Explaining the privatisation boom: public choice versus radical approaches', *Public administration*, 64, Spring, pp.13–34.

Dunleavy, P. and Husbands, C. T. (1985), *British democracy at the crossroads, voting and party competition in the 1980s*, (London: Allen & Unwin).

Dunn, R., Forrest, R. and Murie, A. (1987), 'The geography of council house sales in England 1979–85', *Urban Studies*, 24, pp.47–59.

Engels, F. (1975 edition), *The housing question* (Moscow: Progress Publishers).

Englander, D. (1983), *Landlord and tenant in urban Britain, 1938–1918*, (Oxford: Clarendon Press).

Farmer, M. K. and Barrel, R. (1981), 'Entrepreneurship and government policy: the case of the housing market', *Journal of Public Policy*, 1, pp.307–32.

Field, F. (1975), *Do we need council houses?* Occasional Paper no.2 (London: Catholic Housing Aid Society)

Field, F. (1981), *Inequality in Britain* (London: Fontana).

Fleiss, A. (1985), *Home ownership alternatives for the elderly* (London: HMSO).

Ford, J. (1988), *The Indebted Society: Credit and default in the 1980s* (London: Routledge).

Forrest, R., Lansley, P. and Murie, A. (1984), *A foot on the ladder?* Working Paper no.41, University of Bristol, School for Advanced Urban Studies.

Forrest, R. and Murie, A. (1985), *Housing origins and destinations*, End of award report, Grant No.DUU23/2033, available from the Economic Social Research Council.

Forrest, R. and Murie, A. (1987), 'The affluent home owner: labour market position and the shaping of housing histories', *The Sociological Review*, 35(2), pp.370–403.

Forrest, R. and Murie, A. (1988a), *Selling the welfare state* (London: Routledge).

Forrest, R. and Murie, A. (1988b), 'The affluent home owner: labour market position and the shaping of housing histories', in N. Thrift and P. Williams, (eds), *Class and space* (London: Routledge).

Forrest, R. and Murie, A. (1989a), 'Housing markets, labour markets and housing histories', in C. Hamnett and J. Allen, (eds), *Housing markets and labour markets* (London: Unwin Hyman).

Forrest, R. and Murie, A. (1989b), 'Differential accumulation: wealth, inheritance and housing policy reconsidered', *Policy and Politics*, 17(1), pp.25–39.

Franklin, A. (1986), *Owner occupation, privatism and ontological security: a critical reformulation*, Working Paper no.62, University of Bristol, School for Advanced Urban Studies.

222 Home ownership

Franklin, A. (1989), 'Working class privatism: a historical case study of Bedminster, Bristol', *Environment and Planning D: Society and Space*, 7, pp.93–113.

Gleave, D. and Palmer, D. (1979), 'The relationship between geography and occupational mobility in the context of regional economic growth', in J. Hobcraft and P. Rees (eds), *Regional demographic development* (London: Croom Helm).

Gleave, D. and Sellens, R. (1984), *An investigation into British labour market processes* (ESRC, School Government Publishing Company).

Goldthorpe, J. and Lockwood, D. (1968), *The affluent worker* (Cambridge: Cambridge University Press).

Gray, P. G. (1947), 'The British household', *The social survey* (London: Central Office of Information).

Green, F., Hadjimatheou, G. and Smail, R. (1984), *Unequal fringes* (London: Bedford Square Press).

Griffiths Report (1988), *Community care: agenda for action*, a report to the Secretary of State for Social Services by Sir Roy Griffiths (London: HMSO).

Haddon, R. (1970), 'A minority in a welfare state society: location of West Indians in the London housing market', *The New Atlantis*, 1(2).

Hamnett, C. (1984), 'Housing the two nations: socio-tenurial polarization in England and Wales 1961–1981', *Urban Studies*, 43, pp.389–405.

Hamnett, C. and Randolph, W. (1988), *Cities, housing and profits* (London: Hutchinson).

Hamnett, C., Harmer, M. and Williams, P. (1989), *Housing inheritance and wealth: a pilot study*, End of award report available from the Economic Social Research Council.

Harbury, C. D. and Hitchens, D. W. A. (1979), *Inheritance and wealth inequality in Britain* (London: Allen & Unwin).

Heath, A., Jowell, R. and Curtice, J. (1985), *How Britain votes* (Oxford: Pergamon Press).

Hillyard, P. and Percy-Smith, J. (1988), *The coercive state* (London: Fontana).

Hird, C. and Irvine, J. (1979), 'The poverty of wealth statistics', in J. Irvine, I. Miles and J. Evans (eds), *Demystifying social statistics* (London: Pluto Press), pp.190–211.

Hirsch, F. (1977), *The social limits to growth* (London: Routledge & Kegan Paul).

HM Treasury (1989), *The government's expenditure plans 1989–90 to 1991–1992*, CM 601 to 621 (London: HMSO).

Holmans, A. E. (1986), *Flows of funds associated with house purchase for owner-occupation in the United Kingdom 1977–1984 and equity withdrawal from house purchase finance*, Government Economic Service, Working Paper no.92, Department of Environment.

Holmans, A. E. (1987), *Housing policy in Britain* (London: Croom Helm).

Holme, A. (1985), *Housing and young families in East London* (London: Routledge & Kegan Paul).

References   223

House of Commons (1981), *Third report from the Environment Committee* (London: HMSO).
Howell, D. (1981), *Freedom and capital* (Oxford: Blackwell).
I.D.S. Top Pay Unit (1988), *Executive mobility* Research File no.8.
Jackson, A. A. (1973), *Semi-detached London* (London: Allen & Unwin).
Johnson, C. (1984), 'Borrowing without tears', *Lloyds Bank Economic Bulletin*, no.62.
Johnson, J. H., Salt, J. and Wood, P. A. (1974), *Housing and the migration of labour in England and Wales* (London: Saxon House).
Johnston, R. J. (1987), 'A note on housing tenure and voting in Britain 1983', *Housing Studies*, 2(2), pp.112–21.
Jones, C. (1982), 'The demand for home ownership', in J. English (ed.), *The future of council housing* (London: Croom Helm).

Karn, V., Kemeny, J. and Williams, P. (1985), *Home ownership in the inner city – salvation or despair?* (Aldershot: Gower).
Kelly, I. (1986), *Heading for rubble: the political need for housing finance reform* (London: Catholic Housing Aid Society.
Kemeny, J. (1981), *The myth of home ownership* (London: Routledge & Kegan Paul).
Kemeny, J. and Thomas, A. (1984), 'Capital leakage from owner–occupied housing', *Policy and Politics*, 12(1), pp.1–12.
Kerr, M. (1988), *The right to buy* (London: HMSO).
Kirkham, A. (1983), *Improvement for sale by local authorities (London: HMSO).*

Laing and Cruickshank (1982), *Private housebuilding*, the Stock Exchange, November.
Land Enquiry Committee (1914), *The land*, vol.II (London: Hodder & Stoughton).
Lasch, C. (1977), *Haven in a heartless work* (New York: Basic Books).
Leather, P. (1987), *Making use of home equity in old age*, Draft report of a research project on the Housing Needs of Elderly Owner Occupiers, University of Bristol, School for Advanced Urban Studies: Mimeo.
Levitt, D. (1982), 'Housing standards: space standards are not enough', *Architects' Journal*, November.
Lloyds Bank (1988), 'House price rises peak', *Lloyds Bank Economic Bulletin*, no.116.
London Research Centre (1988), *Quarterly house price bulletin*, no.7, 2nd Quarter.
Lowe, S. and Watson, S. (1989), *Equity Withdrawal from the Housing Market*, Paper presented to BSA Study Group, London, 18 February 1989.
Luria, D. (1976), 'Wealth, capital and power: the social meaning of home ownership', *Journal of Interdisciplinary History*, 2, pp.261–82.

McCulloch, A. (1989), A note on the British Household Survey of 1947, Unpublished paper.
McCulloch, A. (1990), 'A millstone round your neck?' Building Societies in the 1930s and mortgage default, *Housing Studies*, 5, 1, pp. 43–58.

224 *Home ownership*

McPherson, C. B. (1978), *Property* (Oxford: Basil Blackwell).

Madge, C. (1940), 'Wartime saving and spending – a district survey', *Economic Journal*, 200, June–September, pp.327–39.

Marshall, G., Rose, D., Vogler, C., Newby, H. (1985), 'Class, citizenship and distributional conflict in modern Britain', *British Journal of Sociology*, 36, pp.257–84.

Marshall, G., Newby, H., Rose, D. and Vogler, C. (1988), *Social class in modern Britain* (London: Hutchinson).

Massey, D. (1984), *Spatial divisions of labour* (London: Macmillan).

Massey, P. (1942), 'The expenditure of 1360 households in 1938–9', *Journal of the Royal Statistical Society*, 105(3), pp. 159–85.

Means, R. (1988), 'Council housing, tenure polarisation and older people in two contrasting localities', *Ageing and Society*, 8(1), m pp.395–421.

Merrill Lynch Relocation Management International Limited (1986), *Third annual study of employee relocation policies among major UK companies*.

Merrett, S. (1979), *State housing in Britain* (London: Routledge & Kegan Paul).

Merrett, S. (with Fred Gray) (1982), *Owner occupation in Britain* (London: Routledge & Kegan Paul).

Ministry of Labour (1940), 'Weekly expenditure of working class households in the UK in 1937–8', *Ministry of Labour Gazette*, 12, pp.300–5.

Miron, J. and Schiff, M. (1982), 'A profile of the emerging empty nesters household', Center for Urban and Community Studies, Research Paper no.130, University of Toronto.

Moreton, N. and Tate, J. (1986), 'House prices in the older housing stock of Birmingham', *Housing Review*, 35(3), May–June, pp.85–7.

Morrell, J. (1986), *Business forecasts for the housing market to 1991* (London: James Morrell Associates).

Munro, M. (1988), 'Housing wealth and inheritance', *Journal of Social Policy* 17, 4, pp. 417–36.

Munro, M. and Maclennan, D. (1987), 'Intra-urban changes in housing prices: Glasgow 1972–83', *Housing Studies*, 2(2), April, pp.65–81.

Murie, A. (1975), *The sale of council houses: a study in social policy*, Occasional Paper no.35, CURS, University of Birmingham.

Murie, A. (1983), *Housing inequality and deprivation* (London: Heinemann).

Murie, A. (1985), 'What the country can afford? Housing under the Conservatives 1979–83', in P. Jackson (ed.), *Implementing government policy initiatives: the Thatcher administration 1979–1983* (Royal Institute of Public Administration).

Murie, A. (1986), 'Social differentiation in urban areas: housing or occupational class at work?' *Tijdschrift voor Economische en Sociale Geografie*, 77, pp.345–57.

Murie, A. and Forrest, R. (1980a), *Housing market processes and the inner city* (ESRC, School Publishing House).

Murie, A. and Forrest, R. (1980b), 'Wealth inheritance and housing policy', *Policy and Politics* 8(1), pp.1–19.

Murie, A., Hillyard, P., Birrell, D. and Roche, D. (1986), 'New building and housing need', *Progress in Planning*, 6(2), (Oxford: Pergamon).

Murie, A., Niner, P. and Watson, C. (1976), *Housing policy and the housing system* (London: Allen & Unwin).

References

225

Murphy, P. E. and Stopes, W. A. (1979), 'A modernised family life cycle', *Journal of Consumer Research*, 6.

Nationwide Anglia (1988), *House prices: highs and lows – a local view*.
Nationwide Building Society (1985), 'House prices over the past thirty years', April.
Nationwide Building Society (1986), *Housing as an investment*, April.
Nationwide Building Society (1987), 'House prices in 1987'.
Nationwide Anglia Building Society (1989), 'The changing face of mortgage lending, 1968-1988'.
NEDO (1975), *BMRB Housing Consumer Survey, 1975* (London: HMSO).

Offer, A. (1981), *Property and politics, 1870-1914: landownership, law, ideology and urban development in England* (Cambridge: Cambridge University Press).
Office of Population Censuses and Survey (1973), *General Household Survey 1971* (London: HMSO).
OPCS (1979), *General Household Survey 1977* (London: HMSO).
OPCS (1983a), *General Household Survey 1982* (London: HMSO).
OPCS (1983b), *Census 1981: housing and households* (London: HMSO.
OPCS (1987), *Labour Force Survey 1985* (London: HMSO).
OPCS (1989), *General Household Survey, 1986* (London: HMSO).

Packard, V. (1960), *The status seekers* (Harmondsworth: Penguin).
Pahl, R. E. (1970), *Whose city?* (Harmondsworth: Penguin).
Pahl, R. E. (1975), *Whose city?* 2nd edn (Harmondsworth: Penguin).
Parsons, D. (1987), 'Recruitment difficulties and the housing market', *The Planner*, 73(1), pp.30-74.
Pawley, M. (1978), *Home ownership* (London: Architectural Press).
Phillips, B. (1983), 'Profiting from an older market?' *The Housebuilder*, March.
Platt, S. (1986), 'Cashing in on the property boom' *New Society* October 10, pp.10-110.
Pratt, G. (1986), 'Against reductionism: the relations of consumption as a mode of social structuration', *International Journal of Urban and Regional Research*, 10, pp.377-400.
Prescott-Clarke, P., Allen, P. and Morrissey, C. (1988), *Queuing for housing: a study of council house waiting lists* (London: HMSO).
Preteceille, E. (1986), 'Collective consumption, urban segregation and social classes', *Environment and Planning D: Society and Space*, 4, pp.145-54.
Pritchard, R. (1976), *Housing and the spatial structure of the city* (Cambridge: Cambridge University Press).

Randolph, W. (1987), *Social polarisation and residential change in London, 1961-1981*, unpublished PhD thesis, University of London.
Reiss, R. (1919), *The home I want* (London: Hodder & Stoughton).
Reward Regional Surveys (1986), *Cost of living report: regional comparisons*.
Rex, J. and Moore, R. (1967), *Race, community and conflict* (Oxford: Oxford University Press).

Rose, D. (1980), 'Toward a re-evaluation of the political significance of home-ownership in Britain', in Political Economy of Housing Workshop, *Housing, Construction and the State* (London: CSE).

Royal Commission on Friendly and Benefit Societies (1871), 'First report of the Commissioners', *Parliamentary Papers XXV*.

Royal Commission on the Distribution of Income and Wealth, Chairman: Lord Diamond (1977), *Third report on the standing reference*, Cmnd 6999, (London: HMSO).

Runciman, W. G. (1966), *Relative deprivation and social justice* (London: Routledge and Kegan Paul).

Rydin, Y. (1986), *Housing land policy* (Aldershot: Gower).

Salt, J. (1985), 'Housing and labour migration', paper presented at conference on Housing and Labour Market Change, Parsifal College, London 12–13 December.

Salt, J. and Flowerdew, R. (1986), 'Occupational selectivity in labour migration', paper presented to the conference on Comparative Population Geography of the United Kingdom and the Netherlands, St Edmund Hall, Oxford, September.

Saunders, P. (1977), *Housing tenure and class interests*, University of Sussex.

Saunders, P. (1978), 'Domestic property and social class', *International Journal of Urban and Regional Research*, 2, pp.233–51.

Saunders, P. (1984), 'Beyond housing classes: the sociological significance of private property rights in means of consumption', *International Journal of Urban and Regional Research*, 8, pp.202–27.

Saunders, P. (1985), 'The new right is half right', in A. Seldon (ed), *The new right enlightenment* (London: Economic and Literary Books).

Saunders, P. (1986a), 'Comment on Dunleavy and Preteceille', *Environment and Planning D: Society and Space*, 4, pp.155–63.

Saunders, P. (1987), 'Space, the city and urban sociology', in D. Gregory and J. Urry (eds), *Social relations and spatial structures* (London: Macmillan).

Saunders, P. (1988), 'The significance of the home in contemporary English social life', paper given to the conference on the Sociology of Consumption, University of Oslo.

Saunders, P. (1989b), 'A deep and natural desire?'paper given to BSA Study Group Conference, London.

Saunders, P. (1990), *A nation of home owners* (London: Unwin Hyman).

Saunders, P. and Harris, C. (1987), 'Biting the nipple? Consumer preferences and state welfare', paper given to the Urban Change and Conflict Conference, University of Kent.

Saunders, P. and Harris, C. (1988), *Home ownership and capital gains*, Working Paper no.64, Urban and Regional Studies, University of Sussex.

Stewart, A. (1981), *Housing action in an industrial suburb* (London: Academic Press).

Stonehouse, P. (1981), 'The viewpoint of the private housebuilder', *Housing Review*, July/August.

Stretton, H. (1976), *Capitalism, socialism and the environment* (Cambridge: Cambridge University Press).

References

Sullivan, O. and Murphy, M. (1987), 'Young outright owner occupiers in Britain', *Housing Studies*, 2(3), pp.177–91.

Surrey County Council Planning Department (1986), *New house sales surveys 1979-1983* (Surrey County Council).

Swenarton, M. (1981), *Homes fit for heroes: The politics and architecture of early state housing in Britain* (London: Heinemann).

Swenarton, M. and Taylor, S. (1985), 'The scale and nature of the growth of owner occupation in Britain between the wars', *Economic History Review*, 38(3), pp.373–92.

Taylor-Gooby, P. (1982), 'Two cheers for the welfare state', *Journal of Public Policy*, 2, pp.319–46.

Taylor-Gooby, P. (1983), 'Moralism, self-interest and attitudes to welfare', *Policy and politics*, 22, pp.145–60.

Thorns, D. C. (1981), 'Housing policies and the influence of the growth of owner-occupation in social and political change', paper presented to conference on Comparative Urban Research, Essen, 3–5 October.

Townsend, P. (1979), 'Mortgage lending and consumers' expenditure', *The Investment Analyst*, 72, April, pp.3–6.

Usher, D. (1987), 'Housing privatisation: the sale of council estates', Working Paper 67, School for Advanced Urban Studies, University of Bristol.

Valuation Office (1987), *Property market report no.48* (London: Surveyors Publications).

Walker, P. (1977), *The ascent of Britain* (London: Sidgwick & Jackson).

Weeks, G. C. (1980), 'Labour markets, class interests and the technology of production', *Journal of Economic Issues*, 14(2).

Welsh Office (1986), *Welsh house condition survey* (London: HMSO).

Williams, G. (1986), *Meeting the housing needs of the elderly: private initiative or public responsibility*, Department of Town and Country Planning, University of Manchester.

Williams, P. (1982), 'Restructuring urban managerialism: towards a political economy of urban allocation', *Environment and Planning A*, 14, pp.95–105.

Zweig, F. (1976), *The new acquisitive society* (London: Barry Rose).

Index

References in italic are to figures

abandonment 102, 107, 164–5, 212
Abbey National Building Society 68, 203, 215
access 7, 10–11, 42, 99, 105, 161, 181, 186, 207, 209–10
accumulation *see* wealth
age 49
  of first-time buyers 24–5
  of owner-occupiers 32–4, 208, Table 2.4
  of property 20–1, *3.1*
agency 187
  relocation 203, 214
  repairs 205
  services 185, 187, 203–5, 212
  see also estate agency
Alliance 73, 168
annuity schemes 150–2, 205
anti-collectivism 12, 93
arrears *see* mortgage arrears
Australia 26, 44–5, 167
autonomy 47, 88, 95, 175–6, 198, Table 8.1

Ball, M. 14–17, 75, 143, 145, 163–4, 211, 213
banks 43, 201–2
Barrel, R. 154–5
Beckman, Bob 214
Bevan, Ernest 166
Borders, Elsie 72
Bourneville Village Trust 46
Bristol 51, 116–17, 119–24
British Land 68
building 2, 53, 75–6, 190, 199–200, 210–11, 213, 216
  for sale 161
  local authority 64, 71–2, 161, 200
  market segmentation 108–9
  new 5, 14–16, 21, 64–6, 160–1, 181, 184, 192, 199, 207, Table 3.6

  speculative 14–15, 64, 108, 160, 181, 200
building societies 23, 58, 60, 67–8, 72–3, 75, 185, 187, 190–1, 200–4, 214–15
  permanent 181, 200
  terminating 75, 84, 181
  see also mortgage
Building Societies Act (1986) 185, 201
Building Societies Association (BSA) 29, 37, 44, 47, 49, 63
bureaucracy 10–11, Table 1.1

Canada 44
capital 83, 152–4
  leakage 140–1, 143–5, 150, 154, 158, 184, 214
capital gains 17, 50, 87, 130, 134, 154–5, 197, Table 8.1
  tax 73–4, 131, 161
capitalism 3, 12–13, 80–1, 85, Table 1.1
  popular 184
car ownership 32, Table 2.4
caravans 27
Care and Repair 187
Census of Population 55, 62
Chamberlain, Neville 60
choice *see* preference
Churchill, Randolph 69
cities 28
  inner 11, 28, 45, 51, 92, 102
class 5, 12, 16–17, 49, 79–81, 83, 85–8, 90, 94, 134, 148–9, 158, 212, Table 7.1
  housing 10–11, 81, 85, 87, 90, 98, Table 1.1
  occupational 86, 98, 167, 169
  and politics 167–9
commodification 3, 12, 18, 84, 97, 129–30, 191, 198, 203, Table 1.1
Commons, House of Environment Committee 42–3

Index

competition 2, 4, 10–11, 14, 18, 202–3, Table 1.1
concrete cancer 27
Confederation of British Industry (CBI) Employee Relocation Council 114–15
conservatism 67, 166
Conservative Party 67–70, 72–3, 91, 128–9, 167–9
constraints 10–11, 45, 178
construction industry *see* building
consumer protection 212, 216
consumption 4, 13, 16–18, 79–80, 191
  location 87–8
  sector cleavages 4–5, 13, 17, 85–8, 97–8, 158, 196
control 17–18, 170
cooperatives 212
costs, transaction 139, 143, 203, 211
council house sales 19–20, 25, 27, 32, 48, 53–4, 90, 94, 106–7, 134, 161, 170–1, 176, 180, 185, 187–8
  arrears 107
  to developers 109–10
  discounts 162
  Right to Buy 107, 161, 167, 189
council housing 45, 48, 135–6, 163, 166, 180, 188, 209, 211, 216
  home–owner preference for 104, 108, 172–3, 208
  post-war 71–2
  waiting lists 45, 172
council tenants 20, 49, 53, 104, 127, 149, 167–8, 170, 186, 188, *2.1*, Table 2.5
credit 14, 84–5, 141–2, 144, 201, 214, Table 7.1
  institutions 181
cultural practice 172

debt *see* indebtedness
demand 2, 5, 13–14, 18, 42, 45, 53–4, 97, 199–200, Tables 1.1, 8.1
democracy 84, Table 8.1
  property-owning 5, 78–9, 82–4, 128, 184
demographic change 26, 43, 108, 186, 200, 216
Departmental Committee on Valuation for Rates 60
deposits 24, 38–9, 99, Table 2.7
deregulation 14, 163, 189
  financial 24, 203
detached property 20–1, 41
developers 2, 14, 109–10
Diamond, Lord 153

differential subsidies 5, 110
differentiation
  in home ownership 2, 5, 16, 18, 26, 28, 88–91, 95, 101, 130, 184, 192, 198, 208
  in housing market 99–126
  intra–tenure 196
disadvantage 34, 127
discrimination 11, 186
disinvestment *see* equity withdrawal
divorce 23, 26, 34, 43, 94, 108, 173, 186, 208
Doling, J. 30–1
Dunleavy, P. 85

East Anglia 20, 37–8, 49, 100, *4.1*, Tables 2.1, 2.6, 2.7
East Midlands 20, 37, *4.1*, Tables 2.1, 2.6, 2.7
ecological tradition 7
economic groups 63, Table 3.4
education 34, Table 2.4
elderly 23, 26, 32, 34, 43, 102, 104, 127, 151, 164, 172–3, 186, 198, 200, 208
embourgeoisement 80–1
Employee Relocation Council 114–15
employment 51, 114–15, 124–5, 130, 199, 212
Engels, Friedrich 166
England 19, Table 2.1
  see also regions
entrepreneur 92, 154–5, 165
enveloping 162
equity 128
  release schemes 150, 208–9
  sharing 106
  withdrawal 106, 143, 145, 150–1, 184, 187, 199, 214
estate agency 11, 75, 129, 184–5, 202–3, 214–15
ethnic groups 11, 31, 36
Europe, Western 24, 44
European Community 203, 207
exchange value 12, 91, 212
expectations 49

family 4, 22–3, 26, Table 2.2
Farmer, M. K. 154–5
Field, Frank 83
finance, housing 4, 14, 53, 133, 184, 186–7, 190–1, 200–7, Table 7.1
financial institutions 2, 76, 84, 144, 190, 200–3
  banks 43, 201–2

financial institutions (*cont.*)
  insurance companies 201–2
  mortgage companies 201–2
  occupational subsidies 112–13, 199
  see also building societies
first-time buyer 21, 24–5, 30, 109, 143, 161, 189, 206–7
fiscal support *see* tax relief
flats 20, 76, 188
flexible ownership 210
fragmentation 16–17, 198, 208
  housing market 99–126
franchise 68–9
Franklin, A. 172
freedom 17, 47
freehold 19, Table 2.2
  land societies 68

gardens 11, 104
gatekeepers 11–12, Table 1.1
General Household Survey 144, 156
gentrification 184
government
  intervention 2, 4, 7, 10, 12, 68, 179–80, 209, Tables 1.1, 7.1
  policy 2, 4, 7, 14, 44–5, 47, 54, 68–74, 131, 189–90, 201, 206–7
  subsidy 7, 60, 160–6, 185, 204, 206, 215
Greater London *see* London
Griffiths' Report 151
Grossick, G. 93

Hargreaves, Ken 105
Harris, C. 50–1, 137–40, 155, 171
Heseltine, Michael 42, 83
Hird, C. 152–3
Hirsch, F. 89
historical view 45–6, 55–77, 179–88, Tables 3.1–3.3, 7.1
Holman, A. E. 74, 145
Holme, Anthea 171
home 18, 79, 94
  attitudes to 5, 50, 97, 170–9, 197, Table 8.1
home reversion schemes 150
homelessness 103
homesteading 106, 161, 206
house price 5, 10, 14, 21, 50, 64, 99–101, *4.1*, Tables 2.6, 3.5
  collapse 213, Table 8.1
  inflation 37–8, 41, 47, 77, 88, 91, 95, 97, 100, 117, 143, 161, 189–90, 199, 206, 208, 212–13, 216–17
housebuilding *see* building

households 22–6, Table 2.2
  disadvantaged 127
  heads of Table 2.4
  optimum 118
housing 20–1, 27
  condition 27–8, 43, 103–5, 185, 188
  production 4, 13–16, 192, 200, 211
  provision 4, 13, 16
  shortage 43
  sociology of 4
  surplus 42–3, 128
  studies 45–6
  see also council housing
Housing Act (1919) 71
  (1923) 60, 70
  (1980) 161, 189
housing benefit 188–9
housing classes 10–11, 81, 85, 87, 90, 98, Table 1.1
housing market 2–4, 10, 18, Tables 1.1, 7.1
  segmentation 23, 99–126, 198–9, Table 8.1
  slump 14, 100, 213, 215
  volatility 14–15, 97, 188, 213, 215–17
housing policy 216
  Housing Policy Review 110
Howell, David 80
Humberside *see* Yorkshire
Hyndburn 103–5

identity 88, 95, 170, 175–6
improvement
  for sale 106, 161–2, 206
  grants 74, 162–3, 185–7, 205–6
  loans 144, 163, 205–6, 213–14
income 9–10, 34–6, 99, 130, *2.2*
  lower 102, 105, 161, 186, 198, 205, 207, 213
  and MITR 110–11, Table 5.1
Income Tax Act (1952) 73
indebtedness 21, 31, 85, 143, 204, 214, 217
  see also mortgage arrears
inequality 98, 127–8, 133–4, 139, 146, 158, 162, 164, 212
inflation 13, 30, 131, Table 3.5
  see also house price inflation
inheritance 5, 17, 26, 31–2, 38, 91, 130, 134–5, 141, 145–52, 158, 208, 212
insecurity of tenure 30–1
institutions 11–12, Table 1.1
  see also financial institutions

insurance
  companies 201–2
  schemes 204
interest rates 13–14, 22, 29–30, 77, 97,
    130–1, 201, 204, 213–14, 217
investment 5, 12, 17, 49–51, 64, 77, 91,
    97, 129–31, 150, 199–200, 216,
    Table 8.1
  building society 201–2
  strategies 154–7
Irvine, J. 152–3

Johnson, Christopher 141–2
Johnston, R. J. 167–9
joint mortgage 44, 73
Jones, C. 45, 48–9

Karn, V. 51
Kemeny, J. 144–5

labour
  market 5, 114–15, 124–5
  mobility 184, 189–90, 207
  spatial division 37–8
Labour Party 72–3, 167–8
land 14, 82–3, 133, 153
  banks 15, 200
  freehold societies 68
  policy 53
  prices 100
Land Enquiry Committee 59
Land Fit for Heroes Campaign 70
Land Transfer Bill (1887) 69
landlords 2, 66, 76
  absentee 166
  private 2, 67, 166, 179, 199
  residential 24
  see also renting
last-time sellers 144–5
leakage see capital leakage
leasehold 11, 27, 68–70, 77, 213
  enfranchisement bill 69–70
  Reform Act (1967) 27
legal
  rights 174–5
  services 11
life chances 128, 130, 134
loans 24, 60, 144
  beneficial 112–13
  see also mortgage
local authority 71–2, 161, 185, 187, 189,
    210
  building 64, 71–2, 161, 200
  lending 60

services 187
  see also council house sales; council
    housing; council tenants
location 3, 10, 168–9
  consumption 87–8
lodgers 11, 23–4
London, 38, 76, 88, 99–100, 106–7
  Greater 20–1, 37–9, 99, 113, 118, 143,
    181, Tables 2.1, 2.6, 2.7
  Inner 20, 28
low-cost home ownership 105–6, 161,
    185
  schemes 27, 106
Lowe, S. 145
lower-income owners 30, 90, 102, 105,
    107, 161, 164, 186, 198, 205, 207,
    213
Luria, D. 83

McPherson, C. B. 81–2
maintenance see repair
maisonettes 20, 188
marginal owners 5, 27, 29–30, 95, 103,
    141, 152, 167, 184, 207, 209
marginalization 16, 90, 97, 209
marital breakup see divorce
market see housing market; labour
    market
Marshall Aid Plan 72
Mass Observation 46
material interests 197, Table 8.1
Merrett, S. 46–8
middle class 55, 61, 80–1, 89, 93
Midlands see East Midlands: West
    Midlands
MITR see tax relief, mortgage interest
mobility 32, 34, 47–8, 50–1, 112–19, 130,
    139, 150, 158, 184, 197, 205, 212,
    Table 8.1
  labour 184, 189–90, 207
Moore, R. 10–11
mortgage 5, 11, 14, 21–2, 24, 32,
    84–5, 142–3, 198, 201–4, 2.1,
    Table 2.4
  advances & deposits 38–9, 99, 206,
    Table 2.7
  annuity schemes 150–2, 205
  arrears 5, 28–31, 101, 103, 107, 140–1,
    184, 214
  companies 201–2
  multiple 23, 44, 94, 213, Table 2.3
  secondary market 202–4
  see also tax relief
Munro, Moira 147–8

232 *Home ownership*

National Dwelling and Housing Survey 42–3
Neighbourhood Revitalisation Service 187
new building *see* building
non-permanent accommodation 27
non-self-contained accommodation 27
North 20–1, 27, 37, 49, 99–100, 113, 181, *4.1*, Tables 2.1, 2.6, 2.7
North West 20–1, 37, 39, 101, 103, *4.1*, Tables 2.1, 2.6, 2.7
Northern Ireland 37, 100, 181, Tables 2.1, 2.6, 2.7

occupation 17, 34, 61, 83–4, Table 2.5
occupational
  class 86, 98, 167, 169
  subsidy 5, 112–19, 123, 125, 199
Offer, A. 56, 69
older property 20–1, 75
ontological security 5, 170, 174–7, 197, Table 8.1
organization 11, 185, 200–9, 213
outright ownership 11, 20–2, 31–2, 34–6, 94, 147, *2.1, 2.2*, Tables 2.4, 2.5
ownership 19–31, Table 2.1
  flexible 210
  shared 161, 205

parallel tenure 210
political attitude 12, 67–70, 166–70, 197, Table 8.1
political economy 12, 17, Table 1.1
positional goods 89, 198–9, 209
power 5, 68–9, 83–4, 134, 152–4, 158
preference 9–10, 13, 18, 41–55, 64, Table 1.1
Preteceille, E. 86
privatism 160, 170
privatization 97, 129, 163, 185, 189, 192
  building societies 202–3
production, housing 4, 13–16, 192, 200, 211
profit 12, 77, Table 1.1
proletarianization 81, 184
property 5, 68–9, 76, 81–2
  housing as 78–85
  rights 81–3, 175, 179
provision, housing 4, 13, 16–17
public expenditure 7, 165
public sector housing *see* council housing

Reform Acts 68
regions 19–21, 37–9, 48–9, 95, 99–100,
113, 118, 135, 143, 181, 187, *4.1*, Tables 2.1, 2.6, 2.7
  see also individual regions
regulation 10
  building societies 202
  private sector 185, 206
relocation 114–17, Table 5.2
  agency 203, 214
  Employee Relocation Council 114–15
remortgaging 141, 145, 158, 214
removal 143, 156–9, 203–4
Rent Act 91
rental purchase schemes 27, 205, 215
renting 45–6, 114–15, 137–8, 198, 204
  council 20–1, 107, *2.1*, Table 2.8
  private 7, 20–1, 133, 149, 163, 166, 179, 186, 206, 210, *2.1*, Table 2.8
rents 49, 171
  control 71
repair and maintenance 15, 21, 27–8, 32, 102, 151–2, 163, 180, 184–5, 187, 205, 207, 209–11
  agency 187
  decoration 97, 171–2
  improvement grant 163, 185–7, 205
repossession 28–30, 103, 107, 140–1, 173, 203, 214
residence, length of 32, Table 2.4
retirement 32, 36, 43, 109, 117, 151
return, rate of 136–40, 215
Rex, J. 10–11
Right to Buy 31, 107, 161, 167, 189
rights, property 81–3, 175, 179
risk 204–5
Rose, D. 93–4
Royal Commission on Friendly and Benefit Societies 59
Royal Commission on the Distribution of Income and wealth 130, 132, 135–6, 146, 148, 153

Salisbury, Lord 69
Saunders, Peter 4, 50–1, 85–8, 95, 137–40, 155, 158, 170–1, 175–9
saving ratio 142
savings, bonus and loan scheme 206
Scotland 19–21, 37, 39, 49, 100, 149, Tables 2.1, 2.6, 2.7
second-hand market 14, 21, 97, 129, 180, 184, 188, 209
sectoral advantage 113
security *see* ontological security
self-employed 11
self-expression 88, 95, 170, 175–6

Index

233

semi-detached property 20
services 11, 67
  agency 185, 187, 203–5, 212, 215
shared ownership 161, 205
shares 132–3, 152–3
sheltered housing 151, 208
single-parent family 26, 36, 43, 108–9, 186
single-person household 23–6, 43–4, 94, 108–9, 186, Table 2.2
sitting tenant 32, 53, 92–4, 134, 161, 170, 199, 207
Small Dwellings Acquisition Act (1899) 70
social
  class *see* class
  context 4, 17
  groups 10–11, Table 1.1
  housing 48, 108
    polarization 16–17, 188–9
    stability 78
    structure 32–6, 84
    support 212
socialization 160–6
socio-economic groups 34, Table 2.4
sociology
  of consumption 18
  of housing 4
South East 20, 37–9, 88, 99–100, 113, 143, 149, 168, *4.1* Tables 2.1, 2.6, 2.7
South West 20, 38, 49, 100, *4.1*, Tables 2.1, 2.6, 2.7
speculation 154–7
  building 14–15, 64, 108, 160, 181, 200
Stafford, B. 30–1
state *see* government
status 51, 89–90, 93
Stewart, A. 92–3
Stretton, H. 18
structures of provision 4, 13, 16–17
subsidy 2, 5, 7, 12, 24, 60, 73–4, 98, 110, 135, 160–6, 184–6, 188, 204, 206–7, 212, Table 8.1
  building 60
  differential 5, 110
  occupational 5, 112–19, 123, 125, 199
  see also tax relief
suburbia 23, 91–4, 181
supplementary benefit 74, 163, 185–6, 205–6
supply-side factors 53–4, 160, 199–200

tax 2, 12, 74
  capital gains 73, 131, 161

tax relief 2, 12, 204–7
  improvement loan 205–6
  mortgage interest (MITR) 5, 22, 38–40, 52, 68, 73–4, 97, 110–12, 118, 131, 161, 186, 188–9, 204, 206, 213, Table 5.1
tenancy transfers 64, 76
tenants
  lodgers 11, 23–4
  sitting 32, 53, 92–4, 134, 161, 170, 199, 207
  see also council tenants
tenure 5, 7, 10, 17, 26–7, 31, 90, 193, 196–8, *2.1*, Table 2.8
  alternative 210–11
  demand-led 5, 53–4
  history of 45–6, 56–64, 179–88, Table 3.1
  insecurity of 30–1
  parallel 210
  preferences 5, 41–54, Table 2.8
  transfers 21, 64, 76, 180, 184–5
  transitions 6–7, 179–88, 191, Table 7.1
terraced property 11, 20–1, 41, 109
Thatcher government 128
Thomas, A. 144–5
Thorns, D. C. 89
trading-down 28, 140–1, 150–1, 158
trading-up 14, 21, 106, 130, 150
transaction costs 139, 143, 203, 211
transition 6–7, 179–88, 191, Table 7.1

unemployment 29–30, 101, 103, 164–5, 186
United States 26, 44
use value 12, 47–8, 50, 212

voluntary sector 187
voting behaviour 51, 67, 167–8, 217, Table 8.1

Wales 19, 21, 27, 37, 39, 58, 99–100, 103, Tables 2.1, 2.6, 2.7
  House Condition Survey 27
Walker, Peter 210
Watson, S. 145
wealth 5, 16, 18, 32, 68, 83, 127–59, *6.1*, Table 8.1
  accumulation 5, 13, 16, 38, 49, 88–9, 91, 97–8, 127, 130, 134, 143, 154–5, 157–9, 198–9, 209, 212
  distribution 130–4, 150
  inequality 146
  and power 152–4

wealth (*cont.*)
  rates of return 136–40, 215
  realizable 140–5, 157
  redistribution 83, 132, 197
Welsh House Condition Survey 27
West Midlands 37, 100, 118, *4.1*, Tables 2.1, 2.6, 2.7
women 11, 26, 94, 109

working class 12, 51, 58–61, 80–1, 93, 101–2, 105, 135, 167, 180, 184
  voting behaviour 167–9
World Wars 70–2

Yorkshire and Humberside 20, 37, 107, 113, 118, 149, *4.1*, Tables 2.1, 2.6, 2.7
Young, Sir George 105